W9-BDI-717

Hans Hoogendoorn
Brigitte Kristel
Bob Ordish

© **Royal Dutch Touring Club ANWB, The Hague**

All rights reserved.
This book has been written with the utmost care. The ANWB cannot be held responsible, though, for the results of any inaccuracies or faults this book may contain.

ISBN 90 18 01786 8

Third edition 2004

Production: ANWB Uitgeverij Boeken
English text: Brigitte Kristel and Bob Ordish (S. Brouwer Vertalingen, Noordeloos)
Grammar and background information: RomText, The Hague
Cover design: Keja Donia, Schiphol-Oost
Cartography: Softmap, Utrecht
Illustrations: Hilbert Bolland
Desktop Publishing: PSHolland.nl

How to use this phrase book

The various sections of this book each describe particular, standard situations that will offer you the opportunity to try out your Dutch or require you to do so: arrival in the Netherlands or Belgium, at your hotel, travelling around, eating out, shopping, seeing the sights, filling up with petrol, possibly visiting a doctor. The sections - each marked by a small pictogram - then go on to give a large number of phrases and sentences. These are grouped in blocks of three lines: the first line supplies the English sentence (**bold**), the second the Dutch equivalent (**blue**) and the third gives as accurate a rendering as possible of the Dutch pronunciation. In some of the examples the English sentence is preceded by the symbol (◄), indicating that this is the reply or question you can expect to receive from the Dutch person you are talking to. The sections also provide a brief English-Dutch vocabulary relating to the specific situation they describe. Very often you can take different words from the vocabulary and slot them into the sentences shown above. You will find a more extensive vocabulary at the back.

We wish you every success in your attempts to master the Dutch pronunciation. And don't be put off by the widespread Dutch habit of immediately responding to a foreign accent by replying in English. This is well meant but can seriously hinder your progress in the language. If you insist on continuing in Dutch, though, people are sure to respect your efforts. After all, actually speaking a language is the only way of learning it.

Holland or the Netherlands?

Although foreigners often refer to the country as "Holland" its official name is "the Netherlands" - rather in the way that people say "England" when they mean "Britain". It's only comparatively recently that the Dutch themselves started to make the distinction in everyday speech, and this even concerns the name of the language itself. For English speakers there is no problem - we just use the term "Dutch". The Dutch themselves, however, have two terms: the now generally accepted *Nederlands*, and *Hollands*. The latter is somewhat dated but still heard. For a closer understanding of the distinction we need to go back in history.

As early as the Middle Ages the seventeen earldoms (*graafschappen*), duchies (*hertogdommen*) and bishoprics (*bisdommen*) located in the delta formed by the three great rivers - the Rhine (*Rijn*), Meuse (*Maas*) and Scheldt (*Schelde*) - were known as "the Netherlands" (*de Nederlanden*, meaning "the low lands"). Although self-governing, politically these territories were strongly influenced by one or other of their powerful neighbours, the German Empire and France. The existence of these two spheres of influence gave rise to marked cultural and later also religious differences between the northern and southern Netherlands (with the Rhine marking the boundary).

Around 1500 the Netherlands came under the administration of the German Habsburg dynasty, which ruled much of medieval Europe for centuries. After the death of the great emperor, Charles V - "Charles the Wise" - the Netherlands devolved to his son, the king of Spain. By now, however, Protestantism had gained a firm hold in the northern Netherlands and the chasm with Catholic Spain was unbridgeable. This, along with conflicts of commercial interest, triggered the eighty-year war of independence (1568-1648) against the Spaniards. The struggle was waged mainly by the northern Netherlands, with only part of the south making common cause. Following recognition of the independence of the north and their southern partners, the Republic of the United Netherlands (*Republiek der Verenigde Nederlanden*) was set up. The Dutch themselves quickly started to refer to the new state as *Nederland*, using the singular form rather than the plural *Nederlanden* that is the basis of the English term "Netherlands". The earldom of *Holland* (now consisting of the provinces of North and South Holland) played a leading economic and military role in all this, partly because of the many refugees who fled there from the south. When Holland then went on to become a major trading and naval power, for most foreigners its name became synonymous with "the Netherlands" (Nederland). When Napoleon reunited that part of the southern Netherlands which had remained loyal to the Habsburgs - the lion's share - with the north in 1806, he therefore decreed the name "Holland" for the new kingdom that was to be proclaimed. However, following the Congress of Vienna in 1815 (held after Napoleon's defeat at Waterloo), the plural term "Kingdom of the Netherlands" (*Koninkrijk der Nederlanden*) was opted for again although the country's borders were left virtually unchanged. The southern Netherlands, separated from the north for too long to feel comfortable within the union, broke away in 1831 to form the new state of "Belgium" (*België*). The north retained its name, with the Dutch continuing to refer to *Nederland* and almost all foreigners to the familiar-sounding *Holland*. Nor do the Dutch themselves generally have any objection to this - interestingly, they also use the term when they are abroad. In the English edition of this book, we use "Holland" and "the Netherlands" interchangeably.

Introduction to the Dutch language

Dutch is the official language of *the Netherlands*. It is also one of the three official languages of *Belgium* where, very roughly, it is spoken north of an east-to-west line going through Brussels (French and German are spoken elsewhere - see map). Frisian (*Fries*) is officially recognised as a second language in the Dutch province of *Friesland* (and it really is a language in its own right, not just a dialect of Dutch!); The Brussels region is officially bilingual (Dutch and French); in the environs of the Belgian capital, and in individual towns and villages along the "linguistic frontier", the official language is determined by the local authority. This is a situation that has often given rise to discord between the rival language communities.

Dutch is the language of administration and frequently of education in Surinam (*Suriname*) the former colony of Dutch Guiana in South America (other languages, including English, are also widely spoken there). The same applies to the self-governing overseas territories of *Aruba* and the Netherlands Antilles (*Nederlandse Antillen*), in the Caribbean. Finally, there is also a tiny Dutch-speaking minority in French Flanders, in the extreme northwest corner of France. All told, Dutch is used by about twenty-five million people as their everyday language of communication.

The Dutch spoken in Belgium is frequently referred to as Flemish (*Vlaams*). This gives a somewhat misleading impression. The language of government, the media and literature is Dutch, hardly differing from the Dutch spoken in the Netherlands. There are innumerable dialects in Belgium, though, including Western Flemish (*West-Vlaams*) and Eastern Flemish (*Oost-Vlaams*). However, the state border between the Netherlands and Belgium does not mark a rigid border between dialects, which merge into one another gradually. "Flemish" therefore has more validity as a cultural and historical concept than as a linguistic term.

Like English, Dutch is a Germanic language. In other words, it stems from what linguists refer to as "Proto-Germanic", the prehistoric unrecorded language that is the ancestor of all the languages in this group. The Middle Ages gradually saw the development of three distinct branches: North Germanic (consisting of the Scandinavian languages and their dialects), East Germanic (now completely extinct) and West Germanic. The latter gradually divided into two subbranches: the North Sea group, comprising English and Friesian, and the Continental group with Dutch and German. The standard German spoken today crystallised largely out of the "High German" dialects of southern Germany and the Alpine region. The Low German dialects of northern Germany, which are closely related to Dutch and share the same medieval origins, were gradually displaced and do not have official status.

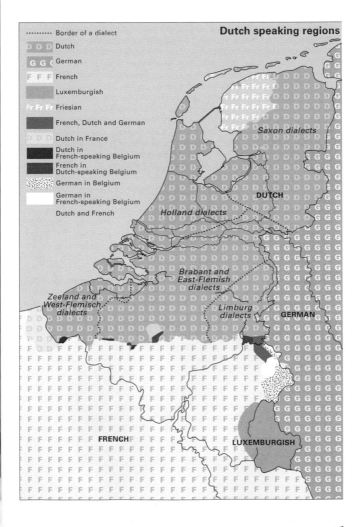

Dutch speaking regions

··········	Border of a dialect
D D D	Dutch
G G G	German
F F F	French
	Luxemburgish
Fr Fr Fr	Friesian
	French, Dutch and German
D D D	Dutch in France
	Dutch in French-speaking Belgium
	French in Dutch-speaking Belgium
	German in Belgium
	German in French-speaking Belgium
	Dutch and French

Saxon dialects

DUTCH

Holland dialects

Brabant and
East-Flemish
dialects

Zeeland and
West-Flemisch
dialects

Limburg
dialects

GERMAN

FRENCH

LUXEMBURGISH

Dutch emigrants and traders spread the use of their language throughout the colonies. The Dutch spoken by colonists in South Africa gave rise to today's *Afrikaans*, which Dutch people find fairly easy to understand.

If you've ever tackled German you'll be pleasantly surprised by Dutch grammar, which is considerably less complicated. Although there are many exceptions to the rules these tend to crop up frequently, so if you make the effort you do get the hang of the exceptions after a while. The greatest obstacle is probably the pronunciation, and some Dutch sounds (g, ch, sch, ui) have no real equivalent in English (Scots will probably have the least trouble, with the likes of "loch", etc). Dutch spelling can also be rather tricky. One thing that will strike you about written Dutch is the profusion of double vowels - aa, ee, oo, uu. These always indicate a "long" sound; single vowels are short, except when at the end of a syllable.

	singular	plural	
(short)	kap	kap-pen	(hood)
(long)	kaap	ka-pen	
(cape)			
(short)	zon	zon-nen	(sun)
(long)	zoon	zo-nen	
(son)			

We provide more such examples in our look at Dutch grammar. For the sentences and vocabularies shown in this book we mark the syllable that has to be stressed in **bold** (condensed) type since there is no single rule on this.

Gender and articles

There are three genders in the Dutch language: masculine, feminine and neuter. In actual practice hardly a distinction is made between masculine and feminine words. The same definite article applies to both: **de** (both singular and plural). Singular neuter words carry the definite article **het**, plural neuter words carry **de**. The indefinite article (singular only) is always **een** (in spoken language usually shortened to '**n**):

	definite article	*indefinite article*
mscl.:	**de** man - the man	**een** man - a man
fem.:	**de** vrouw - the woman	**een** vrouw - a woman
neut.:	**het** kind - the child	**een** kind - a child

The Dutch article is never inflected, with the exception of a limited number of traditional, archaic expressions. In the genitive case the preposition van (of) is added, in the dative case the preposition aan (to) or voor (for) may be added:

Het huis **van de** man - The man's house
Het huis **van de** vrouw - The woman's house
Het huis **van het** kind - The child's house

De man geeft een boek **aan het** kind (more commonly used: geeft **het** kind een boek) - The man gives a book to the child

De vrouw koopt **voor het** kind een boek (less commonly used: De vrouw koopt **het** kind een boek) - The woman buys the child a book

In the case of proper names and a number of nouns the relation of association or ownership can be indicated by adding -**s** (words ending in a vowel get '**s**, except words ending in -**e**).
Monica'**s** fiets - Monica's bicycle
Nederland**s** hoofdstad - the capital of Holland
Vader**s** huis - father's house

Diminutives

The diminutive of a noun can be formed by adding the affix -**tje**; diminutives are **always neuter**:

| (het) wiel | (het) wiel**tje** | (the small) wheel |

Sometimes the last consonant is doubled and followed by -e:

| (de) kar | (het) kar**ret**je | (the small) cart |
| (de) bal | (het) bal**let**je | (the small) ball |

or the **t** is left out:

(de) fiets - (het) fiets**je** - (the small) bicycle

Diminutives of words ending in -**m** are often formed by adding -**pje** (de boom - het boom**pje** - the (small) tree, but: de kam - het kam**metje** - the (small) comb).

Plural

There are three plural noun forms. We start with the most commonly used and work our way down:

1. *plural -en*

| (de) vrouw | (de) vrouw**en** | (the) woman | (the) women |

Because of the pronunciation rules the final consonant may be doubled or a double vowel can be reduced to a single one:

| (de) ma**n** | (de) ma**nnen** (not: manen) | (the) man | (the) men |
| (de) straat | (de) stra**ten** (not: straaten) | (the) street(s) |

There are various plural forms for words ending in -**s**: mens - mens**en** (human being - people), huis - hui**zen** (house - houses), bus - bu**ssen** (bus - busses).

Some words have an irregular plural ending (het kind - de kind**eren** - the child(ren); het ei - de ei**eren**- the egg(s)) or an entirely irregular plural form (de stad - de steden - the city - the cities; het schip - de sch**epen** - the ship(s)).

2. *plural -s*

The plural form of the following word groups is made by adding -**s** instead of -**en**:
a. words ending in an unstressed -**el**, -**em** or -**er**
b. diminutives
c. foreign words ending in a vowel.

(de) lepel	(de) lepel**s**	(the) spoon(s)
(de) bodem	(de) bodem**s**	(the) bottom(s)
(de) meester	(de) meester**s**	(the) master(s)
(het) fietsje	(de) fietsje**s**	(the) small bicycle(s)
(de) auto	(de) auto**'s***	(the) car(s)

* as a result of pronunciation rules the letter -**s** is preceded by an apostrophe if the word ends in a vowel (camera's, ski's, foto's, menu's) unless the final vowel is an **e** (dames - ladies).

3. other irregular endings

There are many words of Greek or Latin origin in the Dutch language; these have their own plural endings, usually taken from the original language:

(het) museum	(de) musea	(the) museum(s)
(het) centrum	(de) centra	(the) centre(s)
(de) basis	(de) bases	(the) base(s)

The adjective

The adjective takes the ending **-e** except when the noun is singular neuter and preceded by the indefinite article;

de oud**e** man	een oud**e** man	de oud**e** mannen
the old man	an old man	the old men
het klein**e** kind	een klein kind	de klein**e** kinderen
the small child	a small child	the small children

A double vowel is reduced to a single one (gr**oot**: de gr**ote** vrouw - large: the large woman), and, again, the final consonant may be doubled (vol: de vol**le** maan - full: the full moon).

The degrees of comparison are formed by adding the affixes **-er** and **-st**:

oud	oud**er**	oud**st**:
de oude man	de oudere man	de oudste man
the old man	the elder/older man	the eldest/oldest man
klein	klein**er**	klein**st**:
het kleine kind	het kleinere kind	het kleinste kind
the small child	the smaller child	the smallest child

The final consonant is often doubled in the comparative: fel - fel**ler** - felst (bright), krom - krom**mer** - kromst (crooked). Words ending in -r receive an additional **d**: zwaar - zwaar**der** - zwaarst (heavy). The **-s** at the end of a word is often changed to a **z**: wijs - wij**zer** - wijst (wise). A number of adjectives, in particular long ones, do not take affixes. In those case the comparative and superlative cases are formed by adding the words meer and meest: gebruikelijk - **meer** gebruikelijk - **meest** gebruikelijk (usual).

Important adjectives which have irregular degrees of comparison are:

veel - meer - meest	(many - more - most)
goed - beter - best	(good - better - best)
weinig - minder - minst	(little - less - least)

The comparative degree is followed by the word dan (than). When both parts are equal the construction even/net zo ... als (just as ... as) is used:

De man is groter **dan** de vrouw (The man is taller than his wife)

De man is **even** groot (**net zo** groot) **als** de vrouw (The man is just as tall as his wife)

The adverb

Adverbs are not inflected but also have degrees of comparison:

De auto rijdt snel - The car rides fast

De auto rijdt snel**ler** (dan ...)

De auto rijdt **het** snel**st**

Het kind tekent mooi - The child is drawing beautifully

Het kind tekent mooi**er** (dan ...)

Het kind tekent **het** mooi**st**

The personal pronoun

Many personal pronouns have two versions: one (a) is used in written language and in stressed positions, whereas the other (b) is used in colloquial, everyday speech and in unstressed positions.

	nom.		gen.		dat.		acc.	
	a	b	a	b	a	b	a	b
singular								
1	ik	'k	mijn	m'n	mij	me	mij	me
2	jij	je	jouw	je	jou	je	jou	je
	u	-	uw	-	u	-	u	-
3	hij	-	zijn	z'n	hem	'm	hem	'm
	zij	ze	haar	d'r	haar	'r	haar	'r
	het	't	zijn	z'n	het	't	het	't
plural								
1	wij	we	ons	-	ons	-	ons	-
2	jullie	-	jullie	-	jullie	-	jullie	-
	u	-	uw	-	u	-	u	-
3	zij	ze	hun	-	hun/hen	ze	hun	ze

U is a polite form of address, that can be used both in the 2nd person singular and plural. Whether you have to use the polite **u** or the more informal **jij** depends on your relationship with the person you speak to. When you are not sure which form to use, use **u**

and wait for the other person to induce you to say **jij** (sg.) or **jullie** (pl.). The possessive pronoun **haar** (her) has an unstressed form (**d'r** in the genitive case, **'r** in the dative and accusative cases), but these forms are restricted to colloquial speech only. **Hun** en **hen** (them) can also apply to women (plural); the formal form **haar** is slightly outdated: De vrouwen eisen **haar** rechten op (The women demand their rights).

There are three ways in which personal pronouns can be made into possessive pronouns (both singular and plural):
a. You may use the above mentioned genitive form.
b. You can use the dative form, preceded by van.
c. (less common) You can use the personal pronoun in a substantive way, adding -e.

a. Dit is **mijn jouw/uw zijn ons jullie hun** huis
    This is my/your/his/our/your/their house
b. Dit huis is **van mij jou/u hem ons jullie hen**
    This house is mine/yours/his/ours/yours/theirs
c. Dit huis is **het mijne jouwe/uwe zijne onze hunne**

Except in the case of c. the possessive pronoun is never inflected. Ons (our) is an exception: it is almost always inflected to **onze** (except when a singular neuter word is used or when it is preceded by van).

Dit is **onze** auto	Dit zijn **onze** auto's
This is our car	These are our cars
Dit is **ons** kind	Dit zijn **onze** kinderen
This is our child	These are our children
Dit huis is **van ons**	Deze huizen zijn van ons
This house is ours	These houses are ours

As in all Germanic languages the possessive pronoun is guided by the gender of the owner and never of the objects owned. When the gender of a person or animal is known, a clear distinction is made between zijn (his) and haar (her):
De man rijdt in **zijn** auto - The man drives his car (the owner is male)
De vrouw pakt **haar** fiets - The woman takes her bicycle (the owner is female)
De man neemt de vrouw **haar** fiets af - The man deprives the woman of her bicycle (the subject is male, but the owner of the bike is female)
Het paard loopt naast **haar** veulen - The horse is walking next to her filly (it may be assumed that the horse is female)

As hardly a distinction can be made between masculine and feminine objects one almost always uses zijn (his): Het land en **zijn** inwoners (the country and its inhabitants). Occasionally a "possessive" inanimate object is regarded as feminine: De stad en **haar** monumenten (the city and its - lit. her - monuments).

The demonstrative pronoun
There are different demonstrative pronouns for persons and things, depending on the distance to the speaker:

	masculine/feminine:	*neuter:*
close by:	**deze** man (this man)	**dit** huis (this house)
	deze mannen (these)	**deze** huizen (these)
further away:	**die** man (that)	**dat** huis (that)
	die mannen (those)	**die** huizen (those)

The relative pronoun
There are different relative pronouns for persons (and animals) and inanimate objects:
persons
Nom.: De boer **die** daar werkt (msc./fem.) - The farmer who works there
Het meisje **dat** hier woont (neut.) - The girl who lives here
Gen.: De slager **van wie** ik dit vlees kocht* - The butcher I bought the meat from
Dat.: De man **aan wie**** ik geld gaf - The man I gave money to
Acc.: De hond **die** hij sloeg (msc./fem.) - The dog he beat
Het kind **dat** zij meebracht (neut.) - The child she brought with her
inanimate objects
Nom.: De auto **die** hier staat (msc./fem.) - The car which stands here
Het huis **dat** aan zee ligt (neut.) - The house which is situated near the sea
Gen.: De fiets **waarvan** het licht kapot is - The bicycle of which the lamp is broken
Dat.: De straat **waarin***** ik loop - The street I walk in
Acc.: De stad **die** ik heb bezocht - The city I visited
Het land **dat** ik binnenkom - The country which I enter

* there is also an older, less commonly used genetive form:
De slager **wiens** vlees ik kocht - The butcher whose meat I bought (masc.)
De vrouw **wier** dochter ik trouwde - The woman whose daughter I married (fem.)
** also: van wie, voor wie, in wie, op wie, etc.
*** also: waarvan, waarvoor, waarop, waaraan, etc.

The interrogative pronoun
Again there are different pronouns for persons and inanimate objects:
persons
Nom.: **Wie** heeft dit gedaan? - Who did this?
Gen.: **Van wie** is deze jas? (archaic: **Wiens** jas is dit?) - Whose coat is this?
Dat.: **Aan wie** is die brief geschreven? - Whom did you write this letter to?
Acc.: **Wie** hebt u daar gezien? - Who did you see there?

inanimate objects

Nom.: **Wat** is er gebeurd? - What happened?
Gen.: **Waarvan** is dit alles betaald? - What did you pay this with? (lit.: of which)
Dat.: **Waaraan** moeten we nog denken? - What do we have to think of?
Acc.: **Wat** hebt u gekocht? - What did you buy?

In everyday speech the forms waarvan, waaraan, waarop, waarin etc. are often divided in two:
Waar is dit alles **van** betaald?
Waar moeten we nog **aan** denken?

The verb

In Dutch there are:
a. weak verbs (the past tense is formed by conjugation);
b. strong verbs (the past tense is formed by a change of vowels);
c. irregular verbs.

The **present tense** consists of the stem of the verb, (usually) followed by an ending:
present tense - stem

rijden	rijd	(to drive - drive)
zingen	zing	(to sing - sing)
maken	m**aa**k (!)	(to make - make)
leven	leef *	(to live - live)

ik	rijd	zing	maak	leef
jij/u	rijd**t****	zing**t**	maak**t**	leef**t**
hij/zij/het	rijd**t**	zing**t**	maak**t**	leef**t**
wij	rijd**en**	zing**en**	mak**en**	lev**en**
jullie***	rijd**en**	zing**en**	mak**en**	lev**en**
zij	rijd**en**	zing**en**	maken	lev**en**

* The stem of a verb can never end in **v** or **z**: leven - leef (to live), verhuizen - verhui**s** (to move).
** When the 2nd person singular is the subject of an interrogative sentence, the ending disappears: rijd jij? (do you drive?) zing jij? (do you sing?)
*** A verb following **u** is conjugated the same way both in singular and plural: u rijdt.
The simplification of vowels (aa-a, ee-e, oo-o, uu-u) and the doubling of consonants again occur in accordance with the rules of pronunciation.
When the stem already ends in -**t**, no extra **t** is added in the 2nd and 3rd person singular; in plural the ending -**ten** is added:
ik zit - jij zit - hij zit - wij zi**tten** - jullie zi**tten** - zij zi**tten** (I sit, etc.)

The **past tense** and the **past perfect** are conjugated in various ways, depending on the type of verb (weak, strong or irregular).

Weak verbs take the ending -**te(n)** when the verb stem ends in -**ch**, -**f**, -**k**, -**p** or -**s**; in all other cases the ending -**de(n)** is used:

infinitive *stem*

la**ch**en	la**ch** (to laugh)
bo**ff**en	bo**f** (to be lucky)
pa**kk**en	pa**k** (to take)
ho**p**en	hoo**p** (!) (to hope)
vi**ss**en	vi**s** (to fish)

ik/jij/u/hij/zij/het (I/you/he/she/it)

lach**te**	bof**te**	pak**te**	hoop**te**	vis**te**	leer**de**

wij/jullie/zij (we/you/they)

lach**ten**	bof**ten**	pak**ten**	hoop**ten**	vis**ten**	leer**den**

Although a **z** or **v** in the infinitive changes into **s** or **f** in the verb stem, the ending will still be **de**: verhuizen - verhuis - verhuis**de** (to move); leven - leef - leef**de** (to live). The past participle is formed by putting **ge-** in front of the verb stem and, according to the same rules mentioned above, -**t** or -**d** at the end: **ge**bof**t**, **ge**pak**t**, **ge**hoop**t**, **ge**vis**t**, **ge**leer**d**, **ge**leef**d**. Verbs prefixed by **be-**, **er-**, **her-**, **ont-** and **ver-** do not take **ge-** in the past participle: verhuis**d**.

In the case of strong verbs a vowel change takes place (and the -**t** or -**d** ending is omitted); the past participle is formed by adding **ge-** to the verb stem (in which the vowel may change) and putting -**en** at the end. For example:

pres. tense	*past tense*	*past part.*
(to drive, ride)		
ik ri**jd**	reed	**ge**red**en**
hij ri**jdt**	reed	
wij ri**j**den	reden	
(to walk)		
ik l**oo**p	liep	**ge**l**o**p**en**
hij l**oo**pt	liep	
wij l**o**pen	liepen	

(to find)		
ik vind	vond	**gevonden**
hij vindt	vond	
wij vinden	vonden	

(to sit)		
ik zit	zat	**gezeten**
hij zit	zat	
wij zitten	zaten	

In many dictionaries you will find a list of the most important strong verbs. Which vowel change may take place is not dictated by clear rules (verbs which have an **ij** in the stem are often strong; in those cases the **ij** is replaced by **e(e)**: rijden - reed - gereden (to drive, ride), blijven - bleef - gebleven (to stay), prijzen - prees - geprezen (to praise), etc.

Irregular verbs are often characterised by a vowel change in the past tense; sometimes the conjugation is totally deviant. The past participle may end both in -**t** and -**en**. We will give a few examples.

The auxiliaries are always irregular (as in most other languages):

	zijn	**hebben**	**mogen**	**kunnen**	**zullen**
	to be	to have	may	can	shall/will
present tense					
ik	ben	heb	mag	kan	zal
jij	bent	hebt	mag	kan	zal
hij	is	heeft	mag	kan	zal
wij	zijn	hebben	mogen	kunnen	zullen
past tense					
ik	was	had	mocht	kon	zou
jij	was	had	mocht	kon	zou
hij	was	had	mocht	kon	zou
wij	waren	hadden	mochten	konden	zouden

The **present perfect** and the **past perfect** are formed by using either zijn (to be) or hebben (to have):

Ik **heb** een boek **gelezen**	I have read a book
Jij **bent** naar Amsterdam **gereisd**	You have traveled to Amsterdam

The **future tense** is formed by using the auxiliary **zullen** (shall/will):

Ik **zal**/Wij **zullen** morgen komen	I/we shall come tomorrow
Ik **zou**/Wij **zouden** morgen komen	I/we would have come tomorrow

Winter in Nederland	Winter in Holland
1 Volkssport nummer 1	The Dutch national sport
2 Een bevroren sloot	A frozen ditch
3 Het aanbinden van schaatsen	Fastening one's skates
4 Warme drankjes te koop	Hot drinks for sale
5 Een flinke sneeuwbui	Heavy snowfall
6 Kale bomen	Bare trees
7 Sinterklaas en Zwarte Piet*	Saint Nicholas and Black Pete

* Sint Nicolaas or Sinterklaas is the Dutch equivalent of Father Christmas/Santa Claus. On December the 5th, on the eve of his birthday, he hands out presents and candy to the children (in fact everyone is buying one another presents). Black Pete is the helper of this great friend of all children.

Vowels

a, aa	short **a**, transcribed as **a**, is pronounced like **a** in f**a**ther; long **a** (before the end of a syllable) and **aa** are pronounced and transcribed like English **ah**
au	is pronounced very much like **ou** in l**ou**d and transcribed as such
e, ee	**e**, when short, is pronounced like **e** in b**e**t and transcribed as **eh**; **e**, when long, and **ee**, like **ay** in s**ay** and transcribed as such; in unstressed syllables **e** is pronounced like **er** in oth**er** and transcribed as **e**
eeu(w)	this combination of vowels is pronounced, very approximately, like ay in s**ay**, followed by **oo** in m**oo**n, so Dutch leeuw (lion) is transcribed as **l**a**yoo**
ei	**ei** in Dutch represents the same sound as Dutch **ij** and is a cross between **eye** and **ee** in sh**ee**p; the sound is transcribed as **aiy**, so Dutch trein (train) is pronounced as tr**aiy**n
eu	as in French "peu" and represented by the symbol **ø**: Dutch leuk (nice) is pronounced l**ø**k
i	when short, like English **i** in h**i**t; when long (before the end of a syllable), like **ee** in b**ee**
ie	like long **i** (see above)
ieu(w)	like **ee** in b**ee**, followed by **oo** in m**oo**n, so nieuw is pronounced n**eeoo**
ij	represents the same sound as Dutch **ei** (see above); IJ is a combination of the letters I en J and like the diphthong 'ei' it is pronounced as *aiy* (like English 'eye', but somewhat shorter). The combination is inseparable, hence the spelling IJsselmeer and not Ijsselmeer. It is no longer the Dutch counterpart of the Y and has lost its position between the letters W and Z in the Dutch alphabet. Names and words beginning with IJ are now listed as Ij.
o, oo	when short, like **o** in dr**o**p; when long, like **oa** in r**oa**d
oe	like **oo** in m**oo**n, so Dutch koe (cow) is pronounced k**oo**
ou	pronounced like **ou** in l**ou**d
u, uu	short **u**: midway between **ew** in n**ew** and **u** in b**u**s, and transcribed as **u**; long **u** (at the end of a syllable) and **uu** as Scottish **ui** in M**ui**r or **u** in c**u**re, and transcribed as **ew** (as in n**ew**), so Dutch muur (wall) is pronounced m**ew**r
ui	approximates to **ow** in Scottish n**ow**, transcribed as **œ**, so Dutch huis (house) is pronounced h**œ**s
b	as in English, but at the end of a word pronounced like **p** in hel**p**
c	before a consonant and a, o, u, like **k** in **k**eep; before e and i like **s** in **s**torm

ch	approximates to Scottish **ch** in Lo**ch** and transcribed as **gh**, so Dutch school (school) is transcribed as s**gh**oal
g	pronounced like Dutch and Scottish **ch** (see above), except in a few words of French origin like rage (mania), when **g** is pronounced like **zh**; in Belgium and the southern parts of the Netherlands the pronunciation of **g** is softer and less guttural than in Standard Dutch
ng	pronounced like English **ng** in si**ng**
j	like **y** in year and transcribed as such; in words of French origin like **zh**, for example lits-jumeaux (twin bed): lee-**zh**ewmoa
n	as in English, although in everyday speech the n in verbs ending in -en (i.e. almost all verbs) is often not pronounced at all
r	should be trilled
sch	pronounced like **s** followed by Dutch **g** or **ch** (see above) except at word ends (usually -isch), when this sound is simply pronounced like **s**, for example fantastisch (fantastic) is pronounced fantastee**s**
t	as in English, but in words ending in -tie pronounced as **ts**, for example politie (police) is transcribed as poalee**ts**ee
th	Dutch th is pronounced like English **t**, for example thee (tea) is transcribed as **t**ay
tj	this combination, which mostly occurs in diminutives, is pronounced as English t followed by **y**, for example kaartje (ticket) is pronounced kahr**ty**e
v	basically as in English, but often pronounced unvoiced, which means it sounds much like **f**
w	pronounced with the lips less rounded than in English, but essentially like English **v** as in **v**ery.

The syllable that has been printed in bold (condensed) type should be stressed. If no syllable has been printed that way, it doesn't matter which syllable is stressed.
If an English word is commonly used in Dutch, we have given no phonetic rendering, but put the English word between inverted commas instead.

A ah	**F** ef	**K** kah	**P** pay	**U** ew	**Z** zet
B bay	**G** ghay	**L** el	**Q** kew	**V** vay	
C say	**H** hah	**M** em	**R** air	**W** way	
D day	**I** ee	**N** en	**S** es	**X** iks	
E ay	**J** yay	**O** oh	**T** tay	**Y** ee-grek	

some basic expressions

everyday words and phrases

yes	ja	yah
no	nee	nay
maybe	misschien	mis**gheen**
please	alstublieft	alstew**bleeft**
here you are	alstublieft	alstew**bleeft**
thank you	dank u wel*	dank ew wehl
thank you very much	hartelijk dank	**har**telek dank
you're welcome	graag gedaan	ghrahg ghe**dahn**
excuse me	neemt u mij niet kwalijk	naymt ew maiy neet **kwah**lek
I'm so sorry	het spijt me*	heht spaiyt me

where?	waar?	wahr?
where is/are ...?	waar is/zijn ...?	wahr is/zaiyn ...?
when?	wanneer?	wa**nayr**?
what?	wat?	wat?
how?	hoe?	hoo?
how much?	hoeveel?	hoo**vayl**?
which?	welk(e)?	**wehlk**(e)?
who?	wie?	wee?
why?	waarom?	wahr**om**?
what do you call this?	hoe heet dit?	hoo hayt dit?
what does this mean?	wat betekent dit?	wat be**tay**kent dit?
it's ...	het is ...	heht is ...
it's not ...	het is niet ...	heht is neet ...
there is/are ...	er is/zijn ...	ehr is/zaiyn ...
there is/are no ...	er is/zijn geen ...	ehr is/zaiyn ghayn ...
is/are there any ...?	is/zijn er ...?	is/zaiyn ehr ...?
is/are there no ...?	is/zijn er geen ...?	is/zaiyn ehr ghayn ...?

* You will be surprised to hear many people say "merci" (the French word) for "dank u"
en "sorry" to express some regret.

across	over	**oa**ver
after	na	nah
already	al	al
always	altijd	altaiyt
and	en	ehn
anyone	iemand	**ee**mant
at once	dadelijk	**dah**delek
behind	achter	**agh**ter
beneath	onder	**on**der
between	tussen	**tus**sen
down	beneden	be**nay**den
downstairs	omlaag	om**lahgh**
during	tijdens	**taiy**dens
for	voor	voar
from	van	van
here	hier	heer
home	thuis	tœs
in	in	in
(to the) left	links(af)	links(af)
near	dicht bij	dight**baiy**
never	nooit	noayt
next to	naast	nahst
no one, nobody	niemand	**nee**mant
not	niet	neet
on top of ...	op	op
of	van	van
or	of	of
outside	buiten	**bœ**ten
overthere	daar	dahr
(to the) right	rechts(af)	rehghts(af)
since	sinds	sints
somebody	iemand	**ee**mant
soon	spoedig	**spoo**degh
then	dan	dan
through	door	doar
to	naar	nahr
until	tot	tot
up	boven	**boa**ven
upstairs	omhoog	om**hoagh**
with	met	meht

without	zonder	**zon**der
with pleasure	graag	ghrahgh

a few adjectives

bad	slecht	slehght
beautiful	mooi	moay
better	beter	**bay**ter
cheap	goedkoop	ghoot**koap**
close by	dichtbij	dight**baiy**
closed	dicht	dight
cold	koud	kout
delicious	heerlijk	**hayr**lek
difficult	moeilijk	**mooy**lek
easy	gemakkelijk	ghe**ma**kelek
empty	leeg	laygh
expensive	duur	dewr
far	ver	vehr
free	vrij	vraiy
full	vol	vol
good	goed	ghoot
heavy	zwaar	zwahr
hot	warm	warm
light	licht	light
new	nieuw	neeoo
occupied	bezet	be**zeht**
old	oud	out
open	open	**oa**pen
quick	snel	snehl
right	juist	yœst
slow	langzaam	**lang**zahm
ugly	lelijk	**lay**lek
warm	warm	warm
wrong	verkeerd	ver**kayrt**
worse	slechter	**slehgh**ter
young	jong	yong

25

language problems

I don't speak Dutch
Ik spreek geen Nederlands
ik sprayk ghayn **nay**derlants

I don't understand you
Ik versta u niet
ik ver**stah** ew neet

Could you repeat that for me?
Kunt u dat nog even herhalen?
kunt ew dat nogh **ay**ven hehr**hah**len?

Does anyone here speak English?
Spreekt hier iemand Engels?
spraykt heer **ee**mant **ehng**els?

I'm English   **I'm Irish**
Ik ben Engels   Ik ben Iers
ik behn **ehng**els   ik behn eers

Dutch is a difficult language
Nederlands is een moeilijke taal
nayderlants is en **mooy**leke tahl

I can't read this
Dit kan ik niet lezen
dit kan ik neet **lay**zen

Could you spell it for me/write it down?
Kunt u het spellen/opschrijven?
kunt ew heht **speh**len/**op**sghraiyven?

I speak only a little Dutch
Ik spreek maar een beetje Nederlands
ik sprayk mahr en **bay**tye **nay**derlants

Could you speak more slowly?
Kunt u wat langzamer praten?
kunt ew wat **lang**zahmer **prah**ten?

Do you speak English?
Spreekt u Engels?
spraykt ew **ehng**els?

I'm foreign (m/f)
Ik ben buitenlander/buitenlandse
ik behn **bœ**tenlander/**bœ**tenlantse

How do you say this in Dutch?
Hoe zeg je dit in het Nederlands?
hoo zehgh ye dit in heht **nay**derlants?

How do you pronounce this?
Hoe spreek je dit uit?
hoo sprayk ye dit œt?

It's going too fast for me
Het gaat mij te snel
heht ghaht maiy te snehl

Could you translate this for me?
Kunt u dit voor mij vertalen?
kunt ew dit voar maiy ver**tah**len?

greetings

Good morning	Goedemorgen	ghoode**mor**ghen
Good afternoon	Goedemiddag	ghoode**mi**dagh
Good evening	Goedenavond	ghooden**ah**vont
Good night/sleep well	Goedenacht/welterusten	ghoode**naght**/wehlte**rus**ten
Welcome	Welkom	**wehl**kom

26

Good bye	Tot ziens	tot zeens
See you later	Tot straks	tot straks
See you tomorrow	Tot morgen	tot **mor**ghen
Have a pleasant journey	Goede reis	**ghoo**de raiys
This is Mr/Mrs ...	Dit is de heer/mevrouw ...	dit is de hayr/me**vrou** ...

How do you do?
Hoe maakt u het?
hoo mahkt ew heht?

◄ **Fine, thank you**
Uitstekend, dank u
œt**stay**kent, dank ew

Nice to meet you
Aangenaam (kennis te maken)
ahnghenahm (**keh**nis te **mah**ken)

Hi! How are things going? (pop.)
Hallo! Hoe gaat het ermee?
ha**loa**! hoo ghaht heht ehr**may**?

◄ **What's your name?**
Hoe is uw naam?
hoo is ew nahm?

My name is ...
Mijn naam is ...
maiyn nahm is ...

This is my ...
Dit is mijn ...
dit is maiyn ...

husband	man	man
wife	vrouw	vrou
son	zoon	zoan
daughter	dochter	**dogh**ter
father	vader	**vah**der
mother	moeder	**moo**der
(boy-)friend/(girl-)friend	vriend/vriendin	vreent/vreen**din**

◄ **Where do you come from?**
Waar komt u vandaan?
wahr komt ew van**dahn**?

I'm from England
Ik kom uit Engeland
ik kom œt **ehng**elant

◄ **Did you have a pleasant journey?**
Hebt u een goede reis gehad?
.hehpt ew en **ghoo**de raiys ghe**hat**?

◄ **Give my regards to ...**
Doet u de groeten aan ...
doot ew de **ghroo**te ahn ...

making friends/dating

◄ **Shall I show you around town?**
Zal ik u de stad laten zien?
zal ik ew de stat **lah**ten zeen?

◄ **Shall we go out tonight?**
Zullen we vanavond uitgaan?
zulen we van**ah**vont œt**gahn**?

Yes, I'd like that/No, thank you
Ja, dat is leuk/Nee, dank je
yah, dat is løk/nay, dank ye

◄ **Shall I pick you up?**
Zal ik je afhalen?
zal ik ye **af**hahlen?

◄ **Shall we meet in front of the hotel/at the camp site?**
Zullen we voor het hotel/bij de camping afspreken?
zulen we voar heht hoa**tehl**/baiy de **kehm**ping **af**sprayken?

Okay, at ... o'clock
Ja/Goed, om ... uur
jah/ghoot, om ... ewr

Leave me alone!
Laat me met rust!
laht me meht rust!

I don't want/like this!
Daar ben ik niet van gediend!
dahr behn ik neet van ghe**deent**!

◄ **May I see you to your hotel/camp site?**
Mag ik je naar het hotel/de camping brengen?
magh ik ye nahr heht hoa**tehl**/de **kehm**ping **brehng**en?

visiting

Does ... live here?
Woont ... hier?
woant ... heer?

◄ **No, he moved out**
Nee, die is verhuisd
nay, dee is ver**hœst**

◄ **Yes, please come in**
Ja, komt u binnen
yah, komt ew **bi**nen

Do you know his new address?
Weet u zijn nieuwe adres?
wayt ew zaiyn **neeoo**-e ah**drehs**?

◄ **He/She is not home right now**
Hij/Zij is momenteel niet thuis
haiy/zaiy is moamehn**tayl** neet tœs

When will he/she be back?
Wanneer komt hij/zij terug?
wa**nayr** komt haiy/zaiy te**rugh**?

Can I leave a message?
Kan ik een boodschap achterlaten?
kan ik en **boat**sghap **agh**terlahten?

◄ **Please sit down**
Gaat u zitten
ghaht ew **zi**ten

May I smoke in here?
Mag ik hier roken?
magh ik heer **roa**ken?

◄ **Of course, go right ahead/I'd rather you wouldn't**
Natuurlijk/Liever niet
nah**tewr**lek/**lee**ver neet

◄ **Would you like anything to drink?**
Wilt u iets drinken?
wilt ew eets **drin**ken?

Here's to your health!
Op uw gezondheid!
op eww ghe**zont**haiyt!

And to yours!
Op de uwe!
op de **ew**we!

◄ **Will you stay for dinner?**
Blijft u eten?
blaiyft ew **ay**ten?

Enjoy your meal!
Eet smakelijk!
ayt **smah**kelek!

I/We should be going
Het is tijd om te gaan
heht is taiyt om te ghahn

Thank you for your hospitality/a lovely meal
Bedankt voor de gastvrijheid/het lekkere eten
be**dankt** voar de ghast**vraiy**haiyt/heht **leh**kere **ay**ten

Dutch etiquette

Good manners are appreciated everywhere and the Netherlands are no exception. And, although this is generally a very relaxed country, the Dutch can still be surprisingly formal on some occasions. For a start, it's far less common to drop in on someone without notice - people appreciate it far more if you phone and arrange things beforehand. If you're visiting someone for the first time you usually bring a small gift. Flowers are a good idea (naturally enough!). The Dutch shake hands more than do, say, the British or Americans, and good friends will embrace and kiss each other three times on the cheeks (i.e. a man and woman or two women but, unlike the Russians, two men much less so).

Although no particular ritual is attached to the evening meal (*avondeten*) it's certainly advisable not to turn up in the middle of it - unless, of course, you've been specifically invited. Bear in mind that most Dutch people sit down to their evening meal rather earlier than the British do - usually between 6 and 7 p.m. Afternoon visitors are offered tea or coffee (the Dutch greatly prefer 'real' coffee to the instant variety) along with a small cake or pastry (*koekje, gebakje*). However, since the Dutch regard restraint as a virtue, hospitality is less lavish than it tends to be in more southerly climes. 'South' in this sense already starts in Belgium - including its Dutch-speaking areas - where the people have a certain flamboyance (it's the French influence).

congratulations

See also the section on "Dates, seasons, months" for special holiday greetings

Happy birthday	Gefeliciteerd met uw verjaardag	ghe**fay**leeseetayrt meht eww ver**yahr**dagh
Happy anniversary	Gefeliciteerd met uw trouwdag	ghe**fay**leeseetayrt meht eww **trou**dagh
Congratulations ...	Gefeliciteerd ...	ghe**fay**leeseetayrt ...
on your marriage	met uw huwelijk	meht eww **heww**lek
on the birth of ...	met de geboorte van ...	meht de ghe**boar**te van ...
All the best!	Het allerbeste!	heht **a**lerbehste!
Good luck!	Succes!/Veel geluk!	sew**xehs**/vayl ghe**luk**!
Take care!	Sterkte!	**stehrk**te!
Have fun!	Veel plezier!	vayl ple**zeer**!
Get well soon	Van harte beterschap	van **har**te **bay**tersghap

0	nul	nul
1	een	ayn
2	twee	tway
3	drie	dree
4	vier	veer
5	vijf	vaiyf
6	zes	zehs
7	zeven	**zay**ven
8	acht	aght
9	negen	**nay**ghen
10	tien	teen
11	elf	ehlf
12	twaalf	twahlf
13	dertien	**dehr**teen
14	veertien	**vayr**teen
15	vijftien	**vaiyf**teen
16	zestien	**zehs**teen
17	zeventien	**zay**venteen
18	achttien	**agh**teen
19	negentien	**nay**ghenteen
20	twintig	**twin**tegh
21	eenentwintig	**ayn**-en-twintegh
22	tweeëntwintig	**tway**-en-twintegh
30	dertig	**dehr**tegh
40	veertig	**vayr**tegh
50	vijftig	**vaiyf**tegh
60	zestig	**zehs**tegh
70	zeventig	**zay**ventegh
80	tachtig	**tagh**tegh
90	negentig	**nay**ghentegh
100	honderd	**hon**dert
101	honderd een	**hon**dert ayn
200	tweehonderd	**tway**hondert
500	vijfhonderd	**vaiyf**hondert
1000	duizend	**dœ**zent
1500	vijftienhonderd	**vaiyf**teenhondert
2000	tweeduizend	**tway**dœzent
10.000	tienduizend	**teen**dœzent
100.000	honderdduizend	**hon**dert-dœzent
1.000.000	(een) miljoen	(ayn) mil**yoon**

Note 1: The Dutch put a comma where the English put a decimal point and the other way around. So Dutch 1.824 = English 1,824 and English 4.56 = Dutch 4,56!

Note 2: An English billion corresponds to a Dutch **miljard** and not to a Dutch **biljoen** (= 1,000,000,000,000).

1/2	een half	en half
1/3	een derde	en **dehr**de
1/4	een kwart/vierde	en kwart/**veer**de
3/4	driekwart	dreekwart
5%	vijf procent	vaiyf proa**sehnt**
first (1st)	eerste (1e, 1ste)	**ayr**ste
second (2nd)	tweede (2e, 2de)	**tway**de
third (3rd)	derde (3e, 3de)	**dehr**de
tenth(10th)	tiende (10e, 10de)	**teen**de
one hundredth (100th)	honderdste (100e, 100ste)	**hon**dertste
2 x 4 = 8	twee keer/maal vier is acht	tway kayr/mahl veer is aght
6 : 2 = 3	zes gedeeld door twee is drie	zehs ghe**daylt** doar tway is dree
4 + 6 = 10	vier plus/en zes is tien	veer plus/ehn zehs is teen
8 - 3 = 5	acht min drie is vijf	aght min dree is vaiyf

I am twenty-five years old
Ik ben 25 (jaar)
ik behn **vaiyf**-en-twintegh (yahr)

There are four of us
We zijn met zijn vieren
we zaiyn meht zen **vee**ren

time

What time is it?
Hoe laat is het?
hoo laht is heht?

◄ **It's ...**
Het is ...
heht is ...

half past three
half vier
half veer

three o'clock
drie uur
dree ewr

a quarter past two
kwart over twee
kwart **oa**ver tway

five to three
vijf voor drie
vaiyf voar dree

five past three
vijf over drie
vaiyf **oa**ver dree

a quarter to four
kwart voor vier
kwart voar veer

twenty past three
tien voor half vier
teen voar half veer

twenty to four
tien over half vier
teen **oa**ver half veer

15.23 hr.
vijftien uur drieëntwintig
vaiyfteen ewr **dree**-en-
twintegh

tomorrow	morgen	**mor**ghen
the day after tomorrow	overmorgen	**oa**vermorghen
tyesterday	gisteren	**ghis**teren
the day before yesterday	eergisteren	ayrghisteren
during the day	overdag	oaver**dagh**
at night	's nachts	snaghts
in the morning	's morgens	**smor**ghens
in the afternoon	's middags	**smi**daghs
in the evening	's avonds	**sah**vonts
this morning	vanmorgen	van**mor**ghen
this afternoon	vanmiddag	van**mi**dagh
tonight, this evening	vanavond	vana**h**vont
last night	gisterenavond	**ghis**teren-ahvont
summer time	zomertijd	**zoa**mertaiyt
local time	plaatselijke tijd	**plaht**seleke taiyt

dates, seasons, months, etc.

2004	tweeduizendvier	twayd**œ**zend**veer**
last year	vorig jaar	**voa**regh yahr
next year	volgend jaar	**vol**ghent yahr
spring	voorjaar, lente	**voar**yahr, **lehn**te
summer	zomer	**zoa**mer
autumn	najaar, herfst	**nah**yahr, hehrfst
winter	winter	**win**ter
January	januari	yanewa**h**ree
February	februari	faybrewa**h**ree
March	maart	mahrt
April	april	ah**pril**
May	mei	maiy
June	juni	**yew**nee
July	juli	**yew**lee
August	augustus	ou**ghus**tes
September	september	sehp**tehm**ber
October	oktober	ok**toa**ber
November	november	noa**vehm**ber
December	december	day**sehm**ber

What's the date today?
Welke datum is het vandaag?
wehlke **dah**tem is heht van**dahgh**?

The Hague, the 25th of May 2004	**on next May 25th/on May 25th last**
Den Haag, 25 mei 2004	op 25 mei aanstaande/jongstleden
dehn hahgh, 25 maiy 2004	op 25 maiy ahn**stahn**de/yongst**lay**den

a year and a half	anderhalf jaar	**an**derhalf yahr
half a year	(een) half jaar	(en) half yahr
a month	een maand	en mahnt
two weeks (a fortnight)	twee weken (veertien dagen)	tway **way**ken (**vayr**teen **dah**ghen)
a week	een week	en wayk

33

Besides a number of religious holidays and the New Year, the Dutch have the following public holidays:

Koninginnedag (30 April) (the Queen's official birthday): 30 April is actually the natural birthday of the Queen Mother, Juliana, but the present queen, Beatrix (whose own birthday is on 31 January) retains the traditional date. This is a full public holiday with children's parties, fairs and markets.

Bevrijdingsdag (5 May): this commemorates the end of the Second World War and the Allied liberation of the Netherlands from Nazi German occupation (1945). The festivities resemble those of "Koninginnedag", but the shops are open,

Sinterklaas (5 December) (Saint Nicholas' Eve): this is a more important festival than Christmas, although the latter is catching on under Anglo-Saxon influence. Sint Nikolaas (or Sinterklaas) arrives from Spain with his helpers, who all bear the name *Zwarte Piet* (Black Pete). Together, "they" distribute presents to all the family (especially the children, of course). The adults write poems to each other (the fiction is that Sinterklaas has written them), and everyone gets a chocolate letter representing their initial.

Oudejaarsavond (31 December) (New Year's Eve): a family occasion lasting till just before midnight. Traditionally, you eat *oliebollen* (rather greasy doughnut balls) and then people flood into the streets to let off fireworks.

There are two additional historical anniversaries in Belgium:

Nationale Feestdag (21 July) (National Holiday)
Wapenstilstandsdag 1918 (11 November)
(Armistice/Remembrance Day)

The following are also recognised public holidays in Belgium:

De Dag van de Arbeid (1 May) (Labour Day)
Maria-ten-hemelopneming (15 August) (Assumption)
Allerheiligen (1 November) (All Saints' Day)

New Year	Nieuwjaar	neeoo-yahr
Twelfth Day	Driekoningen	dree**koa**ningen
Maundy Thursday	Witte Donderdag	**wi**tte **don**derdagh
Good Friday	Goede Vrijdag	**ghoo**de **vraiy**dagh
Easter	Pasen	**pah**sen
Labour Day, May Day	Dag van de Arbeid	dagh van de **ar**baiyt
Ascension Day	Hemelvaartsdag	**hay**melvahrtsdagh

34

Whitsuntide	Pinksteren	**pink**steren
Corpus Christi	Sacramentsdag	**sah**krahmehntsdagh
Assumption	Maria Hemelvaart	mah**ree**yah **hay**melvahrt
All Saints Day	Allerheiligen	aler**haiy**leghen
Christmas	Kerstmis	**kehrst**mis
New Year's Eve	Oudejaarsavond	oude-yahrs-**ah**vont

Merry Christmas and a happy New Year!
Prettige Kerstdagen en een gelukkig Nieuwjaar!
prehteghe **kehrst**dahgen ehn en ghe**lu**kegh neeoo-**yahr**!

Sunday	zondag	**zon**dagh
Monday	maandag	**mahn**dagh
Tuesday	dinsdag	**dins**dagh
Wednesday	woensdag	**woons**dagh
Thursday	donderdag	**don**derdagh
Friday	vrijdag	**vraiy**dagh
Saturday	zaterdag	**zah**terdagh
Sundays and public holidays	zon- en feestdagen	zon ehn **fayst**dahghen
weekdays	werkdagen	**wehrk**-dah-ghen
daily	dagelijks	**dah**gheleks

the weather

What will the weather be like today?
Wat voor weer krijgen we vandaag?
wat voar wayr **kraiy**ghen we van**dahgh**?

◀ **The weather will stay fine/poor**
Het blijft mooi/slecht weer
heht blaiyft moay/slehght wayr

◀ **The weather will be better/worse**
Het wordt beter/slechter weer
heht wort **bay**ter/**slehgh**ter wayr

◀ **A temperature of 15 degrees (below zero)***
Een temperatuur van 15 graden (onder nul)
en tehmpayrah**tewr** van **vaif**teen **ghrah**den (**on**der nul)

◀ **It's going to rain/hail/snow**
We krijgen regen/hagel/sneeuw
we **kraiy**ghen **ray**ghen/**hah**ghel/snayoo

◀ **It's going to freeze/thaw**
Het gaat vriezen/dooien
heht ghaht **vree**zen/**doa**yen

The sky is clouding over, ...
De lucht betrekt, ...
de lught be**trehkt**, ...

The wind is rising/falling
De wind steekt op/gaat liggen
de wint staykt op/ghaht **li**ghen

... it's going to rain/there's going to be a thunderstorm/a gale is blowing up
... het gaat regenen/onweren/stormen
... heht ghaht **ray**ghenen/**on**wayren/**stor**men

It's hot/chilly/sultry/cold today
Het is vandaag warm/koel/drukkend/koud
heht is van**dahgh** warm/kool/**dru**kent/kout

The sky is clear/clouded
De hemel is onbewolkt/bewolkt
de **hay**mel is **on**bewolkt/be**wolkt**

* Note that on the Continent the Celsius system is being used; the degrees used in weather forecasts are always according to the Celsius and never to the Fahrenheit system.

atmospheric pressure	luchtdruk	**lught**druk
changeable	onbestendig	onbe**stehn**degh
depression	lagedrukgebied	lah-ghe-**druk**-ghebeet
drizzle	motregen	**mot**rayghen
easterly wind	oostenwind	**oas**tenwint
fog	mist	mist
frost	vorst	vorst
glazed frost	ijzel	**aiy**zel
heat	hitte	**hi**te
high pressure zone	hogedrukgebied	hoaghe**druk**ghebeet
ice	ijs	aiys
(black) ice on the road	gladheid	**ghlat**haiyt
lightning	bliksem	**blik**sem
northern wind	noordenwind	**noar**denwint
precipitation	neerslag	**nayr**slagh
sea breeze	zeewind	**zay**wint
shower	regenbui	**ray**ghenbœ
southern wind	zuidenwind	**zœ**denwint
storm alarm	stormwaarschuwing	**storm**wahr-sghew-wing
sunny spells	opklaringen	**op**klahringen
thaw	dooi	doay
thunder	donder	**don**der
twilight, dusk, dawn	schemering	**sghay**mering
variable	veranderlijk	ver**an**derlek
variable cloudiness	wisselend bewolkt	**wi**selent be**wolkt**
weather forecast	weersverwachting	**wayrs**verwaghting
western wind	westenwind	**wehs**tenwint
wind	wind	wint

passport control

◄ **May I see your passport/car documents/green card?**
Mag ik uw paspoort/autopapieren/groene kaart zien?
magh ik eww **pas**poart/**ou**toa pahpeeren/**ghroo**ne kahrt zeen?

Here you are
Alstublieft
alstew**bleeft**

◄ **Your passport/visa has expired/is not valid**
Uw pas/visum is verlopen/niet geldig
eww pas/**vee**sem is ver**loa**pen/neet **ghehl**degh

◄ **Your passport will soon expire**
Uw paspoort verloopt binnenkort
eww **pas**poart ver**loapt** binnen**kort**

◄ **You need a visa/transit permit**
U heeft een visum/doorreisvisum nodig
ew hayft en **vee**sem/**doar**raiysveesem **noa**degh

How much is a visa?
Wat kost een visum?
wat kost en **vee**sem?

◄ **How long do you intend to stay in Holland?**
Hoe lang blijft u in Nederland?
hoo lang blaiyft ew in **nay**derlant?

◄ **Are you passing through?**
Bent u op doorreis?
behnt ew op **doar**raiys?

◄ **Are you here for business or pleasure?**
Bent u hier als toerist of voor zaken?
behnt ew heer als too**rist** of voor **zah**ken?

Where can I have passport photos made?
Waar kan ik pasfoto's laten maken?
wahr kan ik **pas**foatoas **lah**ten **mah**ken?

◄ **Would you please fill in this form?**
Wilt u dit formulier invullen?
wilt ew dit formew**leer in**vullen?

◄ **Would you please wait here?**
Wilt u hier even wachten?
wilt ew heer **ay**ven **wagh**ten?

◄ **Would you please follow me?**
Wilt u even meekomen?
wilt ew **ay**ven **may**koamen?

◄ **You cannot enter the country**
U mag ons land niet binnen
ew magh ons lant neet **bi**nen

◄ **We must send you back**
Wij moeten u terugsturen
waiy **moo**ten ew te**rugh**stewren

notices

DOUANE	CUSTOMS
PASCONTROLE	IMMIGRATION
EU-ONDERDANEN	EU CITIZENS
ANDERE NATIONALITEITEN	OTHER NATIONALITIES
NIETS AAN TE GEVEN	NOTHING TO DECLARE
AANGIFTE	ANYTHING TO DECLARE
HIER WACHTEN A.U.B.	WAIT HERE PLEASE
HIER OPSTELLEN	QUEUE HERE
PERSONENAUTO'S	PASSENGER CARS
VRACHTVERKEER	FREIGHT TRAFFIC

customs

◄ **Would you please pull over/dismount?**
Wilt u hier even parkeren/afstappen?
wilt ew heer **ay**ven par**kay**ren/**af**stapen?

◄ **Do you have anything to declare?**
Hebt u iets aan te geven?
hehpt ew eets ahn te **ghay**ven?

◄ **Please open this suitcase**
Wilt u deze koffer openmaken?
wilt ew **day**ze **ko**fer **oa**penmahken?

◄ **You have to pay duty on this**
U moet hiervoor invoerrechten betalen
ew moot heer**voar in**voor-rehghten be**tah**len

◄ **You may proceed/go through**
U kunt doorrijden/doorlopen
ew kunt **doar**raiyden/**doar**loapen

◄ **Do you have a vaccination certificate for your dog/cat?**
Hebt u een inentingsbewijs voor uw hond/poes?
hehpt ew en **in**ehn-tings-bewaiys voar eww hont/poos?

◄ **Would you please open the boot?**
Wilt u de kofferruimte openmaken?
wilt ew de **ko**fer-rœmte **oa**penmahken?

◄ **Is this your suitcase/rucksack/bag?**
Is deze koffer/rugzak/tas van u?
is **day**ze **ko**fer/**rugh**zak/tas van ew?

◄ **It's not allowed to import/export this**
U mag dit niet invoeren/uitvoeren
ew magh dit neet **in**vooren/**œt**vooren

How much do I owe you?
Hoeveel moet ik betalen?
hoovayl moot ik be**tah**len?

◄ **We'll confiscate this property**
Dit nemen we in beslag
dit **nay**men we in be**slagh**

Where can I pay?
Waar kan ik betalen?
wahr kan ik be**tah**len?

transportation

English	Dutch	Pronunciation
(motor) car	auto	**ou**toa
passenger car	personenauto	pehr**soa**nen-outoa
camper	camper	"**cam**per"
car and trailer	auto met aanhanger	**ou**toa meht **ahn**hanger
car and caravan	auto met caravan	**ou**toa meht "caravan"
lorry	vrachtauto	**vraght**outoa
heavy lorry	vrachtauto met aanhanger	**vraght**outoa meht **ahn**hanger
articulated lorry	truck met oplegger	"truck" meht **op**lehgher
containerized truck	truck met container	"truck" meht "container"
van	bestelauto	be**stehl**outoa
minibus	minibus	**mee**neebus
motor cycle	motorfiets	**moa**torfeets
sidecar machine	motor met zijspan *n*	**moa**tor meht **zaiy**span
scooter	step	step
motor scooter	scooter	"scooter"
moped	bromfiets	**brom**feets
bicycle	fiets	feets
racing cycle	racefiets	**rays**feets
tandem	tandem	"tandem"
lady's bike	damesfiets	**dah**mesfeets
gents' bike	herenfiets	**hay**renfeets
child's bicycle	kinderfiets	**kin**derfeets
mountain bike	ATB (mountainbike)	aa tay bay ("mountainbike")
reclining bicycle	ligfiets	**ligh**feets
folding bike	vouwfiets	**vow**feets
BMX	BMX (crossfiets)	bay ehm iks (**kros**feets)
airplane	vliegtuig *n*	**vleegh**tœg
boat	boot	boat
car ferry	autoveerpont	**ou**toa-vayrpont
pleasure boat (city cruises)	rondvaartboot	**ront**vahrtboat
pleasure steamer	cruiseschip *n*	**kroos**-sghip
(local) bus	(stads)bus	(**stats**)bus
(motor) coach	touringcar	**too**ringkar

underground	metro	**may**troa
taxi, cab	taxi	**ta**xee
shared taxi	groepstaxi	**ghroops**taxee
train	trein	traiyn
carriage, coach	koets	koots

car rental

I'd like to hire a car
Ik wil een auto huren
ik wil en **ou**toa **hew**ren

◄ **Which brand/type/class of car do you prefer?**
Hebt u een voorkeur voor een bepaald merk/type/klasse?
hehpt ew en **voar**kør voar en be**pahlt** mehrk/**tee**pe/**klahs**seh?

How much is it per day/week?
Wat kost dit per dag/week?
wat kost dit pehr dagh/wayk?

What's included in the price?
Wat is bij de prijs inbegrepen?
wat is baiy de praiys **in**beghraypen?

comprehensive car insurance	all-riskverzekering	"all risk" ver**zay**kering
fuel	brandstof	**brant**stof
full tank	volle tank	**vol**le "tank"
rate per kilometer	tarief per kilometer	tah**reef** pehr **kee**loamayter
VAT	BTW	bay-tay-way

How much is the deposit?
Hoeveel is de borgsom?
hoo**vayl** is de **borgh**som

Can I use a credit card to pay for the deposit?
Kan ik voor de borg een creditcard gebruiken?
kahn ik voar de borgh ayn "**cre**dit card" ghe**brew**ken

◄ **May I see your driving license?**
Mag ik uw rijbewijs zien?
magh ik eww **raiy**bewaiys zeen?

What kind of fuel does the car use
Wat voor brandstof gebruikt de auto?
wat voar **brahnd**stoff ghe**brœkt** de **ow**to

◄ **Here are the keys/your car papers**
Hier zijn de sleutels/uw autopapieren
heer zaiyn de **slø**tels/eww **ou**toa-pahpeeren

◄ **The car is standing ...**
U vindt de auto ...
ew vint de **ou**toa ...

◄ **The registration number is ...**
Het kenteken is ...
heht **kehn**tayken is ...

Where can I return the car?
Waar kan ik de auto terugbezorgen?
wahr kan ik de **ou**toa te**rugh**-bezorghen?

What time will the office close?
Tot hoe laat is het kantoor open?
tot hoo laht is heht kan**toar oa**pen?

How do I get from here to ...?
Hoe kom ik van hier naar ...?
hoo kom ik van heer nahr ...?

Is this the way to ...?
Is dit de weg naar ...?
is dit de wehgh nahr ...?

Is the road in good condition?
Is de weg goed berijdbaar?
is de wehgh ghoot be**raiyt**bahr?

Do I take the motorway/toll road?
Is dat via de snelweg/tolweg?
is dat **vee**yah de **snehl**wehgh/**tol**wegh?

Is there a scenic route?
Is er een mooie route naar toe?
is ehr en **moa**ye **roo**te nahr too?

Is there a cycle path?
Is er een fietspad?
is ehr en **feets**pat?

Can you point it out on the map?
Kunt u dit op de kaart aanwijzen?
kunt ew dit op de kahrt **ahn**waiyzen?

I'am lost
Ik ben verdwaald
ik behn ver**dwahlt**

◄ **From here you must ...**
U moet van hier af ...
ew moot van heer af ...

go straight on	rechtdoor	rehghtdoar
turn to the right	rechtsaf	rehghtsaf
turn to the left	linksaf	linksaf
turn around	keren	**kay**ren
drive back ...	terugrijden ...	te**rugh**raiyden ...
to the motorway	naar de snelweg	nahr de **snehl**wehgh
to the main road	naar de hoofdweg	nahr de **hoaft**wehgh
and leave the town	de stad uit	de stat œt
and leave the village	het dorp uit	heht dorp œt
through the tunnel	de tunnel door	de **tu**nel doar
and cross the railway	de spoorbaan oversteken	de **spoar**bahn **oa**verstayken
along the river	langs de rivier	langs de ree**veer**
through the woods	door het bos	doar heht bos
through the valley	door het dal	doar heht dal
till the crossing	tot de kruising	tot de **krœ**sing
till the fork	tot de splitsing	tot de **split**sing
till the roundabout	tot de rotonde	tot de roa**ton**de
at the traffic lights	bij de verkeerslichten	by de ver**kehrsl**ighten

Where can I park?
Waar kan ik hier parkeren?
wahr kan ik heer par**kay**ren?

Is there a parking lot/(multi-storey) car park?
Waar is een parkeerplaats/parkeergarage?
wahr is en par**kayr**plahts/par**kayr**-ghah-rah-zhe?

TRAVELLING AROUND

Where can I pay?
Waar moet ik betalen?
wahr moot ik be**tah**len?

Is there a ticket machine/parking meter?
Is er een parkeerautomaat/parkeermeter?
is ehr en par**kayr**-outoamaht/par**kayr**mayter?

◀ **You are not allowed to park here**
U mag hier niet parkeren
ew magh heer neet par**kay**ren

◀ **Your parking time has expired**
Uw parkeertijd is verstreken
eww par**kayr**taiyt is ver**stray**ken

◀ **You will be fined for ...**
U krijgt een bekeuring wegens ...
ew kraiyght en be**kø**ring **way**ghens ...

unauthorized parking	foutparkeren	foutpar**kay**ren
exceeding the parking limit	te lang parkeren	te lang par**kay**ren
speeding	te snel rijden	te snehl **raiy**den
within the built-up area	binnen de bebouwde kom	**bi**nen de be**bou**de kom
dangerous driving	gevaarlijk rijden	ghe**vahr**lek **raiy**den
illegal crossing	verkeerd oversteken	ver**kayrt oa**verstayken
passing through amber	door geel licht rijden	doar ghayl light **raiy**den
jumping the lights	door rood (licht) rijden	doar roat (light) **raiy**den
failing to give right of way	geen voorrang verlenen	ghayn **voa**rang ver**lay**nen
failing to indicate a	geen richting aangeven	ghayn **righ**ting **ahn**ghayven
change of direction		
unauthorized overtaking	verkeerd inhalen	ver**kayrt in**hahlen

◀ **You're not allowed to drive here**
U mag hier niet rijden
ew mahgh heer neet **raiy**den

◀ **The fine is fifty euro**
De boete bedraagt vijftig euro
de **boo**te be**drahght vaiyf**tegh **uh**ro

---

notices

PARKEERVERBOD	NO PARKING
UITRIT	EXIT
NEEM HIER UW PARKEERKAART	TAKE YOUR PARKING CARD
HIER BETALEN	PAY HERE
INWORP	INSERT
... PER UUR	... PER HOUR
WERKDAGEN TOT 18.00 UUR	ON WEEKDAYS UNTIL 6 PM
PARKEERTERREIN VOL	CAR PARK FULL
GERESERVEERD VOOR ...	RESERVED FOR ...
TAXISTANDPLAATS	TAXI RANK

◀ **You can pay to me**
U kunt aan mij betalen
ew kunt ahn maiy be**tah**len

◀ **You must come to the office**
U moet naar het bureau komen
ew moot nahr heht bew**roa koa**men

◀ **I'll only give you a warning this time**
Ik geef u alleen een waarschuwing
ik ghayf ew a**layn** en **wahr**sghew-wing

notices and directions

AFGESLOTEN VOOR ...	CLOSED TO ...
AFSLAG	EXIT
ALLEEN VOOR ...	... ONLY
ALLE RICHTINGEN	ALL DIRECTIONS
BEBOUWDE KOM	BUILT-IN AREA
BROMFIETSERS	MOPED RIDERS
CENTRUM	CENTRE
DOODLOPENDE WEG	DEAD END
DOORGAAND RIJVERKEER GESTREMD	NO THOROUGHFARE
EIGEN WEG	PRIVATE ROAD
ER KAN NOG EEN TREIN KOMEN	ANOTHER TRAIN MAY FOLLOW
FIETSERS	CYCLISTS
FIETSERS OVERSTEKEN	CYCLISTS' CROSSING
FIETSPAD	CYCLE TRACK
FILE(VRIJ)	(NO) TAILBACK
GA TERUG!	GO BACK!
GEEN DOORGAAND VERKEER	NO THROUGH TRAFFIC
GELDT NIET VOOR ...	NOT APPLYING TO ...
GESLOTEN	CLOSED
GEVAARLIJKE STOFFEN	DANGEROUS SUBSTANCES
HIER OPSTELLEN	LINE UP HERE
HIER OVERSTEKEN	CROSS HERE
LANGZAAM RIJDEN	DRIVE SLOWLY
LET OP	ATTENTION
LICHTEN ONTSTEKEN	SWITCH ON LIGHTS
MAXIMUM SNELHEID	SPEED LIMIT
M.U.V.	WITH THE EXCEPTION OF
NA 100 M	AFTER 100 METERS
NIET PARKEREN	NO PARKING
OMLEIDING	DIVERSION
P + R	PARKING FOR RAIL PASSENGERS

POLITIE	POLICE
SCHOOL	SCHOOL
SMALLE WEG	NARROW ROAD
STOPLICHTEN	TRAFFIC LIGHTS
TEGENLIGGERS	ONCOMING TRAFFIC
... TOEGESTAAN	... ALLOWED
TOL	TOLL
TRAM	TRAM, STREETCAR
UIT	EXIT
UITRIT VRIJLATEN	PLEASE KEEP THE EXIT CLEAR
VEERPONT	FERRY
VERBODEN TOEGANG	NO ENTRY
VERBODEN TOEGANG VOOR ONBEVOEGDEN	NO TRESPASSING
VERKEERSDREMPEL	SPEED RAMP
VERKEERSINFORMATIE	TRAFFIC INFORMATION
VOETGANGERS	PEDESTRIANS
VOETGANGERSOVERSTEEKPLAATS	PEDESTRIAN CROSSING
VOLG ROUTE NR. 3	FOLLOW ROUTE NUMBER 3
VOORSORTEREN	GET IN LANE
WEGOMLEGGING	DIVERSION
WERK IN UITVOERING	ROAD WORKS AHEAD
WIELRIJDERS	CYCLISTS
WOONERF	RESIDENTIAL AREA
ZACHTE BERM	SOFT VERGES

hitchhiking

Are we allowed to hitchhike here?
Mogen we hier liften?
moaghen we heer **lif**ten?

◄ **Not alongside the motorway/slip road**
Niet langs de snelweg/oprit
neet langs de **snehl**wehgh/**op**rit

Shall I pay part of the expenses?
Zal ik een deel van de onkosten vergoeden?
zal ik en dayl van de **on**kosten ver**ghoo**den?

Can you take us to ...?
Kunt u ons meenemen naar ...?
kunt ew ons **may**naymen nahr ...?

Thanks for the ride
Bedankt voor de lift
be**dankt** voar de lift

bus, tram, underground

Where is the tube station/central bus terminal?
Waar is het metrostation/centrale busstation?
wahr is heht **meh**troa stahsyon/sehn**trah**le **bus**-stahsyon?

Where is the nearest bus stop?
Waar stopt hier een bus?
wahr stopt heer en bus?

Is there a bus/tram going to ...?
Gaat er een bus/tram naar ...?
ghaht ehr en bus/"tram" nahr ...?

Which number do I take?
Welk nummer moet ik nemen?
wehlk **nu**mer moot ik **nay**men?

What time does the first/last bus/tram leave?
Hoe laat gaat de eerste/laatste bus/tram?
hoo laat ghaht de **ayr**ste/**laht**ste bus/"tram"?

Do I have to change (busses, etc.)?
Moet ik overstappen?
moot ik **oa**verstapen?

return ticket	retour *n*	re**toor**
day ticket	dagkaart	**dagh**kahrt
children's ticket	kinderkaartje *n*	**kin**derkahrtye
monthly season ticket	maandabonnement	**mahnt**-a-bo-ne-mehnt
to stamp	afstempelen	**af**stehmpelen
stamping machine	stempelautomaat	**stehm**pel-outoamaht

Could you notify me when we arrive at ...?
Wilt u mij waarschuwen als we bij ... zijn?
wilt ew maiy **wahr**sghew-wen als we baiy ... zaiyn?

Can I take the dog with me in the bus?
Mag de hond mee in de bus?
magh de hont may in de bus?

◀ **Your ticket please**
Uw plaatsbewijs alstublieft
eww **plahts**bewaiys alstew**bleeft**

◀ **You cannot sit here, this is the first class**
U mag hier niet zitten, dit is de eerste klas
ew magh heer neet **zi**ten, dit is de **ayr**ste klas

◀ **Your ticket has expired**
Uw plaatsbewijs is verlopen
eww **plahts**bewaiys is ver**loa**pen

◀ **Your ticket is not valid**
Uw plaatsbewijs is niet geldig
eww **plahts**bewaiys is neet **ghehl**degh

◀ **You have to pay a fine**
U moet een boete betalen
ew moot en **boo**te be**tah**len

◀ **We stop over for ten minutes**
We houden hier tien minuten pauze
we **hou**den heer teen mee**new**ten **pou**ze

DEUR OPENEN	DOOR BUTTON - PUSH TO OPEN
GEEN UITGANG	NO EXIT
HIER GEEN STAANPLAATSEN	DO NOT STAND HERE
KAARTVERKOOP BIJ DE BESTUURDER	TICKETS CAN BE PURCHASED FROM THE DRIVER
NIET SPREKEN MET DE BESTUURDER	DO NOT SPEAK TO THE DRIVER
NOODREM	ALARM, EMERGENCY BRAKE
VERBODEN TE ROKEN	NO SMOKING

◄ **Terminus, all change here!**
Eindpunt, uitstappen alstublieft
aiyntpunt, **œt**stapen alstew**bleeft**

driver	bestuurder	be**stewr**der
number	(lijn)nummer *n*	(**laiyn**)numer
seat	zitplaats	**zit**plahts
standing room	staanplaats	**stahn**plahts
stop	halte	**hal**te
ticket collector	controleur	kontroa**lør**

train

Where is the station?
Waar is het station?
wahr is heht stah**syon**?

One single to ..., please
Mag ik een enkele reis naar ...?
magh ik en **ehn**kele raiys nahr ...?

Do I have to make a reservation?
Moet ik een plaats reserveren?
moot ik en plahts rayser**vay**ren?

Do I have to transfer?
Moet ik overstappen?
moot ik **oa**verstapen?

Can I take my bicycle with me into the train?
Kan ik mijn fiets in de trein meenemen?
kan ik maiyn feets in de traiyn **may**naymen?

What time does the train to ... leave?
Hoe laat gaat de trein naar ...?
hoo laht ghaht de traiyn nahr ...?

timetable	dienstregeling	**deenst**ray-ghe-ling
arrival	aankomst	**ahn**komst
departure	vertrek *n*	ver**trehk**
change	overstappen	**over**stahppen

The 'strippenkaart'

The Dutch have a unique ticketing system based on the *strippenkaart* ("strip ticket"). This can be used for all buses, trams, the underground and a few overground trains (although usually only on local and short-distance suburban routes). The ticket is divided into a number of "strips", each of which represents a public transport zone. (The entire Netherlands is divided into these zones, and theoretically you could travel from one end of the country to the other using strip tickets.) Calculate how many zones you're travelling through (there'll be a map in the tram or tube, or just ask a helpful local) and stamp the appropriate strip on your ticket. The stamping machines are located in the trams and on the underground and train platforms; in buses (and some trams), tickets are stamped by the driver. If you're travelling, say, three zones you stamp the fourth strip down on your ticket - you don't need to stamp the three sections above. Look at the back of the *strippenkaart* for further instructions.

connection	aansluiting	ahn**slœ**ting
weekdays	werkdagen	**wehrk**dahghen
Sundays and bank holidays	zon- en feestdagen	zon ehn **fayst**dahghen
track	spoor *n*	spoar
platform	perron *n*	peh**ron**
international train	internationale trein	internahshoa**nah**le traiyn
Inter-city train	intercity(trein)	"inter-city"(traiyn)
express train	sneltrein	**snehl**traiyn
local train	stoptrein	**stop**traiyn
through train	doorgaande trein	**doar**ghahnde traiyn
ticket counter	loket *n*	loa**keht**
surcharge	toeslag	**too**slagh
first class	eerste klas	**ayr**ste klas
second class	tweede klas	**tway**de klas
smoking	roken	**roa**ken
non smoking	niet-roken	neet-**roa**ken
reserved	gereserveerd	gherayser**vayrt**
dining compartment	restauratie	rehstoa**rah**tsee
dining car/diner	restauratiewagon	rehstoa**rah**tsee-wahghon
sleeping car/sleeper	slaap-/ligrijtuig *n*	**slahp**-/**ligh**raiytœg
luggage van	bagagerijtuig *n*	bah**ghah**zhe-raiytœgh

ACHTER(STE TREINSTEL)	REAR (TRAIN)
ACHTER/VOOR UITSTAPPEN	GET OUT IN THE BACK/FRONT
BAGAGE(RUIMTE)	LUGGAGE (COMPARTMENT)
BAGAGEKLUIZEN	LOCKERS
BINNENLAND	DOMESTIC
BUITENLAND	INTERNATIONAL
DAMES	LADIES
D-TREIN MET TOESLAG	INTER-CITY EXPRESS WITH SURCHARGE
EERSTE KLASSE	FIRST CLASS
FIETSENSTALLING	BICYCLE SHED
GEEN TOEGANG	NO ENTRY
HEREN	GENTS
INGANG	ENTRANCE
INLICHTINGEN	INFORMATION
KAARTVERKOOP	TICKET OFFICE
METRO	UNDERGROUND
MET TOESLAG	WITH A SURCHARGE
NIET INSTAPPEN	DO NOT GET IN
NIET OPENEN VOORDAT DE TREIN STILSTAAT	DO NOT OPEN UNTIL THE TRAIN HAS COME TO A COMPLETE STOP
NIET ROKEN	NO SMOKING
NOODREM	EMERGENCY BRAKE
NOODUITGANG	EMERGENCY EXIT
OPENEN	OPEN
OP VOL BALKON NIET ROKEN	NO SMOKING WHEN PLATFORM IS FULL
OVERSTAPPEN	CHANGE HERE
ROKEN	SMOKING
SLUIT AUTOMATISCH	DOOR CLOSES AUTOMATICALLY
SLUITEN	CLOSE
SPOOR	TRACK (PLATFORM)
STATIONSRESTAURATIE	STATION RESTAURANT
STOPT NIET IN ...	DOES NOT STOP IN ...
STOPT OP VERZOEK	REQUEST STOP
TOILETTEN	TOILETS
UITGANG	EXIT
VOOR(STE TREINSTEL)	FRONT (TRAIN)
WACHTKAMER	WAITING ROOM

berth	couchette	koo**sheht**
seat	zitplaats	**zit**plahts
corridor	gangpad *n*	**ghang**pat
luggage rack	bagagerek *n*	bah**ghah**zhe-rehk
ticket collector	conducteur	konduk**tør**
engine driver	machinist	mashee**nist**

◀ **The train only stops at/does not stop at ...**
De trein stopt alleen/niet in ...
de traiyn stopt a**layn**/neet in ...

◀ **You're in the wrong train**
U zit in de verkeerde trein
ew zit in de ver**kayr**de traiyn

◀ **You're sitting in the wrong seat**
U zit op de verkeerde plaats
ew zit op de ver**kayr**de plahts

◀ **You're in the first-class section**
U zit in de eerste klasse
ew zit in de **ayr**ste **kla**se

◀ **Your ticket isn't valid**
Uw kaartje is niet geldig
eww **kahr**tye is neet **ghehl**degh

◀ **The train has a 30 minutes delay**
De trein heeft 30 minuten vertraging
de traiyn hayft **dehr**tegh mee**new**ten ver**trah**ghing

plane

I would like to book a flight to London
Ik wil graag een vlucht reserveren naar Londen
ik wil ghragh en vlught rayser**veh**ren nahr londen

Where is the information desk?
Waar is de informatiebalie?
wahr is de infor**maht**see-**bah**lee

I would like to book a return flight to Liege
Ik wil graag een retourvlucht boeken naar Luik
ik wil ghragh en re**toor**vlught **boo**ken nahr lœk

◀ **Can I see your passport?**
Mag ik uw paspoort zien?
mahgh ik ew **pahs**poort zeen

I would like to cancel this flight
Ik wil deze vlucht annuleren
ik wil **day**ze vlught ahnnew**lay**ren

◀ **Your ticket is not valid**
Uw ticket is ongeldig/niet geldig
ew "ticket" is on**ghel**digh/neet **ghel**digh

Where is the check-in counter for the 8 p.m. flight to Amsterdam?
Waar is de incheckbalie voor de vlucht van 20.00 uur naar Amsterdam?
wahr is de "incheck"-**bah**lee voar de vlught vahn **twin**tigh ewr nahr ahmster**dahm**

◀ **Please put your metal objects here**
Metalen voorwerpen alstublieft hier neerleggen
may**tah**len **voar**werpen alstew**bleeft** heer **legh**ghen

◀ **Your boarding card please**
Uw instapkaart alstublieft
ew **in**stapkahrt alstew**bleeft**

UITGANG	EXIT
NGANG	ENTRANCE
NIETS AAN TE GEVEN	NOTHING TO DECLARE
ROOKRUIMTE	SMOKING AREA
VERBODEN TE ROKEN	NO SMOKING
BAGAGE OPHALEN	BAGGAGE CLAIM AREA
BAGAGEBAND	ONVEYOR BELT
VERTREK	DEPARTURE(S)
AANKOMST	ARRIVAL(S)
BINNENLANDSE VLUCHTEN	DOMESTIC FLIGHTS
INTERNATIONAAL	INTERNATIONAL FLIGHTS

◄ **Would you please open your bag?**
Wilt u uw tas openmaken?
wilt ew ew tahs **o**penmahken

◄ **Your plane will leave from gate A12**
Uw vliegtuig vertrekt van gate A12
ew **vleegh**tœgh ver**trek**t van "gate" ah twahlf

◄ **The flight to Amsterdam is delayed by one hour**
De vlucht naar Amsterdam heeft een vertraging van een uur
de vlught nahr ahmster**dahm** hayft en ver**trah**ghing van ayn ewr

◄ **The flight to Brussels has been cancelled**
De vlucht naar Brussel is geannuleerd
de vlught nahr **brus**sel is gheannew**lehrd**

Is this a non-smoking flight?
Is deze vlucht rookvrij?
is **day**ze vlught roak**vraiy**

I would like a seat by the window
Ik wil graag bij het raam/het gangpad zitten
ik wil ghrahgh by het rahm/het **ghahng**pahd **zit**ten

We would like to sit next to each other
Wij willen graag naast elkaar zitten
waiy **wil**len ghrahgh nahst el**kahr zit**ten

◄ **There are technical problems**
Er zijn technische problemen
er zaiyn **tegh**nieese pro**blay**men

I have a fear of flying
Ik heb last van vliegangst
ik heb last van **vleegh**ahngst

Would you call a doctor, please?
Wilt u een dokter waarschuwen?
wilt ew en **dok**ter **wahr**sghewen

My suitcase/rucksack has disappeared
Mijn koffer/rugzak is verdwenen
maiyn **kof**fer/**rugh**zahk is ver**dway**nen

airline company	vliegmaatschappij	**vleegh**-mahtsghappaiy
air port tax	luchthavenbelasting	**lught**hahven-be**las**ting
arrival/departure hall	aankomsthal/vertrekhal	**ahn**komsthahl/ver**trek**hahl

captain	gezagvoerder	ghe**zagh**voorder
customs	douane	doo**wah**ne
detection gate	detectiepoortje	day**tek**seepoartye
emergency exit	nooduitgang	**noad**œtghangh
emergency landing	noodlanding	**noad**lahnding
hand luggage	handbagage	hahndba**gha**zhe
landing	landen	**lahn**den
life vest	zwemvest	**zwem**vest
luggage control	bagagecontrole	ba**gha**zhe-con**troh**le
passport control	paspoortcontrole	**pahs**poart-con**troh**le
pilot	piloot	pee**loat**
purser	purser	"**pur**ser"
safety regulations	veiligheidsvoorschriften	**vaiy**lighhaiyds-**voars**ghriften
seat belt	stoelriem	**stool**reem
stewardess, air hostess	stewardess	"stewar**dess**"
stop	tussenlanding	tussen**lahn**ding
take off	opstijgen	**op**staiyghen
tax free shopping	belastingvrij winkelen	be**lahs**tingvraiy **win**kelen
terminal	terminal	"**ter**minal"
turbulence	turbulentie	turbew**len**tsee

boat service

I'd like to have a ticket to ...
Ik wil een kaartje naar ...
ik wil en **kahr**tye nahr ...

How much for a car and two passengers?
Wat kost het vervoer van een auto met 2 inzittenden?
wat kost heht ver**voor** van en **ou**toa meht tway in**zit**tenden?

I'd like to reserve a reclining seat/cabin
Ik wil een slaapstoel/hut reserveren
ik wil en **slahp**stool/hut rayser**vay**ren

on the outside	aan de buitenzijde	ahn de **bœt**enzaiyde
on the inside	aan de binnenzijde	ahn de **bi**nenzaiyde
with a shower	met douche	meht doosh
for three people	voor 3 personen	voar dree pehr**soa**nen

Can I take my bike aboard?
Kan de fiets mee op de boot?
kan de feets may op de boat?

When will the next boat sail?
Wanneer vaart de eerstvolgende boot af?
wahnnayr vahrt de **ayrst**volghende boat af?

How long does the passage take?
Hoe lang duurt de overtocht?
hoo lang dewrt de **oa**vertoght?

◀ **Follow the crew's instructions**
U moet de aanwijzingen van de bemanning volgen
ew moot de **ahn**waiyzingen van de be**ma**ning **vol**ghen

HIER OPSTELLEN	QUEUE HERE
MOTOR AFZETTEN	SWITCH OFF YOUR MOTOR
REDDINGSVESTEN	LIFE JACKETS
REDDINGSBOTEN	LIFEBOATS
ALLEEN PASSAGIERS	PASSENGERS ONLY
BENEDENDEK	LOWER DECK
TUSSENDEK	BETWEEN DECK
BOVENDEK	UPPER DECK
GEEN TOEGANG	NO ENTRY
NAAR HET AUTODEK	TO THE CAR DECK

cab

Could you call a cab for me?
Kunt u voor mij een taxi bellen
kunt ew voar maiy en **ta**xee **beh**len?

Is there a taxi rank around?
Waar is hier een taxistandplaats?
wahr is heer en **ta**xee-stantplahts?

To the ... please
Naar de/het ... alstublieft
nahr de/heht ... alstew**bleeft**

airport	vliegveld n	**vleegh**vehlt
railway station	(trein)station n	(**traiyn**)stahsyon
centre	centrum n	**sehn**trum
"Phoenix" Hotel	Hotel n "Phoenix"	hoa**tehl fø**niks
museum	museum n	mew**say**-yum
hospital	ziekenhuis n	**zee**kenhœs

Could you bring me to this address?
Wilt u mij naar dit adres brengen?
wilt ew maiy nahr dit ah**drehs brehng**en?

How much for the ride?
Wat gaat de rit kosten?
wat ghaht de rit **kos**ten?

Could you stop here?
Wilt u hier stoppen?
wilt ew heer **sto**pen?

How much do I owe you?
Hoeveel ben ik u schuldig?
hoovayl behn ik ew **sghul**degh?

Keep the change
Laat maar zitten
laht mahr **zi**ten

Can I have a receipt?
Mag ik een kwitantie?
magh ik en kwee**tan**see?

at the petrol station

Fill her up/Five litres* please
Voltanken/Vijf liter alstublieft
voltehnken/vaiyf **lee**ter alstew**bleeft**

Would you please check the ...?
Wilt u de/het ... even nakijken?
wilt ew de/heht ... **ay**ven **nah**kaiyken?

brake fluid	remvloeistof	**rehm**vlooystof
front lights	verlichting vóór	ver**ligh**ting voar
oil level	oliepeil *n*	**oa**leepaiyl
rear lights	verlichting achter	ver**ligh**ting **agh**ter
tyre pressure	bandenspanning	**ban**denspaning
water level	waterpeil *n*	**wah**terpaiyl

Do you have a road map?
Heeft u een wegenkaart?
hayft ew en **way**ghenkahrt?

Are there any toilets here?
Is hier een toilet aanwezig?
is heer en twah**leht** ahn**way**zegh?

notices

EURO LOODVRIJ 95	UNLEADED 95
SUPER PLUS LOODVRIJ 98	SUPER UNLEADED 98
SUPER MET LOODVERVANGER 98	LRP
DIESEL	DIESEL
LPG	LPG
MENGSMERING	PETROIL/TWO-STROKE MIXTURE
LUCHT	AIR
WATER	WATER
ZELFBEDIENING	SELF-SERVICE
AUTOWASSEN/WASTUNNEL	CAR WASH

* the common fluid measure (5 litres = 1.1 gallon)

Could you please ...?
Kunt u ...?
kunt ew ...?

fill this petrol can	deze jerrycan vullen	**day**ze "jerry can" **vu**len
repair this tyre	deze band reparen	**day**ze bant raypah**ray**ren
change this tyre	deze band verwisselen	**day**ze bant ver**wi**selen
pump/inflate the tyres	de banden oppompen	de **ban**den **op**-pompen
clean the windows	de ruiten schoonmaken	de **rœ**ten **sghoan**mahken
clean the windscreen	de vooruit schoonmaken	de **voar**œt **sghoan**mahken
give me a receipt	een kwitantie geven	en kwee**tan**see **ghay**ven
wash the car	de auto wassen	de **ou**toa **wa**sen
charge the battery	de accu vullen	de **a**kew **vu**len
change the oil	de olie ververssen	de **oa**lee ver**vehr**sen
change the sparking plugs	de bougies verwisselen	de boo**zhees** ver**wi**selen
call a breakdown van/truck	een takelwagen bellen	en **tah**kelwahghen **beh**len

Where is the nearest garage/bicycle repair shop?
Waar is een garage/fietsenmaker?
wahr is en ghah**rah**zhe/**feet**senmahker?

I have trouble with the ...
Ik heb een defect aan de/het ...
ik hehp en de**fehkt** ahn de/heht ...

I am losing oil/petrol
Ik verlies olie/benzine
ik ver**lees oa**lee/behn**zee**ne

I have a flat front/rear tyre
Ik heb een lekke voorband/achterband
ik hehp en **leh**ke **voar**bant/**ahght**erbant

I hear a strange noise
Ik hoor een vreemd geluid
ik hoar en vraymt ghe**lœt**

The car won't start
De wagen wil niet starten
de **wah**gen wil neet **star**ten

The engine is overheated
De motor raakt oververhit
de **moa**tor rahkt oaverver**hit**

The battery is flat
De accu is leeg
de **a**kew is laygh

Could you repair/change the ...?
Kunt u de/het ... repareren/verwisselen?
kunt ew de/heht ... raypah**ray**ren/ver**wi**selen

Do you have the parts in stock?
Hebt u de onderdelen in voorraad?
hehpt ew de **on**derdaylen in **voa**raht?

I can have the parts sent in from Britain/America
Ik kan onderdelen uit Engeland/Amerika laten overkomen
ik kan **on**derdaylen œt **ehng**elant/ah**may**reekaa **lah**ten **oa**verkoamen

When will the car/motorcycle/bicycle be ready?
Wanneer is de auto/motor/fiets weer klaar?
wanayr is de **ou**toa/**moa**tor/feets wayr klahr?

Till what time can I pick it up?
Tot hoe laat kan ik hem afhalen?
tot hoo laht kan ik hehm **af**hahlen?

Do you have any idea how much it will be?
Heeft u een idee hoeveel het gaat kosten?
hayft ew en ee**day** hoovayl heht ghaht **kos**ten?

I have come to pick up my car/motorcycle/bicycle
Ik kom mijn auto/motor/fiets afhalen
ik kom maiyn **ou**toa/**moa**tor/feets **af**hahlen

Have you found the defect?
Heeft u het mankement kunnen vinden?
hayft ew heht **man**kemehnt **ku**nen **vin**den?

Can I pay with a traveller's letter of credit?
Kan ik betalen met de reis- en kredietbrief?
kan ik be**tah**len meht de raiys- ehn kre**deet**breef?

car parts

The parts indicated by * are not shown in the illustration (page 56-58)

23	**accelerator pedal**	gaspedaal *n*	**ghas**pedahl
52	**backrest**	rugleuning	**rugh**løning
2	**battery**	accu	**a**kew
*32	**bearing**	lager	**lah**gher
34	**bonnet**	motorkap	**moa**torkap
28	**boot**	kofferruimte	**ko**fer-rœmte
*27	**boot lid**	kofferdeksel *n*	**ko**ferdehksel
46	**brake, brake pedal**	rem, rempedaal *n*	**rehm**, **rehm**pedahl
47	**brake calliper**	remklauw	**rem**klow
49	**brake disc**	remschijf	**rehm**sghaiyf
48	**brake light, stoplight**	remlicht *n*	**rehm**light
10	**bumper**	bumper	"bumper"
	front bumper	voorbumper	**voar**bumper
	rear bumper	achterbumper	**agh**ter-bumper

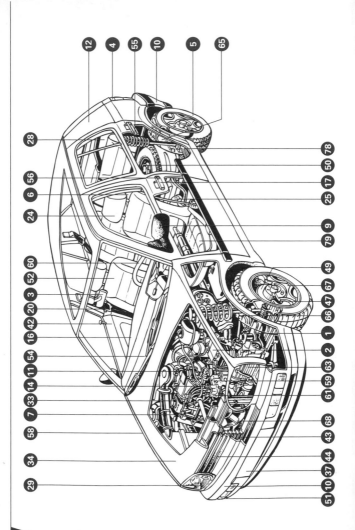

*29	camshaft	nokkenas	**no**ken-as
25	catalyst	katalysator	kahtahlee**sah**tor
11	carburettor	carburateur	karbew**rah**tor
42	car door	portier n	por**teer**
*13	chassis	chassis n	sha**see**
30	clutch pedal	koppelingpedaal n	**ko**pelingpedahl
*12	coachwork	carrosserie	ka-ro-se-**ree**
*21	connecting rod	drijfstang	**draiyf**stang
26	cooling water pipe	koelwaterleiding	**kool**wahterlaiyding
*31	crankshaft	krukas	**kruk**as
*13	cylinder crankcase	cilinderblok n	see**lin**derblok
*14	cylinder head	cilinderkop	see**lin**derkop
16	dashboard	dashboard n	"dashboard"
*75	defroster vent	voorruitverwarming	**voa**-rœt-ver-war-ming
*19	distribution belt	distributieriem	distri**bewt**seereem
*18	dipped beam	dimlicht n	**dim**light
17	door handle	deurkruk	**dør**kruk
1	drive shaft	aandrijfas	**ahn**drive-as
22	dynamo	dynamo	dee**nah**mo
23	engine mounting	motorophanging	**moa**tor-ophanging
65	exhaust	uitlaat	**œt**laht
*64	exhaust valve	uitlaatklep	**œt**lahtklehp
68	fan	ventilator	vehntee**lah**tor
71	fan belt	ventilatorriem	vehntee**lah**tor-reem
*69	fan clutch for viscous drive	ventilatorkoppeling	vehntee**lah**tor-kopeling
*74	flywheel	vliegwiel n	**vleegh**weel
8	fuel supply line	brandstofleiding	**brant**stof-laiyding
*73	(multi-speed) gearbox	versnellingsbak	ver**sneh**lings-bak
63	gearing	transmissie	trans**mi**see
72	gear (lever)	versnelling(shandle)	ver**sneh**ling(s-"handle")
29	headlight	koplamp	**kop**lamp
24	headrest	hoofdsteun	**hoaft**støn
*15	horn	claxon	**klak**son
16	ignition distributor	stroomverdeler	**stroam**verdayler
51	indicator light	richtingaanwijzer	**righ**ting-ahnwaiyzer
3	inside rear-view mirror	achteruitkijkspiegel	aghter**œt**kaiyk-speeghel
41	ignition	ontsteking	ont**stay**king
56	lock	slot n	slot
37	number plate	nummerplaat	**num**merplaht
*38	oil filter	oliefilter	**oa**leefilter
*39	oil pipe	olieleiding	**oa**leelaiyding

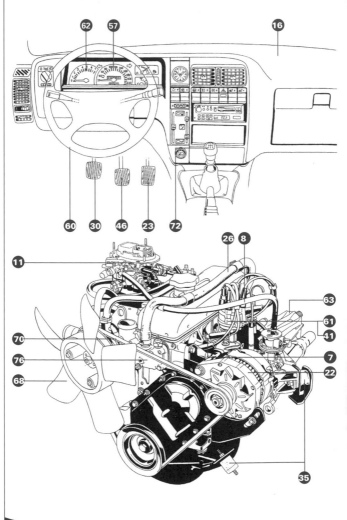

*40	oil pump	oliepomp	**oa**leepomp
6	petrol tank	benzinetank	behn**zee**ne-"tank"
*80	piston	zuiger	**zœ**gher
43	radiator	radiator	rah-dee**yah**tor
44	radiator grill	radiatorgrill	rah-dee**yah**tor-ghril
*45	reflector	reflector	re**flehk**tor
62	rev counter	toerenteller	**too**renteller
4	reversing light	achteruitrijlicht *n*	aghter-**œt**-raiy-light
67	rim	velg	vehlgh
79	seat	zitting	**zi**ting
	front seats	voorzitting	**voar**ziting
	rear seats	achterziting	**agh**ter-ziting
55	shock absorber	schokdemper	**sghok**dehmper
50	spare wheel	reservewiel *n*	re**sehr**ve-weel
7	sparking plug	bougie	boo**zhee**
57	speedometer	snelheidsmeter	**snehl**haiyts-mayter
59	starter	startmotor	**start**motor
60	steering wheel	stuurwiel *n*	**stewr**weel
66	strut unit	veerpoot	**vehr**poat
*71	suspension	vering	**vay**ring
20	three-point seat belt	driepuntsgordel	**dree**puntsghordel
5	tyre	band	bant
76	water pump	waterpomp	**wah**terpomp
77	wheel	wiel *n*	weel
	front wheel	voorwiel *n*	**voar**weel
	rear wheel	achterwiel *n*	**agh**ter-weel
78	wheel suspension	wielophanging	**weel**ophahnging
53	window	ruit	rœt
	windscreen	voorruit	**voar**rœt
	side window	zijruit	**zaiy**rœt
	rear window	achterruit	**agh**te-rœt
54	windscreen wiper	ruitenwisser	**rœ**tenwisser
58	wing	spatbord *n*	**spat**bort
9	wing mirror	buitenspiegel	**bœ**ten-speeghel

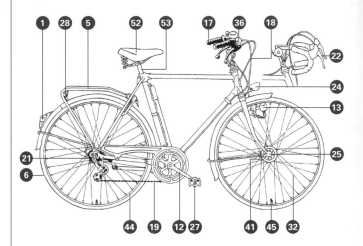

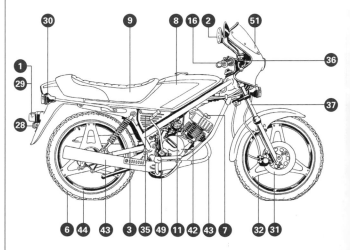

The parts indicated by * are not shown in the illustration.

4	axle	as	as
39	back-pedal brake	terugtraprem	te**rught**rap-rehm
*23	ball race	kogellager	**koa**ghel-lahgher
15	bicycle lock	fietsslot *n*	**feets**-slot
14	bicycle pump	fietspomp	**feets**pomp
52	bicycle saddle	zadel *n*	**zah**del
18	cable	kabel	**kah**bel
	brake cable	remkabel	**rehm**kahbel
	gear cable	versnellingskabel	ver**sneh**lings-kahbel
	throttle cable	gaskabel	**ghas**kahbel
11	carburettor	carburator	karbew**rah**tor
5	(luggage) carrier	bagagedrager	bah**ghah**zhe-drahgher
19	chain	ketting	**keh**ting
20	chain guard	kettingkast	**keh**tingkast
21	chain wheel	kettingwiel *n*	**keh**tingweel
31	disc brake	schijfrem	**sghaiy**frehm
41	drum brake	trommelrem	**tro**mel-rehm
13	dynamo	dynamo	dee**naa**moa
43	exhaust	uitlaat	**œt**laht
49	footrest	voetsteun	**voot**støn
*47	four-stroke engine	viertaktmotor	**veer**taktmoator
8	fuel tank	brandstoftank	**brant**stof-"tank"
*46	gear-change, gear shift	versnelling	ver**sneh**ling
22	hand brake	knijprem	**knaiyp**rehm
36	handlebars	stuur *n*	stewr
17	handles	handvatten	**hant**vatten
24	headlamp	koplamp	**kop**lamp
25	hub	naaf	nahf
30	indicator (light)	richtingaanwijzer	**righ**ting-ahnwaiyzer
34	kick stand	standaard	**stan**dahrt
33	mudguard	spatbord *n*	**spat**bort
*26	oil tank	olietank	**oa**lee-"tank"
27	pedal	pedaal *n*	pe**dahl**
12	pedal crank	crank	"crank"
9	racing-style twin seat	buddyseat	"buddy seat"
3	rear fork	achtervork	**agh**tervork
1	rear light	achterlicht *n*	**agh**terlight
2	rear-view mirror	achteruitkijkspiegel	agh-ter-**œt**-kaiyk-speeghel
28	reflector	reflector	reflehktor

*40	rev counter	toerenteller	**too**rentehler
44	rim	velg	vehlgh
53	seat pillar	zadelpen	**zah**delpehn
7	spark plug	bougie	boo**zhee**
32	spoke	spaak	spahk
35	starter	starter	**star**ter
29	tail light	remlicht *n*	**rehm**light
37	telescopic shock absorber	telescoopvork	tayles**koap**vork
16	throttle twist grip	gashandel	**ghas**-"handle"
10	tubular frame	buisframe *n*	**bœs**fraym
42	two-stroke engine	tweetaktmotor	**tway**taktmoator
6	tyre	band	bant
	front tyre	voorband	**voar**bant
	rear tyre	achterband	**agh**terbant
	(inner) tube	binnenband	**bi**nenbant
	tyre	buitenband	**bœ**tenbant
45	valve, valve tube	ventiel *n*, ventielslang	vehn**teel**, vehn**teel**slang
50	wheel	wiel *n*	weel
	front wheel	voorwiel *n*	**voar**weel
	rear wheel	achterwiel *n*	**agh**terweel
51	windscreen	windscherm *n*	**wint**sghehrm
*48	wing/butterfly nut	vleugelmoer	**vlø**ghelmoor

nature of the damage

blocked, clogged	verstopt	ver**stopt**
broken	gebroken	ghe**broa**ken
burnt-out	doorgebrand	**doar**ghebrant
burst	gebarsten	ghe**bars**ten
dirty	vuil	vœl
frozen	bevroren	be**vroa**ren
jammed	geblokkeerd	gheblo**kayrt**
makes a noise	maakt lawaai	mahkt lah**wahy**
not properly set/aligned	verkeerd afgesteld	ver**kayrt af**ghestehlt
overheated	oververhit	oaverver**hit**
punctured	lek	lehk
rusty	verroest	ve**roost**
short-circuits	maakt kortsluiting	mahkt **kort**slœting
stuck	klemt	klehmt
vibrates	trilt	trilt
worn out	versleten	ver**slay**ten

(see also "Problems encountered in town" and "Medical assistance")

There has been an accident!
Er is een ongeluk gebeurd!
ehr is en **on**gheluk ghe**børt**!

There is only material damage
Er is alleen materiële schade
ehr is a**layn** mah-tay-ree-**yay**-le **sghah**de

May I please call the police?
Kan ik hier de politie bellen?
kan ik heer de poa**lee**tsee **beh**len?

Don't touch him/her
Raak hem/haar niet aan
rahk hehm/hahr neet ahn

◄ **Who is the driver?**
Wie is de bestuurder?
wee is de be**stewr**der?

◄ **I'll have to book you**
Ik moet een proces-verbaal opmaken
ik moot en proa**sehs**-ver**bahl op**mahken

The other party made a mistake
De ander heeft een fout gemaakt
de **an**der hayft en fout ghe**mahkt**

◄ **You have ...**
U hebt/bent ...
ew hehpt/behnt ...

There are (no) casualties
Er zijn (geen) gewonden
ehr zaiyn (ghayn) ghe**won**den

Call the police/an ambulance
Waarschuw de politie/een ambulance
wahrsghew de poa**lee**tsee/en ambew**lan**se

Wait for the doctor/ambulance
Wacht op een dokter/ambulance
waght op en **dok**ter/ambew**lan**se

◄ **May I see your driving license/insurance papers?**
Mag ik uw rijbewijs/verzekeringspapieren zien?
magh ik ew **raiy**bewaiys/ver**zay**kerings-pahpeeren zeen?

◄ **Are there any witnesses?**
Zijn er getuigen?
zaiyn ehr ghe**tœ**ghen?

◄ **You are (not) to blame for this accident**
U hebt (geen) schuld aan dit ongeval
ew hehpt (ghayn) sghult ahn dit **on**gheval

been speeding	te snel gereden	te snehl ghe**ray**den
cut in	verkeerd ingevoegd	ver**kayrt in**ghevoogt
failed to give way	geen voorrang verleend	ghayn **voa**rang ver**laynt**
incorrectly overtaken	onjuist ingehaald	on**yœst in**ghe-hahlt
jumped the lights	door rood (licht) gereden	doar roat (light) ghe**ray**den

◀ **You will be fined for this**
U krijgt hiervoor een bekeuring
ew kraiyght heer**voar** en be**kø**ring

◀ **You'll have to come to the office**
U moet even mee naar het bureau
ew moot **ay**ven may nahr heht bew**roa**

◀ **You will have to undergo a breathalyzer/blood test**
U moet een blaastest doen/bloedproef laten afnemen
ew moot en **blah**stest doon/**bloowd**proof **lah**ten **af**naymen

◀ **You may/are not allowed to drive on**
U mag (niet) verder rijden
ew mahgh (neet) **vehr**der **raiy**den

◀ **You can settle the matter amicably**
U kunt de zaak onderling schikken
ew kunt de zahk **on**derling **sghi**ken

◀ **Your car will be confiscated for inspection**
Uw auto wordt voor controle in beslag genomen
eww **ou**toa wort voar kon**tro**le in be**slagh** ghe**noa**men

I would like to have your details for insurance purposes
Ik wil graag uw gegevens voor de verzekering
ik wil ghrahgh eww ghe**ghay**vens voar de ver**zay**kering

◀ **Would you sign here?**
Wilt u dit tekenen?
wilt ew dit **tay**kenen?

I can't read this
Ik kan dit niet lezen
ik kan dit neet **lay**zen

third-party insurance	WA-verzekering	way-ah ver**zay**kering
comprehensive insurance	all-riskverzekering	"all-risk" ver**zay**kering
road patrol	wegenwacht	**way**ghenwaght
emergency telephone	praatpaal	**praht**pahl

A accommodation

asking for directions

Where is the "Phoenix" Hotel?
Waar is hotel "Phoenix"?
wahr is hoa**tehl fø**niks?

Is there a hotel/guesthouse around?
Is hier in de buurt een hotel/pension?
is heer in de bewrt en hoa**tehl**/pehn**syon**?

Is there a camping site nearby?
Is hier in de buurt een camping?
is heer in de bewrt en **cam**ping?

Can we camp on private property?
Kunnen wij op een privéterrein kamperen?
kunnen waiy op en pree**vay**-terraiyn kahm**peh**ren

Where is the 'Zeezicht' camping site?
Waar is camping 'Zeezicht'?
wahr is de **cam**ping **zay**zihght

Where is the tourist information office
Waar is het VVV-kantoor?
wahr is het vay-vay-**vay**-kahntoar

Could you show it on the map?
Kunt u het op de kaart aanwijzen?
kunt ew het op de kahrt **ahn**waiyzen

checking in

I have a room reservation
Ik heb een kamer gereserveerd
ik hehp en **kah**mer gerayser**vayrt**

My name is ...
Mijn naam is ...
maiyn nahm is ...

Are there any vacancies?
Heeft u nog kamers vrij?
hayft ew nogh **kah**mers vraiy?

◄ **Do you have a voucher/confirmation?**
Hebt u een voucher/reserveringsbevestiging?
hehpt ew en "voucher"/rayser**vay**rings-be-veh-ste-ghing?

◄ **No, the hotel is fully booked**
Nee, het hotel is vol(geboekt)
nay, heht hoa**tehl** is **vol**(ghebookt)

I'd like to have a ...
Ik wil graag een ...
ik wil ghrahgh en ...

single room	eenpersoonskamer	**ayn**-per-soans-kah-mer
double room	tweepersoonskamer	**tway**-per-soans-kah-mer
apartment	appartement *n*	a**par**temehnt

with a bath	met bad n	meht bat
with a shower	met douche	meht doosh
with a toilet	met toilet n	meht twah**leht**
with running water	met stromend water n	meht **stroa**ment **wah**ter
with a kitchenette	met kitchenette	meht "kitchenette"
with a double bed	met tweepersoonsbed	meht **tway**-per-soans-beht
with twin beds	met lits-jumeaux	meht lee-zhew**moa**
with an extra bed	met een extra bed	meht en **ehx**trah beht
with a cot	met een kinderbedje n	meht en **kin**derbehtye
with air conditioning	met airconditioning	meht "air conditioning"
with a telephone	met telefoon	meht tayle**foan**
with a radio	met radio	meht **rah**deeyoa
with a television	met televisie	meht tayle**vee**see
with a minibar	met een minibar	met en "**mi**nibar"
with a balcony	met balkon n	meht bal**kon**
with a terrace	met terras n	meht teh**ras**
overlooking/with a view of the sea	met zeezicht n	meht **zay**zight
facing the street	aan de straatzijde	ahn de **straht**zaiyde
at the back	aan de achterzijde	ahn de **agh**terzaiyde
on the ground floor	op de begane grond	op de be**ghah**ne ghront
on a low floor	op een lage verdieping	op en **lah**ghe ver**dee**ping
on a high floor	op een hoge verdieping	op en **hoa**ghe ver**dee**ping

I/We will be staying for only one night/... nights
Ik blijf/we blijven alleen deze nacht/... nachten
ik blaiyf/we **blaiy**ven a**layn day**ze naght/... **nagh**ten

notices

RECEPTIE	RECEPTION
SLEUTELBORD	KEY RACK
KASSIER	CASHIER
ONTBIJTZAAL	BREAKFAST ROOM
RESTAURANT	RESTAURANT
ADMINISTRATIE	ADMINISTRATION
DAMES	LADIES
HEREN	GENTS
KAPPER	HAIRDRESSER
REISBUREAU	TRAVEL AGENCY
LIFT	LIFT

I'd like to have ...
Ik wil graag ...
ik wil ghrahgh ...

accommodation only	alleen logies	a**layn** loa**zhees**
bed and breakfast	logies en ontbijt	loa**zhees** ehn ont**baiyt**
half board	half pension	half pehn**syon**
full board	volledig pension	vo**lay**degh pehn**syon**

How much is the room ...?
Hoeveel kost de kamer ...?
hoovayl kost de **kah**mer ...?

a night	per nacht	pehr naght
a week	per week	pehr wayk
a fortnight	per 2 weken	pehr tway **way**ken

Can I pay with a credit card?
Kan ik betalen met een creditcard?
kan ik be**tah**len meht en "creditcard"?

◄ **Would you please fill in this form?**
Wilt u dit formulier invullen?
wilt ew dit formew**leer in**vullen?

◄ **May I have your passport?**
Mag ik uw paspoort (hebben)?
magh ik eww **pas**poart (**heb**ben)?

◄ **Your room number is ...**
Uw kamernummer is ...
eww **kah**mernumer is ...

◄ **Unfortunately, your room is not ready yet**
De kamer is helaas nog niet vrij
de **kah**mer is hay**lahs** nogh neet vraiy

◄ **Your room will be ready at .. o'clock**
U kunt vanaf .. uur op uw kamer terecht
ew kunt van**af** .. ewr op eww **kah**mer te**rehght**

◄ **Here is your key**
Hier is uw sleutel
heer is eww **slø**tel

◄ **It's on the ... floor**
Het is op de ... verdieping
heht is op de ... ver**dee**ping

◄ **The lift is over there**
Daar vindt u de lift
dahr vint ew de lift

Can anybody help me with my luggage?
Kan iemand mij met mijn bagage helpen?
kan **ee**mant maiy meht maiyn bah**ghah**zhe **hehl**pen?

◄ **Your luggage will be brought to your room**
Uw bagage wordt gebracht
eww bah**ghah**zhe wort ghe**braght**

At what time is breakfast being served?
Om hoe laat kan ik ontbijten?
om hoo laht kan ik ont**baiy**ten?

Where will breakfast be served?
Waar wordt het ontbijt geserveerd?
wahr wort heht ont**baiyt** gesehr**vayrt**?

Could I have my key? Number ...
Mag ik mijn sleutel hebben? Nummer ...
magh ik maiyn **slø**tel **heh**ben? **Nu**mer ...

I would like to check out
Ik wil uitchecken
ik wil **œt**shehken

Could I have the bill, please?
Wilt u de rekening voor mij opmaken, alstublieft?
wilt ew de **ray**kening voar maiy **op**mahken, alstew**bleeft**?

disabled travellers

Is there an entrance for wheelchairs?
Is er een rolstoelingang?
is er en **roll**stool-**in**ghang

Is this building accessible to wheelchairs?
Is dit gebouw toegankelijk voor rolstoelen?
is dit ghe**baow** too**ghahn**kelik voar **roll**stoolen

I am ...
Ik ben ...
ik ben

phisically/mentally handicapped	lichamelijk/verstandelijk gehandicapt	li**gha**melik/**verstahn**delik ghe**han**dicapt
hard of hearing	slechthorend	sleght**hoa**rend
partially sighted	slechtziend	sleght**zeend**
depending on a wheelchair	afhankelijk van een rolstoel	ahf**hahn**kelik vahn en **roll**stool
epileptic	epileptisch	aypee**lep**tees

I am suffering from ...
Ik heb .../Ik lijd aan ...
ik heb/ik laiyd ahn

ME/fatigue symptoms	ME/een vermoeidheids-ziekte	em-ay/en ver**mooyd**haiyds-**zeek**te
RSI	rsi	er-es-ee

Would you please speak a bit slower/louder?
Wilt u alstublieft wat langzamer/duidelijker praten?
wilt ew alstew**bleeft** waht **lahng**zahmer/**dœ**deliker **prah**ten

Would you please hold the door open for me?
Wilt u de deur alstublieft voor mij open houden?
wilt ew de duhr alstew**bleeft** voar my **o**pen **how**den

Would you please get me ... ?
Wilt u ... even voor mij pakken?
wilt ew ... **ay**ven voar my **pahk**ken

The door is too narrow
De deur is te smal
de duhr is te smahl

Where is the nearest elevator?
Waar is de dichtstbijzijnde lift?
wahr is de **dightst**-baiyzaiynde lift

Is there a toilet/bathroom foor disabled persons?
Is er een invalidentoilet/wasruimte?
is er en invale**ee**den-twa**let**/**wahs**rœmte

point	aanwijzen	**ahn**waiyzen
logo for disabled persons	invalidenvignet	invah**lee**den-vin**yet**
parking for the disabled	parkeerplaats voor invaliden	pahr**kehr**plahts vaor invah**lee**den
ground level	gelijkvloers	ghelaiyk**vloors**
guide dog	blindengeleidehond	**blin**den-ghe**laiy**dehond
automatic door	automatische deur	owto**mah**teese duhr
ramp for a wheelchair	(rolstoel)oprit	(**roll**stool)oprit
slope	helling	**hel**ling

information, service, complaints

Where can I park my car?
Waar kan ik de auto parkeren?
wahr kan ik de **ou**toa par**kayr**en?

◄ **We have our own car park (indoors/outdoors)**
We hebben een eigen parkeerterrein/parkeergarage
we **heh**ben en **aiy**ghen par**kayr**tehraiyn/par**kayr**-ghah-rah-zhe

◄ **That will cost an extra ... euros a day**
Dat kost u ... euro extra per dag
dat kost ew ... **uh**ro **ehx**trah pehr dagh

Can I use room service?
Kan ik gebruik maken van de roomservice?
kan ik ghe**brœk mah**ken van de "roomservice"?

Do you have a map of the town?
Heeft u een plattegrond van de stad?
hayft ew en platte**ghront** van de stat?

Do you have a list of events?
Heeft u een evenementenlijst?
hayft ew en ayvene**mehn**tenlaiyst?

Could you order a taxi for me?
Kunt u voor mij een taxi bestellen?
kunt ew vaor maiy en **tax**ee be**stehl**en?

I would like to make a phone call to ...
Ik wil graag een telefoongesprek met ...
ik wil ghrahgh en tayle**foan**ghesprehk meht ...

I would like an outside line
Ik wil graag een buitenlijn
ik wil ghrahgh en **bœ**tenlaiyn

Could you wake me tomorrow at ...?
Wilt u mij morgen wekken om ...?
wilt ew maiy **mor**ghen **weh**ken om ...?

Can I have breakfast/lunch/dinner in my room?
Kan ik op de kamer ontbijten/lunchen/dineren?
kahn ik op de **kah**mer ont**baiy**ten/**lun**shen/dee**nay**ren?

Has anyone left a message for me?
Is er een boodschap voor mij achtergelaten?
is ehr en **boat**sghap voar maiy **agh**ter-ghelahten?

I am expecting a visitor
Ik verwacht een bezoeker
ik ver**waght** en be**zoo**ker

I'll wait ...
Ik wacht ...
ik waght ...

here	hier	heer
in the bar	in de bar	in de bar
in the lounge	in de lounge	in de "lounge"
in the restaurant	in het restaurant	in heht rehstoa**rant**
in my room	op mijn kamer	op maiyn **kah**mer

Could you put this in the safe?
Kunt u dit in de safe bewaren?
kunt ew dit in de "safe" be**wah**ren?

Can I leave my luggage here?
Kan ik deze bagage hier laten staan?
kan ik **day**ze bah**ghah**zhe heer **lah**ten stahn?

The room has not been cleaned
De kamer is niet schoongemaakt
de **kah**mer is neet **sghoan**ghemahkt

The bed linen has not been changed
Het beddengoed is niet verschoond
heht **beh**de(n)ghoot is neet ver**sghoant**

I have no ...
Ik heb geen ...
ik hehp ghayn ...

towel	handdoek	**han**dook
bath towel	badhanddoek	**bat**handook
soap	zeep	zayp
plug	afvoerstop	**af**voorstop
toilet paper	toiletpapier *n*	twah**leht**pahpeer
wastepaper basket	prullenbak	**prul**-en-bak
pillow case	kussensloop *n*	**kus**-en-sloap
coat hangers	klerenhangers	**klay**ren-hangers

The ... doesn't/don't work
Er is een defect aan de/het ...
ehr is en de**fehkt** ahn de/heht ...

air conditioning	airconditioning	"air conditioning"
heating	verwarming	ver**war**ming
lights	verlichting	ver**ligh**ting
television set	televisietoestel *n*, t.v.	tayle**vee**see-toostehl, tay-vay
shower	douche	doosh
drainage	afvoer	**af**voor

The window cannot be opened/closed
Het raam kan niet open/dicht
heht rahm kan neet **oa**pen/dight

I would like to have an extra blanket/pillow
Ik wil graag een extra deken/kussen
ik wil ghrahgh en **eh**xtrah **day**ken/**kus**en

Could you send up a chambermaid/repairman?
Kunt u een kamermeisje/reparateur sturen?
kunt ew en **kah**mermaiysye/raypahrah**tør** stew**ren?

My room has been broken into/Something has been stolen
Er is bij mij ingebroken/Er is iets gestolen
ehr is baiy maiy **in**ghebroaken/ehr is eets ghe**stoa**len

I would like to have another room
Ik wil graag een andere kamer
ik wil ghrahgh en **an**dere **kah**mer

I am moving into another hotel
Ik neem een ander hotel
ik naym en **an**der hoa**tehl**

on the camp site

Good morning/Good afternoon/Good evening
Goedemorgen/Goedemiddag/Goedenavond
ghoode**mor**ghen/ghooden**mid**dagh/ghooden**ah**vond

I am looking for a spot to put ...
Ik zoek een plaats voor ...
ik zook en **plahts** voar

a (small) tent	een (kleine) tent	en (**klaiy**n) tent
two tents	twee tenten	tway **ten**ten
a car with a caravan	een auto met caravan	en **ow**to met "**ca**ravan"
a car and a trailer tent	een auto met vouwwagen	en **ow**to met **vow**waghen
a camper/camper van	een camper/een kampeerbus	en "camper"/en kahm**pehr**bus

◄ **I'm sorry, the camp site is full**
Het spijt me, de camping is vol
het spaiyt meh, de "**cam**ping" is vol

◄ **That is possible**
Dat is mogelijk
daht is **mo**ghelik

◄ **This is a private/members only camp site**
Dit is een besloten camping
dit is en be**slow**ten "camping"

Do you accept the CCI?
Accepteert u de CCI?
ahksep**tehrt** ew de say-say-ee

We do not know yet how long we shall be staying
Wij weten nog niet hoe lang wij hier blijven
waiy **way**ten nogh neet hoo lahng waiy heer **blaiy**ven

We shall be staying here for ...
Wij blijven hier ...
waiy **blaiy**ven heer

one night	één nacht	ayn naght
two nights	twee nachten	tway **nagh**ten
three nights	drie nachten	dree **nagh**ten
four nights	vier nachten	veer **nagh**ten
one week	een week	en wayk
two weeks (a fortnight)	twee weken	tway **way**ken

What is the price per site?
Wat is de prijs per plaats?
waht is de praiys per plahts

What does the price include?
Wat is bij de prijs inbegrepen?
waht is baiy de praiys inbe**ghray**pen

How much will it be per/for each ... ?
Wat kost het per ... ?
waht kost het per

night	nacht	naght
week	week	wayk
person	persoon	per**soan**
adult	volwassene	vol**wahs**sene
child	kind	kihnd
tent	tent	tent
caravan	caravan	"**ca**ravan"
car	auto	**ow**to
motorcycle/bicycle	motor/fiets	**mo**tor/feets

◀ **May I see your camping card/membership card?**
Mag ik uw kampeercarnet/lidmaatschapskaart zien?
magh ik ew kahm**pehr**-karnet/**lid**mahtsghaps-kahrt zeen

Do I get a discount with this?
Krijg ik hiermee korting?
kraiygh ik **heer**may **kohr**ting

◀ **Could you fill this in please?**
Wilt u dit invullen?
wilt ew dit **in**vullen

May we park the car next to the tent?
Mag de auto bij de tent staan?
magh de **ow**to baiy de tent stahn

May I choose a place myself?
Mag ik zelf een plaats uitzoeken?
makh ik zelf en plahts **œt**zooken

Where am I allowed to camp?
Waar mag ik staan?
wahr magh ik stahn

Can we camp together?
Mogen wij bij elkaar staan?
mowghen waiy baiy el**kahr** stahn

Does the site have a number?
Heeft de plek een nummer?
hayft de plek en **num**mer

Is there a bicycle shed?
Is er een fietsenstalling?
is er en **feet**sen-**stahl**ling

◄ Yes, but only if on a lead
Ja, maar alleen aan de lijn
yah, mahr ahl**layn** ahn de laiyn

◄ With a key/security card
Met een sleutelkaart/magneetkaart
met en **slø**telkahrt/magh**nayt**kahrt

Is the camp site guarded?
Is de camping bewaakt?
is de "**cam**ping" be**wahkt**

Are dogs allowed on the camp site?
Mag de hond op de camping?
magh de hond op de "**cam**ping"

How do you raise the barrier?
Hoe gaat de slagboom omhoog?
hoo ghaht de **slagh**boam om**hoagh**

What is the latest we have to be back?
Tot hoe laat kunnen wij nog binnenkomen?
tot hoo laht **kun**nen waiy nogh **bin**nenkohmen

May I attach an awning to the caravan?
Mag ik aan de caravan een voortent zetten?
magh ik ahn de "**ca**ravan" en **voar**tent **zet**ten

Can I rent a tent/bungolow/caravan/linen here?
Kan ik hier een tent/bungalow/caravan/linnengoed huren?
kan ik heer en tehnt/"bungalow"/"caravan"/**lin**ne(n)ghoot **hew**ren?

Is there any electricity here?
Is er een aansluiting voor elektriciteit?
is ehr en **ahn**slœting voar ay-lehk-tree-see-**taiyt**?

Can I hire a ...?
Kan ik een ... huren?
kahn ik en ... **hew**ren

bicycle	fiets	feets
motor scooter	scooter	'scooter'
mountain bike	mountainbike	'mountainbike'
tent	tent	tent
canoe	kano	**kah**no
rowing boat	roeiboot	**rooy**boot
sailing boat	zeilboot	**zaiyl**boot

Can I have my gas cylinders filled/replaced here?
Kan ik hier gasflessen laten vullen/omwisselen?
kan ik heer **ghas**flehsen **lah**ten **vul**en/**om**wisselen?

Are we allowed to make campfires/barbecue on the camp site?
Mogen wij op de camping vuur maken/barbecuen?
moghen waiy op de "**cam**ping" vewr **mah**ken/"**bar**becue"-en

We are leaving, can I have the bill please?
Wij gaan vertrekken, mag ik afrekenen?
waiy ghahn ver**trehk**ken, magh ik af**ray**kenen

◄ **Here is your bill**
Hier is uw rekening
heer is ew **ray**kening

Do you accept credit cards?
Neemt u een creditcard aan?
naymt ew en "**cre**ditcard" ahn

◄ **Thank you very much. Have a safe journey!**
Dank u wel. Goede reis!
dahnk ew wel. **ghoo**de raiys

camping along the road

Is unauthorized camping allowed here?
Mag je hier vrij kamperen?
mahgh ye heer vraiy kahm**peh**ren

◄ **No, only on an official camp site**
Nee, alleen op een officiële camping
nay, ahl**layn** op en offi**sjay**le "**cam**ping"

◄ **Yes, if the landowner gives his permission**
Ja, met toestemming van de eigenaar van de grond
yah, met **too**stemming vahn de **aiy**ghenahr vahn de ghrond

May we put up our tent/park our caravan here?
Mogen wij hier een tent opslaan/de caravan neerzetten?
mohghen waiy heer en tent **op**slahn/de "**ca**ravan" **op**zetten

Is it allowed to spend the night in the car/caravan?
Mogen wij hier in de auto/caravan overnachten?
mohghen waiy heer in de **ow**to/"**ca**ravan" over**nagh**ten

◄ **No, this is a nature reserve**
Nee, dit is een natuurgebied
nay, dit is en nah**tewr**ghebeed

Who is the owner of this land?
Wie is de eigenaar van de grond?
wee is de **aiy**ghenahr van de ghrond

May we spend the night on your property?
Mogen wij op uw terrein overnachten?
mohghen waiy op ew ter**raiyn** over**nagh**ten

We are staying for just one night
Wij blijven maar één nacht
waiy **blaiy**ven mahr ayn naght

How much do we owe you?
Hoeveel zijn wij u schuldig?
hoovayl zaiyn waiy ew **sghul**digh

Where can we wash?
Waar kunnen wij ons wassen?
wahr **kun**nen waiy ons **wahs**sen

◄ **You are not allowed to camp here**
U mag hier niet kamperen
ew magh heer neet kahm**peh**ren

camping equipment

The numbers refer to the illustrations on pages 76 and 78

10	air mattress	luchtbed	**lught**bed
	bottle opener	flesopener	**fless**opener
	bucket	emmer	**em**mer
4	butane gas	butagas	**bew**taghas
	camping stove	primus	**pree**mus
14	clothes pegs	wasknijpers	**wahs**knaiypers
8	coolbox	koelbox	**kool**box
	corkscrew	kurkentrekker	**kur**kentrekker
	cup	kopje	**kop**ye
2	cutlery	bestek	be**stek**
	deckchair	ligstoel	**ligh**stool
	first-aid-kit	verbandkist	vehr**bahnd**kist
6	folding chair	klapstoel	**klahp**stool
7	folding table	klaptafel	**klahp**tahfel
	fork	vork	vork
5	gas burner	gasbrander	**ghahs**brahnder
11	inflator	luchtpomp	**lught**pomp
9	lamp	lamp	lahmp
	lantern	lantaarn	lahn**tahrn**
1	mug	beker	**bay**ker
	pan	pan	pahn
3	plate	bord	bord
16	pocketknife	zakmes	**zahk**mess
	rope	touw	taow
12	rucksack	rugzak	**rugh**zahk
	saucer	schotel	**sgho**tel
	(pair of) scissors	schaar	sghahr
	spoon	lepel	**lay**pel
13	thermos flask	thermosfles	**ter**mosfles
	tin opener	blikopener	**blik**opener
15	torch	zaklamp	**zahk**lahmp
	travelling bag	reistas	**raiys**tahs

tent and caravan

	axle	as	ahs
29	awning	luifel	**lœ**fel
	brake cable	remkabel	**rem**kahbel
	brake drum	remtrommel	**rem**trommel

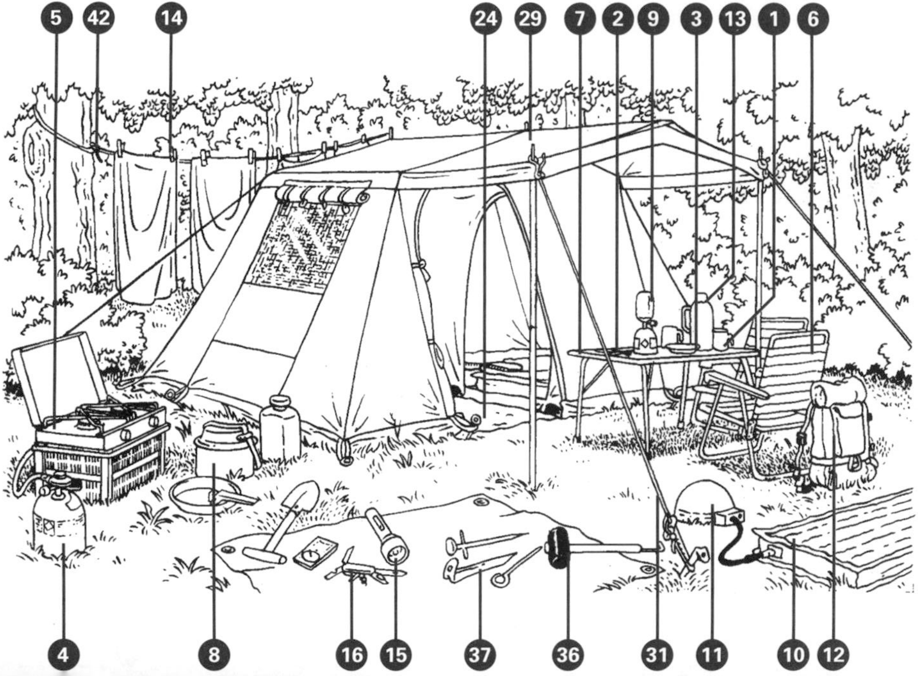
5
42
14
24
29
7
2
9
3
13
1
6
4
8
16
15
37
36
31
11
10
12

	brake light	remlicht	**rem**light
	chemical toilet	chemisch toilet	**ghay**mees twa**let**
42	clothes line	waslijn	**wahs**laiyn
28	clutch	koppeling	**kop**pehling
	cooling element	koelelement	**kool**aylement
	earthing switch	aardlekschakelaar	**ahrd**lek-**sghah**kelahr
	electric wiring	elektrische bedrading	ay**lek**treese be**drah**ding
41	floor	vloer	vloor
27	fridge	koelkast	**kool**kahst
	fuse	zekering	**zay**kering
	gas cylinder	gasfles	**ghahs**fles
23	gas pipe	gasslang	**ghahs**slahng
24	groundsheet	grondzeil	**ghrond**zaiyl
31	guy	scheerlijn	**sghehr**laiyn
25	handbrake	handrem	**hahnd**rem
26	handbrake cable	handremkabel	**hahnd**remkahbel
40	heating	verwarming	ver**wahr**ming
	indicator	richtingaanwijzer	**right**ing-ahn**waiy**zer
	light bulb	gloeilamp	**ghlooy**lahmp
32	lock	slot	slot
36	mallet	tenthamer	**tent**hahmer
33	mirror	spiegel	**spee**ghel
30	nose wheel	neuswiel	**nøs**weel
18	outer wall	buitenwand	**bœ**tenwahnd
	overrun brake	oplooprem	**op**loaprem
34	plug	stekker	**stek**ker
22	pole	dissel	**dis**sel
	rear light	achterlicht	**ahght**erlihght
19	roof	dak	dahk
	shock absorber	schokbreker	**sghok**brayker
	side light	zijlicht	**zaiy**lihght
20	skylight	dakluik	**dahk**lœk
35	socket	stopcontact	**stop**kontahkt
37	tent peg	tentharing	**tent**hahring
38	tent pole	tentstok	**tent**stok
	towbar	trekhaak	**trek**hahk
17	tyre	band	bahnd
	water pump	waterpomp	**wah**terpomp
	water tank	watertank	**wah**ter-'tank'
43	wheel	wiel	weel
39	window	raam	rahm
	windshield	windscherm	**wind**sgherm

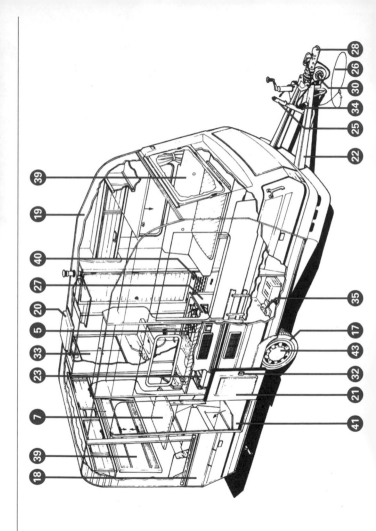

Eating habits

A Dutch breakfast (*ontbijt*) usually consists of sandwiches (*boter-hammen*) - white or brown bread (*wit of bruin brood*) with butter (*boter*), *margarine* or *halvarine* (low-fat margarine) and something savoury like cheese (*kaas*), *ham* and sausage (*worst*) or sweet such as *jam* or honey (*honing*). You can even sprinkle *hagelslag* - chocolate "hailstorm" - on your bread! More familiarly, you can order an egg (*ei*) - hard-boiled (*hardgekookt*), soft-boiled (*zachtgekookt*) or fried (*gebakken*, also known as *spiegelei*). In many hotels you will be served an English or American breakfast with toast, bacon, etc. on request. Besides cornflakes you'll also see many other types of cereal, muesli and crispbreads (often UK imports). Coffee (*koffie*) or tea (*thee*) and fruit juice (*vruchtensap*) will also be served. Lunch (*middageten*) is between 12.30 and 1.30 p.m. Most working people generally take sandwiches (although many large firms have their own canteens). The evening meal (*avondeten*) is on the early side - usually between 6 and 7 p.m. It generally consists of two or three hot courses.

places to eat and drink

broodjeszaak	snack bars specialising in rolls and sandwiches. See snacks below;
bruin café	("brown café")these resemble British pubs; you find them in the big cities and they are highly popular with the locals. They are called "brown" after the colour of the wooden wall covering; while sipping your (alcoholic) drink you can play billiards, darts or cards; small snacks are also available;
café	a cross between a simple bar (serving alcohol, mainly beer) and a coffee shop;
cafetaria	a snack bar or small restaurant, usually self-service and relatively cheap; hot meals available;
croissanterie	French-inspired café-type establishments specialising in croissants and French bread, coffee and tea;
eetcafé	(eating house) usually relatively inexpensive and simple restaurants;

haringkraam	(herring stall)fish stall in the street; you can eat your purchase on the spot (hold the fish by the tail and swallow it) or take it away. A speciality in late spring is fresh, young herring (Hollandse nieuwe or nieuwe haring) - relatively expensive, especially in the first few days after the catch, but delicious. The herring are eaten raw, usually with chopped onions (uitjes);
koffieshop	(coffee shop)usually in shopping centres or department stores serving coffee, tea, soft drinks, cakes and pastries; in several big cities - notably Amsterdam - many coffee shops (most using the English term) sell soft drugs. Strictly speaking the trade is illegal but tolerated by the authorities in the interests of separating the markets for soft and hard drugs;
pannenkoeken-huisje	(pancake house) these restaurants might be small but the pancakes are enormous (served with savoury or sweet toppings); popular with children;
patatkraam	(chip/fries stall) besides chips (cut in the French way) also serving other snacks (to eat on the spot or take away); the Flemish often use the term frituur;
restaurant	restaurants in Holland are high quality and generally cheaper than in the UK, and some also offer an inexpensive Tourist Menu. There are also lots of very good foreign restaurants: Chinees-Indisch (see above), Surinaams (from Surinam, the former Dutch Guiana), Grieks (Greek), Turks (Turkish), Italiaans (Italian), Spaans (Spanish), etc.;
snackbar	wide selection of fast food to take away or consume on the premises. Many of these snackbars have fruit machines;

Do you have a table for us?
Heeft u een tafel vrij?
hayft ew een **tah**fel voar ons vraiy?

A table for two please
Een tafel voor 2 personen alstublieft
en **tah**fel voar tway pehr**soa**nen alstew**bleeft**

◄ **Do you have a reservation?**
Heeft u gereserveerd?
hayft ew gerayser**vayrt**?

I made a reservation for a table for two
Ik heb een tafel voor 2 personen gereserveerd
ik hehp en **tah**fel voar tway pehr**soa**nen gerayser**vayrt**

◄ **Unfortunately all tables are occupied**
We hebben helaas geen tafel meer vrij
we **heh**ben hay**lahs** ghayn **tah**fel mayr vraiy

◄ **You can come back in half an hour**
U kunt over een half uur terugkomen
ew kunt **oa**ver en half ewr te**rugh**koamen

◄ **The restaurant does not open until seven**
Het restaurant gaat pas om zeven uur open
heht rehstoa**rant** ghaht pas om **zay**ven ewr **oa**pen

◄ **The kitchen is already closed**
De keuken is al gesloten
de **køken** is al ghe**sloa**ten

The menu/wine list please
De menukaart/wijnkaart alstublieft
de me**new**kahrt/**waiyn**kahrt alstew**bleeft**

Can you recommend anything?
Kunt u iets aanbevelen?
kunt ew eets **ahn**bevaylen?

Could you open this bottle for me?
Wilt u deze fles voor mij openen?
wilt ew **day**ze flehs voar maiy **oa**penen?

◄ **Did you enjoy your meal?**
Heeft het gesmaakt?
hayft heht ghe**smahkt**?

Waiter!   **The bill please**
Ober!   De rekening alstublieft
oaber!   de **ray**kening alstew**bleeft**

We'd like to have separate bills
We willen graag apart betalen
we **wi**len ghrahgh a**part** be**tah**len

I only eat vegetarian dishes
Ik eet alleen vegetarische maaltijden
ik ayt a**layn** vayghe**tah**reese **mahl**taiyden

We'd like small portions for our children
Voor onze kinderen graag een kinderportie
voar **on**ze **kin**deren ghrahgh en **kin**derporsee

◄ **Enjoy your meal!**
Eet smakelijk!
ayt **smah**kelek!

◄ **Can I clear the table?**
Kan ik afruimen?
kan ik **af**rœmen?

I would like to pay
Ik wil graag betalen
ik wil ghrahgh be**tah**len

Where's the toilet/cloakroom?
Waar is het toilet/de garderobe?
wahr is heht twah**leht**/de gharde**ro**be?

EATING OUT

some useful expressions

ashtray	asbak	**as**bak
bottle	fles	flehs
cutlery	bestek *n*	be**stehk**
fork	vork	vork
glass	glas *n*	ghlas
knife	mes *n*	mehs
napkin	servet *n*	sehr**veht**
salt and pepper	peper- en zoutstel *n*	**pay**per- ehn **zout**stehl
spoon	lepel	**lay**pel

Enjoy your meal!	Eet smakelijk!	ayt **smah**kelek!
Cheers, here's to your health!	Proost! Op uw gezondheid!	proast! op eww ghe**zont**hayt!
And here's to you!	Op de uwe!	op de **ew**we!
I hope you have enjoyed your meal!	Moge het u wel bekomen!	**moa**ghe heht ew wehl be**koa**men!

VOORGERECHTEN	STARTERS
ganzenleverpastei	pâté de foie gras
garnalencocktail	prawn cocktail
gevulde eieren	stuffed eggs
(Ardenner) ham	(Ardennes) ham, a very tasty kind of ham
haring	herring, a Dutch delicacy, usually eaten salted, sometimes pickled
huzarensalade	a salad consisting of meat (usually ham), vegetables, potatoes and mayonnaise
mosselen	mussels, usually eaten boiled or fried
oesters	oysters
omelet	omelette
pasteitje	a pastry shell stuffed with hot ragout
paté	pâté

SOEPEN	SOUPS
aspergesoep	asparagus soup
bouillon	broth
erwtensoep	(trad.; winter) a typical Dutch delicacy: a thick soup made of green peas, leek, celeriac, pork and smoked sausage
groentesoep	vegetable soup
kerriesoep	curry soup
kervelsoep	chervil soup
kippensoep	chicken soup
koninginnensoep	cream of chicken soup
ossenstaartsoep	oxtail soup
soep van de dag	soup of the day
tomatensoep	tomato soup
uiensoep	onion soup
vissoep	fish soup

VIS EN SCHAALDIEREN	FISH AND SEAFOOD
baars	perch
bokking	smoked herring, comparable to kippers
forel	trout
garnalen	shrimps, prawns
haring	(trad.) herring, a typical Dutch delicacy, for example maatjesharing (young herring, Hollandse nieuwe (new herring), rolmops (pickled herring), panharing (fried herring)
heilbot	halibut

inktvis	squid, octopus
kabeljauw	cod
karper	carp
kreeft	lobster
makreel	mackerel, usually eaten smoked
mosselen	mussels, usually eaten boiled or fried
paling	(trad.) eels, a real specialty, for example gerookte paling (smoked eels), paling in het groen (a typical Belgian dish, consisting of stewed eels served in chervil sauce)
snoekbaars	pikeperch
stokvis	stockfish, cured cod or haddock
tarbot	turbot
tong	sole
tonijn	tuna
wijting	whiting
zalm	salmon
zeekreeft	lobster
zeetong	sole

WILD EN GEVOGELTE	**GAME AND FOWL**
duif	pigeon
eend	duck
fazant	pheasant
gans	goose
haantje	chicken
haas	hare
hazepeper	jugged hare, hare stew
kalkoen	turkey
kip	chicken, for example gebraden kip (fried chicken), kippenborst (chicken breast), kipfilet (fillet of chicken), kippenlevertjes (chicken liver)
konijn	rabbit
patrijs	partridge
reerug	venison

VLEESGERECHTEN	**MEAT**
biefstuk	steak: biefstuk van de haas (fillet steak), biefstuk tartaar (steak tartare)
blinde vink	(trad.) slice of veal rolled up and stuffed with minced meat
entrecote	entrecôte, rib steak
filet	fillet, tenderloin
gehaktbal	meat ball, a very common dish, usually not served in

	resaurants but only eaten at home
hachee	hash, a meat stew with lots of onions
jachtschotel	meat casserole with mashed potatoes and apples
kalfsvlees	veal, for example kalfsborst (breast of veal), kalfsbout (leg of veal), kalfsoester (veal escalope), kalfsschenkel (knuckle of veal)
karbonade	pork chop
kotelet	cutlet
lamsvlees	lamb
lendenstuk	sirloin
lever	liver
nieren	kidneys
ossenhaas	tenderloin
pastei	pie
pens	tripe
ragout	ragout
rollade	rolled meat
rolpens	spiced minced meat in tripe
rookworst	(trad.) smoked sausage, eaten with almost all typical Dutch winter dishes
rosbief	roast beef
rundvlees	beef, for example: runderlapje (braised slice of beef), run derrollade (rolled beef, a popular dish at Christmas)
schapenvlees	mutton
spek	bacon
tong	tongue, for example ossetong (ox tongue), rundertong (beef tongue)
tournedos	fillet steak
varkensvlees	pork, for example varkenshaas (pork tenderloin), varkens-karbonade (pork chop), varkenspoot (pettitoes)

CHINEES-INDONESISCHE GERECHTEN	CHINESE AND INDONESIAN DISHES

A small selection (the spelling may vary):

atjar tjampoer	a side dish: a sweet-and-sour vegetable mixture
babi pangang	grilled pork in a sweet-and-sour sauce
bami goreng	fried noodles and vegetables, pork and omelette, sometimes served with "saté"
foe jong hai	omelette with vegetables, sometimes also with meat
gado gado	a variety of vegetables covered with a peanut sauce
kroepoek	a side dish: prawn crackers

mie goreng	fried noodles
nasi goreng	fried rice with meat, onions, chicken, prawns and a fried egg on top
nasi rames	a mini "rijsttafel" (see "rijsttafel")
oedang	prawns
pisang goreng	fried bananas
rijsttafel	(min. 2 pers.) a sumptuous meal, a remnant of Dutch colonial times in Indonesia, consisting of white rice served with numerous small meat and vegetable dishes
sambal	(sometimes extremely) hot pepper paste
saté (sateh) babi/ajam	grilled cubes of pork or chicken on skewers, served with a peanut sauce
tjap tjoy	chop suey, vegetables served in a special sauce

methods of preparation

aan het spit	roasted on the spit, barbecued
gaar	done
gebakken	fried: goed doorbakken (well-done), half doorbakken (medium), in de oven gebakken (baked)
gebraden	roasted
gegarneerd met ...	garnished with ...
gegrild	grilled
gehakt	chopped
gekookt	boiled
gekruid	spicy
gelardeerd met ...	larded with ...
gemarineerd	marinated
gepaneerd	breaded
gerookt	smoked
geroosterd	broiled
gesmoord	braised
gestoofd	stewed
gestoomd	steamed
gevuld met ...	stuffed with ...
gezouten	salted
koud	cold
mager	lean
rauw	raw
scherp	spicy, hot
vers	fresh

GROENTEN	VEGETABLES
andijvie	endive
artisjokken	artichoke
(rode) bietjes	beetroot
bloemkool	cauliflower
boerenkool met worst	(trad.; winter) dish of kale and potatoes, served with smoked sausage
(witte/bruine) bonen	(haricot/kidney) beans
champignons	mushrooms
(dop)erwten	(green) peas
hutspot met klapstuk	(trad.; winter) boiled potatoes, carrots and onions mixed together, served with boiled beef
kapucijners	marrow peas
komkommer	cucumber
peulen	sugar peas, mangetout
prei	leek
radijs	radishes
rode kool	red cabbage
selderij	celery
sla	lettuce
snijbonen	sliced green beans
sperziebonen	French beans
spinazie	spinach
spruitjes	Brussels sprouts
tomaten	tomatoes
uien	onions
zuurkool met spek	(trad.; winter) sauerkraut and potatoes mixed together, served with bacon

SAUSEN, KRUIDEN E.D.	SAUCES, HERBS, ETC.
azijn	vinegar
bieslook	chives
citroen	lemon
dille	dill
gelei	jelly, aspic
kaassaus	cheese sauce
kaneel	cinnamon
ketchup	(tomato) ketchup
knoflook	garlic
komijn	cummin
kruiden	herbs
kruidnagel	cloves

laurierbladeren	bay leaves
mayonaise	mayonnaise
mierikswortel	horseradish
mosterd(saus)	mustard (sauce)
nootmuskaat	nutmeg
olie	oil
olijven	olives
paprika(poeder)	paprika
peterselie	parsley
peper	pepper
room	cream
rozemarijn	rosemary
rozijnen	raisins
slagroom	whipped cream
witte wijnsaus	sauce made of white wine, flour and cream
zout	salt

NAGERECHTEN/DESSERTS DESSERTS

fruit	fruit, for example appels (apples), peren (pears), bananen (bananas), perziken (peaches), pruimen (prunes), mandarijnen (tangerines), sinaasappels (oranges), grapefruits (grapefruits), ananas (pineapple), aardbeien (strawberries), meloen (melon), bosbessen (blueberries), bramen (blackberries), druiven (grapes), dadels (dates) etc.
gebak, koekjes	pastry, cookies, usually served with coffee or tea at the end of a meal; a few Dutch specialities are: amandelgebak, appelgebak/appelpunt met slagroom, tompoes, moorkop, bitterkoekjes, kokosmakronen, Arnhemse meisjes, bokkenpootjes
ijs	various kinds of icecream; for children you could order the kinderijsje, a small portion of ice cream, usually accompanied by a small gift or surprise
kaas	cheese; in restaurants at the end of a meal one usually serves French and Swiss geitenkaas or schapenkaas; Dutch cheese is labelled either jonge kaas, belegen kaas or oude kaas according to its age; most kinds of cheese are named after the town in which they used to be traded in the old days: Goudse kaas, Edammer kaas, Leidse kaas (the latter contains komijn) or the region where they are made Texelaar, Maaslander, Friese nagelkaas
pannenkoeken	pancakes, if so desired served with stroop (syrop), gember

(ginger) or some other ingredient; small, thin pancakes are called flensjes; tiny, thick ones are called poffertjes and are served with butter and icing sugar

pudding	milk pudding
vlaai	a speciality from the southern province of Limburg: a large flat pie filled with fruit (cherries, strawberries, prunes, apricots, etc.)
vruchtencompote	stewed fruit
yoghurt	yoghurt

DRANKEN	DRINKS
Alcoholische dranken	Alcoholic drinks
advocaat	a typical ladies' drink: egg liqueur served with whipped cream, which can't be drunk but is eaten with a small spoon
Berenburg	a strong herbal gin from the northern province of Friesland
bier	beer, the most popular kind being lager, called Pilsener bier in Dutch or pils in short; other kinds of beer are bokbier (a seasonal beer), moutbier (malt beer) and oud bruin (a dark, sweet stout); Dutch beer brands (Amstel, Heineken, Grolsch, Bavaria) are renowned, but many connoisseurs prefer beer from the southern provinces of Holland and especially from Belgium (this beer can be bought in many Dutch cafés nowadays), for example geuzenlambiek, kriekenlambiek (cherry-flavoured beer) and trappist (a malt beer brewed in Trappist monasteries)
borrel(tje)	almost synonymous with "jenever", but also the term used to indicate alcoholic drinks in general or even a small five o'clock party during which alcoholic drinks are served
brandewijn (met suiker)	brandy (served with sugar)
jenever	a juniper-flacoured spirit, comparable to gin; there are several kinds, like oude jenever or jonge jenever, popularly referred to as oude/jonge klare; there are also flavoured kinds like bessenjenever (blackcurrant gin, especially popular with women) and citroenjenever (lemon gin, popularly also called: citroentje met suiker)
likeur	liqueur; the Curaçao (orange-flavoured liqueur) is renoned
wijn	wine; you can buy almost all kinds of wine in Holland: Frans (French), Italiaans (Italian), Duits (German), Spaans; (Spanish); you have a choice of rode wijn (red wine), witte wijn (white wine), rosé (rosé), droge wijn (dry

wine), zoete wijn (sweet wine), mousserende wijn
(sparkling wine), port(wijn) (port), sherry (sherry), etc.

cognac, rum and *whisky* have no Dutch names

Niet-alcoholische dranken	Non-alcoholic drinks
alcoholvrij bier	low alcohol beer (brand names: Bavaria Malt, Amstel Malt, Grolsch Malt etc.)
chocolademelk	chocolate-flavoured milk; warme chocolademelk (hot chocolate) can be served if one so wishes with slagroom (whipped cream); koude chocolademelk (cold chocolate-flavoured milk) is usually referred to as Chocomel (a brand name)
frisdranken	soft drinks; numerous kinds of soft drinks and all well-known international brands are available
koffie	coffee; you can choose from bonenkoffie, filterkoffie or oploskoffie (instant coffee); if you don't want any cream in your coffee you must order zwarte koffie (black coffee), although nowadays the cream is usually served separately; koffie verkeerd is coffee with a lot of hot milk, koffie met slagroom is coffee with whipped cream; espresso, cappuccino, Wiener melange and other foreign specialities are available in most restaurants and coffee bars nowadays; Dutch people like to have some kind of pastry with their coffee (see desserts), whereas Belgium is renowned for its bonbons/pralines, chocolates of an exceptionally high quality
melk	milk; milk is subdivided according to fat content in volle melk, halfvolle melk or magere melk; other dairy products are karnemelk, kwark, (Duitse) hüttenkäse and umer, which are more often eaten or drunk at breakfast than as a dessert
mineraalwater	mineral water, almost always carbonated; the most popular brand is "Spa", named after the Belgian town of that name and all waiters will know exactly what you mean if you order een spaatje; (Spa rood is carbonated, Spa blauw is not; the colour refers to the colour of the label and not to the colour of the water, which is clear, although coloured Spa with blueberry, orange or apple flavour is becoming popular)
thee	tea, can be sterk (strong) or slap (weak), just like coffee, and is being served without milk, unless you explicitly ask

	for thee met melk; tea with lemon is called thee met citroen; in the major cities you will find theehuizen which serve numerous kinds of tea
tomatensap	tomato juice
vruchtensap	fruit juice; the most popular being jus d'orange (orange juice), but you can also buy appelsap (apple juice), citroensap (lemon juice), grapefruitsap or druivensap (grape juice), or a combination of various kinds of juice.

SNACKS	SNACKS
patat (patates frites)	chips, served with mayonaise or pindasaus (peanut sauce). You could also try patat speciaal (chips covered with tomato ketchup, mayonnaise and onions)
croquet/kroket	meat croquettes
frikadel	sausage made of minced meat and, if so desired, served with mayonnaise, tomato ketchup and onions
bal gehakt	meatball
bamischijf	(Indon.) kind of square, flat croquette made of chow mein
milkshake	milkshake
nasibal	(Indon.) kind of square, flat croquette made of fried rice with meat, spices and vegetables
hamburger	hamburger
loempia	(Indon./Chin.) spring roll
saté	(Indon.) meat on a skewer, served with a peanut sauce

Most snack bars and cafeterias also serve a wide variety of belegde broodjes (rolls stuffed with various fillings): you can choose from broodje ham (roll stuffed with ham), kaas (cheese), ei (egg), gezond (a health-food roll stuffed with ham, cheese, lettuce, tomato, cucumber), lever (liver), tartaar (minced steak) or halfom (a popular combination of liver and salted meat).

Do you have a list of events/theatre performances?
Heeft u een lijst met evenementen/theatervoorstellingen?
hayft ew en laiyst meht ayvene**mehn**ten/tay-**ah**-ter-voar-steh-ling-en?

Is there anything special going on in town today/tonight?
Is er vandaag/vanavond iets bijzonders te zien in de stad?
is ehr van**dahgh**/van**ah**vont eets bee**zon**ders te zeen in de stat?

ballet	ballet *n*	ba**leht**
bar	bar	'bar'
café	café	ka**fay**
cinema	bioscoop	bee-yos**koap**
circus performance	circusvoorsteling	**sir**kus-voarstehling
concert hall	concertzaal	kon**sehrt**zahl
discotheque	discotheek	diskoa**tayk**
film	film	film
folkloristic performance	folkloristische voorstelling	folkloa**ris**teese **voar**stehling
loungebar	loungebar	'loungebar'
musical	musical	"musical"
open-air cinema	openluchtbioscoop	oapen**lught**-beeyoskoap
open-air concert	openluchtconcert	oapen**lught**konsehrt
open-air theatre	openluchttheater	oapen**lught**-tay-ah-ter
opera	opera	**oa**pe-rah
operetta, light opera	operette	oape**reh**te
outdoor café	terras	ter**rahs**
parade, pageant	optocht	**op**toght
performance of ...	optreden van ...	**op**trayden van ...
play	toneelstuk *n*	toa**nayl**stuk
rock concert, gig	popconcert *n*	**pop**konsehrt
theatre	schouwburg, theater *n*	**sghou**burgh, tay-**ah**ter
variety show	variété *n*	vah-ree-yay-**tay**

GOING OUT

Is there a cinema nearby?
Is hier in de buurt een bioscoop?
is heer in de bewrt en beeyos**koap**?

Are foreign films being dubbed?
Worden buitenlandse films nagesynchroniseerd?
worden **bœ**tenlantse films **nah**ghe-sin-ghroa-nee-sayrt?

◄ **No, they come with Dutch subtitles***
Nee, ze hebben Nederlandse ondertitels
nay, ze **heh**ben **nay**derlantse **on**derteetels

* In Belgium films often get both Dutch and French subtitles; in the French speaking regions many foreign films are being imported from France, where they have been dubbed.

What's on tonight?	**What kind of film is it?**
Wat draait er vanavond?	Wat is het voor een soort film?
wat drahyt ehr van**ah**vont?	wat is heht voar en soart film?

American	Amerikaans	ahmayree**kahns**
adventure film	avonturenfilm	ahvon**tew**renfilm
cartoon	tekenfilm	**tay**kenfilm
children's film	kinderfilm	**kin**derfilm
comedy	komedie	koa**may**dee
crime/action film	misdaadfilm	**mis**dahtfilm
Dutch	Nederlands	**nay**derlants
English	Engels	**ehng**els
French	Frans	frans
Italian	Italiaans	ee-tah-lee-**ahns**
musical	musical	"musical"
psychological drama	psychologisch drama	pseegho**loh**ghees **dra**ma
romantic movie	romantische film	ro**mahn**teese film
science fiction	science fiction	"science fiction"
thriller	thriller	"thriller"
tragedy	drama	**drah**mah

What time does the performance start?
Hoe laat begint de voorstelling?
hoo laht be**ghint** de **voar**stehling?

Is the film ...
Is de film ...
is de film

| **U-rated** | voor alle leeftijden | voar **al**le **layf**taiyden |
| **X-rated** | voor 16 jaar en ouder | voar **zes**teen yahr en **ow**der |

Is there a play in any other language than Dutch?	**Who are performing?**
Is er een toneelstuk in een andere taal dan Nederlands?	Wie treedt er op?
is ehr en toa**nayl**stuk in en **an**dere tahl dan **nay**derlants?	wee trayt ehr op?

Where can I buy tickets?
Waar kan ik kaarten krijgen?
wahr kan ik **kahr**ten **kraiy**ghen?

◄ **At the box office/booking office**
Aan de kassa/bij het bespreekbureau
ahn de **ka**sah/baiy heht be**sprayk**bewroa

Two tickets for tonight's show, please
Twee kaartjes alstublieft voor de voorstelling van vanavond
tway **kahr**tyes alstew**bleeft** voar de **voar**stehling van van**ah**vont

in the back	achteraan	agh-ter-ahn
in the front	vooraan	voar**ahn**
in the middle	in het midden	in heht **mid**den
box, loge	loge	**loa**zhe
gallery	balkon	bal**kon**
stalls	zaal	zahl

intermission	pauze	**pow**ze
cloakroom	garderobe	gharde**roh**be
box office	kassa	**kahs**sa
premiere	première	prim**yeh**re

◄ **The show is sold out**
De voorstelling is uitverkocht
de **voar**stelling is **œt**verkoght

discotheque and nightclub

Is there a nice discotheque around?
Is hier een leuke disco(theek)?
is heer en **lø**ke diskoa(**tayk**)?

◄ **This is a private club**
Dit is een besloten club
dit is en be**sloa**ten klup

Do they charge an admission fee?
Moet er entree betaald worden?
moot ehr ehn**tray** be**tahlt wor**den?

What kind of music do they usually play?
Wat voor muziek wordt er meestal gedraaid?
wat voar mew**zeek** wort ehr **mays**tal ghe**draiyd**?

Is there live music?
Is het live muziek?
is heht "live" mew**zeek**?

Is there a good d.j.?
Is er een goede d.j.?
is ehr en **ghoo**de "d.j."?

Would you like to go to the disco?
Ga je mee naar de disco?
ghah ye may nahr de **dis**koa?

Would you care for a drink?
Wil je iets drinken?
wil ye eets **drin**ken

The music is far out/smashing/cool
Wat een leuke/toffe/coole muziek
what en **lø**keh/**tof**feh/**kooh**leh mew**zeek**

Let's step out
Laten we naar buiten gaan
lahten we nahr **bœ**ten ghahn

Let's go somewhere/someplace else
Laten we ergens anders heen gaan
lahten we **ehr**ghens **an**ders hayn ghahn

Shall I take you home/to the hotel?
Zal ik je naar huis/het hotel brengen?
zal ik ye nahr hœs/heht hoa**tehl** **brehng**en?

Thank you for a lovely evening
Bedankt voor de leuke avond
be**dankt** voar de **lø**ke **ah**vont

Can we go ballroom-dancing here as well?
Kunnen we hier ook stijldansen?
kunen we heer oak **staiyl**dansen?

May I have this dance, please?
Mag ik deze dans van u?
magh ik **day**ze dans van ew?

Hello, can I sit here?
Hallo, mag ik erbij komen zitten?
hahl**lo**, magh ik ehr baiy **koh**men **zit**ten

◄ **Rather not/This seat is taken**
Nee, liever niet/Deze plek is al bezet
nay, **lee**ver neet/**day**ze plek is ahl be**zet**

Do you like it here?
Vind je het hier leuk?
vind ye het heer lø

◄ **Yeah, groovy!/No, it's boring**
Ja, helemaal te gek!/Nee, ik verveel me
yah, **hay**lemahl te ghek/nay, ik ver**vayl** meh

Do you have a light for me?
Heb je een vuurtje voor me?
heb ye en **vewr**tye voar meh

I can't hear/understand you
Ik kan je niet verstaan
ik kahn ye neet ver**stahn**

It's hot/crowded/boring in here.
Het is hier warm/vol/saai.
het is heer wahrm/vol/sigh

Shall we go outside?
Zullen wij naar buiten gaan?
zullen waiy nahr **bœ**ten ghahn

◄ **No, I'd rather stay here**
Nee, ik blijf liever hier
nay, ik blaiyf **lee**ver heer

◄ **Yes, that's OK**
Ja, dat is goed
yah, daht is ghood

I have to go now.
Ik moet helaas gaan.
ik moot hay**lahs** ghahn.

Shall we meet again?
Zullen wij iets afspreken?
zullen waiy eets **ahf**sprayken

Do you have any plans for tomorrow/tonight
Heb je al plannen voor morgen/vanavond?
heb ye ahl **plahn**nen voar **moar**ghen/vahn**ah**vond

Shall we have a bite/drink together?
Zullen wij samen iets eten/drinken?
zullen waiy **sah**men eets **ay**ten/**drin**ken

◀ **Let's meet at nine at .../at the doors of ...**
Laten wij afspreken om negen uur bij .../voor de ingang van ...
lahten waiy **ahf**sprayken om **nay**ghen ewr baiy .../voar de **in**ghahng vahn ...

Do you have a steady friend?
Heb je vaste verkering?
heb ye **vahs**te ver**keh**ring

◀ **I am married. I have children**
Ik ben getrouwd/Ik heb kinderen
ik ben ghe**trowd**/ik heb **kin**deren

◀ **I am gay/lesbian/heterosexual**
Ik ben homo/lesbisch/hetero
ik ben **ho**mo/**les**bees/**hay**tero

Are you alone here or ith other people?
Ben je hier alleen of met anderen?
ben ye heer al**layn** of met **ahn**deren

I am jealous
Ik ben jaloers
ik be yah**loors**

Where are you from?
Waar kom je vandaan?
wahr kom ye van**dahn**

What do you do for a living?
Wat doe je voor werk?
waht do ye voar wairk

What are you studying?
Wat studeer je?
waht stew**dehr** ye

How old are youy?
Hoe oud ben je?
hoo owd ben ye

◀ **You're fooling me**
Je houdt me voor de gek
ye howd me voar de ghek

Do you come here often?
Kom je hier vaker?
kom ye heer **vah**ker

What kind of music do you like?
Wat voor muziek vind je leuk?
waht voar mew**zeek** vind ye løk

Do you want to dance with me?
Wil je met me dansen?
wil ye met me **dahn**sen

How long will you be staying in ... ?
Hoe lang blijf je nog in ...?
hoo lahng blaiyf ye nogh in ...

May I give you a compliment?
Mag ik je een complimentje geven?
magh ik ye en complee**ment**ye ghayven

You're looking fine
Je ziet er goed uit
ye zeet er ghood œt

◄ You're making me shy
Je maakt me verlegen
ye mahkt me ver**lay**ghen

That blush suits you well
Die blos staat je goed
dee bloss staht ye ghood

I like your smile
Wat lach je leuk
waht lahgh ye løk

◄ Stop teasing me!
Plaag me niet zo!
plahgh me neet zo

You have beautiful eyes/hair
Wat heb je mooie ogen/haar
waht heb ye **moh**ye **oh**ghen

◄Thank you
Dank je (wel)
dahnk ye (wel)

I think we are getting closer
Volgens mij klikt het wel tussen ons
volghens maiy klikt het well **tus**sen ons

I fancy you/think you're attractive
Ik vind je leuk/aantrekkelijk
ik vihnd ye løk/ahn**trek**kelik

I like you very much
Ik vind je erg aardig
ik vihnd ye airgh **ahr**digh

I think I am in love with you
Ik geloof dat ik verliefd op je ben
ik ghe**loaf** dat ik ver**leefd** op ye ben

I am thinking about you all day
Ik moet de hele dag aan je denken
ik moot de **hay**le dagh ahn ye **den**ken

◄Really?
Echt waar?
eght wahr

I love you
Ik hou van je
ik how vahn ye

◄I love you, too
Ik (hou) ook van jou
ik (how) oak vahn yow

I'm mad about you
Ik ben gek op je
ik ben ghek op ye

◄ Please go!
Ga alsjeblieft weg!
gha alsye**bleeft** wegh

◄ Keep your hands off me!
Blijf van me af!
blaiyf vahn me ahf

Shall we go to the hotel/my room?
Zullen we samen naar het hotel/mijn kamer gaan?
zullen we **sah**men nahr het hotel/maiyn **kah**mer ghahn

◄ Not here
Niet hier
neet heer

I want to sleep with you
Ik wil met je naar bed
ik will met ye nahr bed

◄ No, that's out of the question
Nee, geen sprake van
nay, ghayn **sprah**ke vahn

◄ You're going too fast
Je loopt te hard van stapel
ye loapt te hard vahn **stah**pel

◄ Maybe some other time
Misschien een andere keer
mis**sgheen** en **ahn**dere kehr

◄ **I only want to have safe sex**
Ik wil alleen veilig vrijen
ik will ahl**layn vaiy**ligh **vrai**yen

Do you have a condom?
Heb je een condoom bij je?
heb ye en con**doam** baiy ye

Did you like it?   ◄ **It was great**
Vond je het leuk/lekker? Het was geweldig
vond ye het løk/**lek**ker het was ghe**wel**digh

◄ **I don't want to see you again**
Ik wil je niet meer zien
ik will ye neet mehr zeen

I liked it, but I don't want any further contact
Ik vond het leuk, maar ik hoef verder geen contact
ik vond het løk, mahr hoof **ver**der ghayn kon**tahkt**

Thank you for a wonderful evening/night
Bedankt voor de leuke avond/nacht
be**dahnkt** voar de **lø**ke **ah**vond/naght

I shall miss you
Ik zal je missen
ik zahl ye **mis**sen

See you tomorrow/See you soon
Tot morgen/Tot gauw
tot **mor**ghen/tot ghaow

Can I have your address?
Mag ik je adres?
magh ik ye ah**dres**

◄ **That's OK/No, I won't do that**
Dat is goed/Nee, daar begin ik niet aan
daht is ghood/nay, dahr be**ghin** ik neet ahn

I will get in touch with you
Ik neem wel contact op met jou
ik naym well kon**takt** op met yow

AIDS	aids	"aids"
chlamydia	chlamydia	kla**mee**dia
condom	condoom	con**dohm**
HIV	HIV	hah-ee-vay
come	klaarkomen	**klahr**komen
I'm having my period	ik ben ongesteld	ik ben onghe**steld**
penis	penis	**pay**nis
pill	pil	pil
caress	strelen	**stray**len
vagina	vagina	**vah**gheena
contraceptive	voorbehoedsmiddel	**voar**behoods-middle
making love	vrijen	**vrai**yen

Is there a nice place for children to go to?
Is er iets leuks voor de kinderen?
is ehr eets løks voar de **kin**deren?

Do you have a children's menu?
Hebt u een kindermenu?
hebt ew en **kin**dermenew

Is there a day-care centre?
Is hier een crèche?
is heer en crash

I will pick up my child at 5 o'clock
Ik kom mijn kind om vijf uur ophalen
ik kom maiyn kind om vaif ewr **op**hahlen

babyphone	babyfoon	baby**foan**
changing unit	commode	com**moh**de
bottle	fles	fles
dummy	fopspeen	**fop**spayn
high chair	kinderstoel	**kin**derstool
bib	slabbetje	**slabb**betye
teat	speen	spayn

amusement park	pretpark *n*	**preht**park
aquarium	aquarium *n*	ah-**kwah**-ree-yum
children's museum	museum *n* voor kinderen	mew**say**-um voar **kin**deren
circus	circus *n*	**sir**kus
miniature town	miniatuurstad	meeneeyah**tewr**stat
mini zoo	kinderboerderij	**kin**derboorderaiy
play area	speelweide	**spayl**waiyde
playground	speeltuin	**spayl**tœn
round trip by plane	rondvlucht	**ront**vlught
sightseeing cruise	rondvaart	**ront**vahrt
steam train	stoomtrein	**stoam**traiyn
swimming pool	zwembad *n*	**zwehm**bat
swimming pool and leis ure centre	waterpretpark *n*	**wah**terprehtpark
terrarium	terrarium *n*	teh**rah**reeyum
Wild West village	wildwestdorp *n*	wilwehstdorp
zoo	dierentuin	**dee**rentœn

asking for directions

Could you show me the way to the/a ... ?
Kunt u mij de weg wijzen naar de/het/een ... ?
kunt ew maiy de wehgh **waiy**zen nahr de/heht/en ...?

English	Dutch	Pronunciation
amusement park	pretpark *n*	**preht**park
bank	bank	bank
bus stop	bushalte	**bus**hahlte
bus terminal	busstation *n*	**bus**-stahsyon
cathedral	kathedraal, dom	ka-te-**drahl**, dom
centre	centrum *n*	**sehn**trum
doctor	dokter	**dok**ter
exit	uitgang	**œt**ghang
hospital	ziekenhuis *n*	**zee**kenhœs
market	markt	markt
museum	museum *n*	mew**say**-um
open-air museum	openluchtmuseum *n*	oa-pen-**lught**-mew-say-um
police station	politiebureau *n*	poa**lee**tsee-bewroa
post office	postkantoor *n*	**post**kantoar
this address	dit adres	dit ah**drehs**
station	station *n*	stah**syon**
tourist information	VVV-kantoor *n*	vay-vay-vay-kan**toar**
underground station	metrostation	**may**tro-sta**shon**

◄ **No, I'm afraid I'm a stranger here**
Nee, ik ben hier helaas niet bekend
nay, ik behn heer hay**lahs** neet be**kehnt**

◄ **From here you go ...**
U gaat hier...
ew ghaht heer ...

English	Dutch	Pronunciation
straight on	rechtuit	**rehght**œt
to the right	rechtsaf	**rehghts**af
to the left	linksaf	**links**af
round the corner	de hoek om	de hook om

◄ **as far as/up to ...**
... en dan tot aan ...
... ehn dan tot ahn ...

the crossing	de kruising	de **krœ**sing
the large square	het grote plein	heht **ghroa**te plaiyn
the roundabout	de rotonde	de roa**ton**de
the bridge	de brug	de brugh
the church	de kerk	de kehrk
the first turning on the right	de eerste zijstraat rechts	de **ayr**ste **zaiy**straht rehghts
the third turning on the left	de derde zijstraat links	de **dehr**de **zaiy**straht links
on your left	aan uw linkerhand	ahn eww **lin**kerhant
on your right	aan uw rechterhand	ahn eww **rehgh**terhant
right in front of you	recht vóór u	rehght voar ew
across the road and a little to the left/right	schuin (links/rechts) aan de overzijde	sghœn (links/rehghts) ahn de **oa**verzaiyde
behind/beyond that	daarachter	dahr**agh**ter
next to that	daarnaast	dahr**nahst**
200 meters* from here/there	na 200 meter	nah **tway**hondert **may**ter
half an hour on foot	een half uur lopen	en half ewr **loa**pen
around the corner	om de hoek	om de hook

◄ **You'd better ask again from there**
Vraag het dan nog maar een keer
vrahgh heht dan nogh mahr en kayr

How far is it on foot?
Hoe ver is het lopen?
hoo vehr is heht **loa**pen?

Is it far from here?
Is het ver van hier?
is heht vehr van heer?

◄ **You had better take bus number 4****
U kunt beter met bus nummer 4 gaan
ew kunt **bay**ter meht bus **nu**mer veer ghahn

◄ **You had better take a taxi/cab**
U kunt beter een taxi nemen
ew kunt **bay**ter en **ta**xi **nay**men

I am lost
Ik ben de weg kwijt
ik behn de wehgh kwaiyt

◄ **You have taken the wrong way**
U bent verkeerd gelopen
ew behnt ver**kayrt** ghe**loa**pen

◄ **They've sent you in the wrong direction**
Men heeft u de verkeerde weg gewezen
mehn haiyft ew de ver**kayr**de wehgh ghe**way**zen

---

* On the continent **meters** and **kilometers** are used instead of feet, yards and miles
(1 kilometre = 0.62 miles).
**All bus and tram services are indicated by numbers; the underground is named after
its destination (for example "Gaasperplas").

Can you show me on the map where I am now?
Kunt u op de plattegrond aanwijzen waar ik nu ben?
kunt ew op de pla-te-**ghront ahn**waiyzen wahr ik new behn?

◄ **You are now here**
U staat nu hier
ew staht new heer

Could you walk part of the way with me?
Kunt u een eindje met mij meelopen?
kunt ew en **aiyn**tye meht maiy **may**loapen?

accidents/police

A fire has broken out/There has been an accident
Er is brand uitgebroken/Er is een ongeluk gebeurd
ehr is brant **œt**ghebroaken/ehr is en **on**gheluk ghe**børt**

I urgently need help
Ik heb snel hulp nodig
ik hehp snehl hulp **noa**degh

Would you please call the police/an ambulance/the fire brigade?
Wilt u de politie/ambulance/brandweer bellen?
wilt ew de poa**lee**tsee/ambew**lan**se/**brant**wayr **bel**en?

Help! Stop thief!
Help! Houd de dief!
hehlp! hout de deef!

Where is the police station?
Waar is het politiebureau?
wahr is heht poa**lee**tseebewroa?

I'd like to report (a/an) ...
Ik wil aangifte doen van ...
ik wil **ahn**ghifte doon van ...

arson	brandstichting	**brant**stichting
assault	aanranding	**ahn**randing
battery	mishandeling	mis**han**deling
breaking and entering	inbraak	**in**brahk
damage	schade	**sghah**de
fraud	oplichting	**op**lichting
loss	verlies *n*	ver**lees**
pickpocketing	zakkenrollerij	**zak**-en-rol-e-raiy
rape	verkrachting	ver**kragh**ting
robbery/theft	beroving/diefstal	be**roa**ving/**deef**stal
shoplifting	winkeldiefstal	**win**keldeefstal
that my car has been broken into	openbreken van de auto	**oa**penbrayken van de **ou**toa
vandalism	vernieling	ver**nee**ling

My ... has been stolen/I lost my ...
Ik ben beroofd van mijn .../Ik ben mijn ... verloren
ik behn be**roaft** van maiyn .../ik behn maiyn ... ver**loa**ren

bank card	pinpas	**pin**pahs
banker's card	betaalpas	be**tahl**pas
camera	fototoestel *n*	**foa**toa-toostehl
car radio	autoradio	**ou**toa-rahdeeyoa
cell phone	mobiele telefoon	moh**bee**le tele**foan**
cheques	cheques	shehks
credit card	creditcard	"creditcard"
digital camera	digitale camera	**dee**gheetahle **kah**mera
hand bag	handtasje *n*	**hant**-ta-sye
luggage	bagage	bah**ghah**zhe
passport	paspoort *n*	**pas**poart
purse	portemonnee	portemo**nay**
suitcase	koffer	**kof**er
travel documents	reisdocumenten	**raiys**doa-kew-mehn-ten
videocamera	videocamera	**vee**dayokahmera
wallet	portefeuille	porte**fœ**ye

My car/bicycle/caravan/trailer/motor scooter has been stolen
Mijn auto/fiets/caravan/aanhanger/scooter is gestolen
maiyn **ou**toa/feets/"caravan"/**ahn**hanger/"scooter" is ghe**stoa**len

I have been harassed
Ik ben lastiggevallen
ik behn **las**tegh ghe**val**en

I am being followed
Ik word achtervolgd
ik wort aghter**volght**

◄ **Do you want to report a crime/make a statement?**
Wilt u aangifte doen/een verklaring afleggen?
wilt ew **ahn**ghifte doon/en ver**klah**ring **af**lehghen?

◄ **We will make a report**
Wij zullen proces-verbaal opmaken
waiy **zul**en proa**sehs**-vehrbahl **op**mahken

◄ **Are there any witnesses?**
Hebt u getuigen?
hehpt ew ghe**tœ**ghen?

◄ **We can't do anything just yet**
Wij kunnen er voorlopig niets aan doen
waiy **kun**en ehr voar**loa**pegh neets ahn doon

◄ **We will take the matter into investigation**
Wij zullen de zaak onderzoeken
waiy **zul**en de zahk onder**zoo**ken

◄ **You can inquire at the lost and found office**
U kunt navraag doen bij het bureau voor gevonden voorwerpen
ew kunt **nah**vrahgh doon baiy heht bew**roa** voar ghe**von**den **voar**wehrpen

◄ **Would you fill in/sign this form?**
Wilt u dit formulier invullen/ondertekenen?
wilt ew dit formew**leer in**vulen/onder**tay**kenen?

I can't read it Ik kan het niet lezen ik kan heht neet **lay**zen	**I'd like to have an interpreter/see a police woman** Kan er een tolk/vrouwelijke agent bijkomen? kan ehr en tolk/vrou-we-le-ke ah**ghehnt baiy**koamen?
I can't sign this Ik kan dit niet ondertekenen ik kan dit neet onder**tay**kenen	**I retract my report/statement** Ik trek de aangifte/verklaring in ik trehk de **ahn**ghifte/ver**klah**ring in

◄ **Your car has been towed away**   ◄ **You can collect it there**
Uw auto is weggesleept   U kunt hem daar afhalen
eww **ou**toa is **wehgh**-gheslaypt   ew kunt hehm dahr **af**hahlen

◄ **You are suspected of .../arrested for ...**
U wordt verdacht van .../gearresteerd wegens ...
ew wort ver**daght** van .../ghe-arehs**tayrt** wayghens ...

an act of violence	geweldpleging	ghe**wehlt**playghing
being guilty of causing an accident	schuld aan een ongeval	sghult ahn en **on**gheval
having illegally entered the country	illegale grens-overschrijding	ee**lay**-ghah-le **ghrehns**-oaver-sghraiyding
possesion of drugs	bezit van verdovende middelen	be**zit** van ver**doa**vende **mid**-e-len
public drunkenness	openbare dronkenschap	**oa**penbahre **dron**kensghap
smuggling	smokkel	**smok**el
theft	diefstal	**deef**stal
vandalism	vernieling	ver**nee**ling
violation of the public order	verstoring van de openbare orde	ver**stoa**ring van de **oa**penbahre **or**de

◄ **May I see your passport/driving license/ID?**
Mag ik uw paspoort/rijbewijs/een legitimatie zien?
magh ik eww **pas**poart/**raiy**bewaiys/en lay-ghee-tee**mah**tsee zeen?

◄ **You must come along to the police station**
U moet mee naar het bureau
ew moot may nahr heht bew**roa**

◄ **You are trespassing**
U bevindt zich op verboden terrein
ew be**vint** zigh op ver**boa**den teh**raiyn**

◄ **You're not allowed to take pictures here**
U mag hier niet fotograferen
ew magh heer neet foa-toa-ghrah**fay**ren

I'd like to see a lawyer/someone from the embassey
Ik wil een advocaat/iemand van de ambassade spreken
ik wil en atvoa**kaht**/**ee**mant van de am-ba-**sah**-de **spray**ken

◄ **We're placing you under arrest**
Wij nemen u in voorlopige hechtenis
waiy **nay**men ew in voar**loa**peghe **hehgh**tenis

◄ **We're taking you into custody**
Wij nemen u in hechtenis
waiy **nay**men ew in **hehgh**tenis

◄ **You will have to go to court**
U wordt voorgeleid
ew wort **voar**ghelaiyt

I'm innocent/have nothing to do with this
Ik ben onschuldig/heb hier niets mee te maken
ik behn on**sghul**degh/hehp heer neets may te **mah**ken

accused, defendant	beklaagde	be**klahgh**de
criminal investigation department	recherche	re**syehr**sye
judge	rechter	**rehgh**ter
magistrate in a juvenile court	kinderrechter	**kin**der-rehghter
public prosecutor	officier van justitie	of-ee-**seer** van jus**tee**tsee
suspect	verdachte	ver**dagh**te
traffic police	verkeerspolitie	ver**kayrs**poaleetsee
vice squad	zedenpolitie	**zay**denpoaleetsee

medical care

asking for help

I (urgently) need a doctor/dentist
Ik heb (dringend) een dokter/tandarts nodig
ik hehp (**dring**ent) en **dok**ter/**tant**arts **noa**degh

What is the emergency number?
Wat is het alarmnummer?
waht is het a**larm**nummer

Could you call a doctor/ambulance for me?
Kunt u voor mij een dokter/ambulance bellen?
kunt ew voar maiy en **dok**ter/ambew**lan**se **be**len?

I have to get to a hospital quickly
Ik moet snel naar een ziekenhuis
ik moot snehl nahr en **zee**kenhœs

Where can I find a first-aid post/outpatients' clinic?
Waar is een eerstehulppost/de polikliniek?
wahr is en **ayr**ste hulp-post/de **poa**lee-kleeneek?

I'd like to make an appointment with the/a ...
Ik wil een afspraak maken met de/een ...
ik wil en **af**sprahk **mah**ken meht de/en ...

dentist	tandarts	**tant**arts
dermatologist	huidarts	**hœt**arts
doctor	arts	arts
ear, nose and throat specialist	keel-, neus- en oorarts	kayl-, nøs- ehn **oar**arts
general practitioner, GP	huisarts	**hœs**arts
gynaecologist	gynaecoloog	**ghee**naykolohgh
internist	internist	inter**nist**
neurologist	zenuwarts	**zay**neww-arts
ophthalmologist	oogarts	**oagh**arts
paediatrician	kinderarts	**kin**der-arts
surgeon	chirurg	shee**rurgh**
urologist	uroloog	ewroa**loagh**

When is the surgery open?
Hoe laat heeft de dokter spreekuur?
hoo laht hayft de **dok**ter **sprayk**ewr?

Is the doctor in?
Is de dokter aanwezig?
is de **dok**ter ahn**way**zegh?

MEDICAL CARE

Does the doctor speak English?
Spreekt de dokter Engels?
spraykt de **dok**ter **eng**els?

◀ **Would you please take a seat in the waiting room?**
Wilt u in de wachtkamer plaats nemen?
wilt ew in de **waght**kahmer plahts **nay**men?

in the doctor's/dentist's office

I suffer from ...
Ik heb last van ...
ik hehp last van ...

My ... is hurting
Ik voel pijn in mijn ...
ik vool paiyn in maiyn ...

I can't move my ...
Ik kan mijn ... niet bewegen
ik kan maiyn ... neet be**way**ghen

I have been bitten by a dog/an insect
Ik ben gebeten door een hond/insect
ik behn ghe**bay**ten doar en hont/in**sehkt**

I am a diabetic/have a heart condition/am allergic to ...
Ik ben diabeticus/hartpatiënt/allergisch voor ...
ik behn dee-yah-**bay**-tee-kus/**hart**pah-syehnt/a**lehr**ghees voar ...

I have been treated/operated for this before
Ik ben al eerder behandeld/geopereerd hiervoor/hieraan
ik behn al **ayr**der be**han**delt/ghe-oa-pe-**rayrt** heer**voar**/heer**ahn**

◀ **How long have you been suffering from this?**
Hoe lang hebt u hier al last van?
hoo lang hehpt ew heer al last van?

◀ **Do you use any medication?**
Gebruikt u medicijnen?
ghe**brœkt** ew maydee**saiy**nen?

◀ **Where does it hurt?**
Waar doet het pijn?
wahr doot heht paiyn?

◀ **Does this hurt?**
Doet dit pijn?
doot dit paiyn?

◀ **Take a deep breath**
Zucht eens diep
zught ayns deep

◀ **Breathe in, than slowly breathe out**
Inademen en langzaam uitademen
inah-de-men ehn **lang**zahm **œt**ah-de-men

◀ **You should have an X-ray**
U moet een röntgenfoto laten maken
ew moot en "**rönt**gen"-foatoa **lah**ten **mah**ken

◀ **I have to refer you to a specialist**
Ik moet u naar een specialist verwijzen
ik moot ew nahr en **spay**syah-list ver**waiy**zen

◀ **You are suffering from ...**
U lijdt aan ...
ew laiyt ahn ...

◀ **I shall write out a prescription**
Ik zal u een recept geven
ik zal ew en re**sehpt ghay**ven

◄ You need to go to a hospital ...
U moet hiermee naar een ziekenhuis ...
ew moot heer**may** nahr en **zee**kenhœs ...

for a blood test	voor een bloedproef	voar en **bloot**proof
for a urinalysis	voor een urinetest	voar en ew**ree**netest
for further examinations	voor nader onderzoek	voar **nah**der **on**derzook

◄ You may not use/move this for a few days
U mag dit een paar dagen niet gebruiken/bewegen
ew magh dit en pahr **dah**ghen neet ghe**brœ**ken/be**way**ghen

◄ It's nothing serious
Het is niets ernstigs
heht is neets **ehrn**steghs

◄ I'll give you a painkiller/a sedative/sleeping pills
Ik geef u een pijnstiller/een kalmerend middel/een slaapmiddel
ik ghayf ew en **paiyn**sti-ler/en kal**may**rent **mi**del/en **slahp**mi-del

◄ You must take a tablet ...
U moet een tablet nemen ...
ew moot en tah**bleht nay**men ...

on an empty stomach	op de nuchtere maag	op de **nugh**tere mahgh
three times a day	driemaal daags	**dree**mahl dahghs
before each meal	vóór elke maaltijd	voar **ehl**ke **mahl**taiyt
after each meal	na elke maaltijd	nah **ehl**ke **mahl**taiyt
before you go to bed	vóór het slapengaan	voar heht **slahp**enghahn
with some water	met wat water	meht wat **wah**ter

I have .../You have ...
Ik heb ... /U hebt ...
ik hehp .../ew hehpt ...

a toothache	kiespijn/tandpijn	**kees**paiyn/**tant**paiyn
bleeding gums	bloedend tandvlees *sg.*	**bloo**dent **tant**vlaiys
an inflammation of the gums	ontstoken tandvlees *sg.*	ontstoaken **tant**vlays
caries	een gaatje/.. gaatjes	en **ghah**tye/.. **ghah**tyes
neuritis	een zenuwontsteking	en **zay**new-ontstayking
a broken tooth	een afgebroken tand	en **af**ghebroaken tant

I lost a filling/I broke my dentures
Ik heb een vulling verloren/Ik heb mijn kunstgebit gebroken
ik hehp en **vul**ing ver**loa**ren/ik hehp maiyn **kunst**ghebit ghe**broa**ken

◄ I'll have to pull/fill/drill this tooth
Ik moet deze kies trekken/vullen/boren
ik moot **day**ze kees **treh**ken/**vul**en/**boa**ren

◄ Rinse your mouth with this
U moet hiermee de mond spoelen
ew moot **heer**may de mont **spoo**len

◄ I'll give you a(n) ...
Ik geef u een ...
ik ghayf ew en ...

anaesthetic	verdoving	ver**doa**ving
crown	kroon	kroan
fluoride rinse	fluorspoeling	**flew**or-spooling
injection	injectie	in**jehk**see
temporary filling	noodvulling	**noat**vul-ing
root canal treatment	wortelkanaalbehandeling	**wor**tel-kahnahl-be**han**deling
root canal work	zenuwbehandeling	**zay**new-behandeling

◄ Consult your GP/dentist/specialist on returning home
U moet na thuiskomst uw huisarts/tandarts/specialist raadplegen
ew moot nah **toes**komst eww **hoes**arts/**tant**arts/**spay**shah-list **raht**playghen

◄ You must pay cash	Could I have a receipt for the insurance company?
U moet contant betalen	Kan ik een bewijsje krijgen voor de verzekering?
ew moot kon**tant** be**tah**len	kan ik en be**waiys**ye **kraiy**ghen voar de ver**zay**kering?

symptoms

abscess	abces *n*	ap**sehs**
aids	AIDS	"aids"
allergy	allergie	ahller**ghee**
angina	angina	ahn**ghee**na
appendicitis	blindedarmontsteking	blinde**darm**ontstayking
asthma	astma	**as**mah
backache	rugpijn	**rugh**paiyn
bellyache	buikpijn	**boek**paiyn
bleeding, haemorrhage	bloeding	**bloo**ding
bruise	bloeduitstorting	**bloot**oetstorting
burns	brandwond	**brant**wont
cold	verkoudheid	ver**kout**haiyt
concussion	hersenschudding	**hehr**sen-sghu-ding
constipation	verstopping	ver**sto**ping
cramp, spasm	kramp	kramp
depression	neerslachtigheid	nayr-**slagh**-tegh-haiyt
diarrhoea	diarree	dee-ya-**ray**
earache	oorpijn	**oar**paiyn
fever	koorts	koarts
flu	griep	ghreep

food poisoning	voedselvergiftiging	**voot**sel-vergifteghing
gastroenteritis	buikgriep	**bœk**ghreep
graze	schaafwond	**sghahf**wont
haemorrhoids	aambeien	**ahm**baiy-en
headache	hoofdpijn	**hoaft**paiyn
infection	infectie	in**fehk**see
inflammation of the jaw	kaakontsteking	**kahk**ont-stay-king
insect bite	insectenbeet	in**sehk**ten-bayt
insomnia	slapeloosheid	slahpe**loas**haiyt
itch	jeuk	yøk
laryngitis	keelontsteking	**kayl**ont-stay-king
lumbago	spit	spit
nausea	misselijkheid	**mi**-se-lek-haiyt
ophthalmia	oogontsteking	**oagh**ontstayking
pneumonia	longontsteking	**long**ont-stay-king
qualms	braakneigingen	**brahk**naiy-ghing-en
(the) shivers	rillerigheid *sg.*	**ri**-le-regh-haiyt
sinusitis	voorhoofdsholteontsteking	**voar**hoafts-holte-ont**stay**king
sore muscles	spierpijn *sg.*	**speer**paiyn
stomachache	maagpijn	**mahgh**paiyn
sunburn	zonnebrand	**zo**-ne-brant
sunstroke	zonnesteek	**zo**-ne-stayk
tick sting	tekenbeet	**tay**kenbayt
toothache	kiespijn	**kees**paiyn
ulcer	maagzweer	**mahgh**zwayr
wound	wond	wont

◄ **This bone has been fractured/cracked/injured**
Dit bot is gebroken/gescheurd/gekneusd
dit bot is ghe**broa**ken/ghe**sghørt**/ghe**knøst**

◄ **You've torn/pulled a muscle**
De spier is gescheurd/verrekt
de speer is ghe**sghørt**/veh**rehkt**

◄ **This must be ...**
Dit moet worden ...
dit moot **wor**den ...

bandaged	verbonden	ver**bon**den
operated on	geopereerd	ghe-oa-pe-**rayrt**
removed	verwijderd	ver**waiy**dert
rubbed	ingesmeerd	**in**ghe-smayrt
splint	gespalkt	ghe**spalkt**
stitched	gehecht	ghe**hehght**

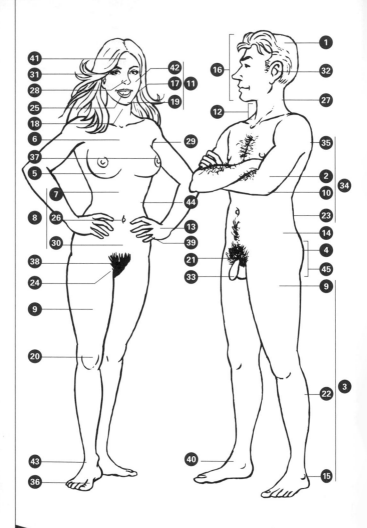

8	abdomen	buik	bœk
*	anus	anus	**ah**nus
2	arm	arm	arm
29	armpit	oksel	**ok**sel
34	back	rug	rugh
5	breast	borst	borst
4	buttock	bil	bil
45	buttocks, backside	zitvlak *n*	**zit**vlak
22	calf	kuit	kœt
42	cheek	wang	wang
6	chest	borstkas	**borst**kas
19	chin	kin	kin
21	crotch	kruis *n*	krœs
32	ear	oor *n*	oar
10	elbow	elleboog	**eh**-le-boagh
31	eye	oog *n*	oagh
11	face	gezicht *n*	ghe**zight**
39	finger	vinger	**ving**er
44	flank	zij	zaiy
38	foot	voet	voot
41	forehead	voorhoofd *n*	**voar**hoaft
24	groin	lies	lees
13	hand	hand	hand
16	head	hoofd *n*	hoaft
15	heel	hiel	heel
14	hip	heup	høp
41	instep	wreef	wrayf
17	jaw	kaak	kahk
20	knee	knie	knee
3	leg	been *n*	bayn
23	loin	lende	**lehn**de
30	lower abdomen	onderbuik	**on**derbœk
25	mouth	mond	mont
27	nape	nek	nehk
26	navel	navel	**nah**vel
12	neck	hals	hals
36	nipple	tepel	**tay**pel
28	nose	neus	nøs
1	occiput	achterhoofd *n*	**agh**terhoaft
33	penis	penis	**pay**nis

35	shoulder	schouder	**sghou**der
9	thigh	dij	**daiy**
18	throat	keel	kayl
36	toe	teen	tayn
7	upper abdomen, epigastrium	bovenbuik	**boa**venbœk
38	vagina	vagina	**vah**gheena

internal organs

4	appendix	blinde darm	**blin**de darm
2	bladder	blaas	blahs
3	bowel, intestine	darm	darm
7	gall bladder	galblaas	**ghal**blahs
8	heart	hart *n*	hart
9	heart valve	hartklep	**hart**klehp
14	kidney	nier	neer
5	large intestine	dikke darm	**di**ke darm
10	liver	lever	**lay**ver
11	lung	long	long
*1	pancreas	alvleesklier	**al**vlayskleer
6	small intestine	dunne darm	**du**ne darm
13	spleen	milt	milt

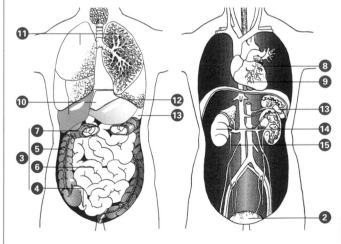

| 12 stomach | maag | mahgh |
| 15 ureter | urineleider | ew-**ree**-ne-laiy-der |

bones, joints, muscles

abdominal muscle	buikspier	**bœk**speer
Achilles tendon	achillespees	a-**ghi**-les-pays
cervical vertebra	halswervel	**hals**wehrvel
cheekbone	jukbeen n	**juk**bayn
chest, thorax	borstkas	**borst**kas
collar bone	sleutelbeen n	**slø**telbayn
dorsal muscle	rugspier	**rugh**speer
fibula	kuitbeen n	**kœt**bayn
gluteus maximus	bilspier	**bil**speer
gullet	slokdarm	**slok**darm
metacarpal bone	middenhandsbeentje n	**mi**-den-hants-bayn-tye
metatarsus	middenvoetsbeentje n	**mi**-den-voots-bayn-tye
muscle, muscular system	spier, spierstelsel n	speer, **speer**stehlsel
nasal bone	neusbeen n	**nøs**bayn
nasal cavity	neusholte	**nøs**holte
patella	knieschijf	**knee**sghaiyf
pelvis	bekken n	**beh**ken
phalanx (finger)	vingerkootje n	**ving**er-koatye
phalanx (toe)	teenkootje n	**tayn**-koatye
rib	rib	rip
scapula, shoulder blade	schouderblad n	**sghou**derblat
skull	schedel	**sghay**del
spine	wervelkolom	**wehr**velkolom
sural muscle	kuitspier	**kœt**speer
thighbone, femur	dijbeen n	**daiy**-bayn
tibia, shinbone	scheenbeen n	**sghayn**-bayn
tongue	tong	tong
tympanic membrane	trommelvlies n	**tro**melvlees
upper arm	bovenarm	boavenarm

at the pharmacy

(for items which can be bought without prescription, see "Toiletries and medicines" in the chapter on "Shopping")

Could you prepare this prescription for me?
Kunt u dit recept voor mij klaarmaken?
kunt ew dit re**sehpt** voar maiy **klahr**mahken?

What time can I pick it up?
Wanneer kan ik het afhalen?
wanayr kan ik heht **af**hahlen?

◄ **It can be prepared while you're waiting**
U kunt erop wachten
ew kunt ehr**op wagh**ten

Can you make out a receipt?
Wilt u een kwitantie uitschrijven?
wilt ew en kwee**tan**see **œt**sghraiven?

notices

DIT MIDDEL BEÏNVLOEDT	THIS MEDICINE AFFECTS
DE RIJVAARDIGHEID	YOUR ABILITY TO DRIVE
BUITEN BEREIK VAN	KEEP OUT OF REACH OF
KINDEREN HOUDEN	CHILDREN
NIET OM IN TE NEMEN	DO NOT INGEST/SWALLOW

hospital

◄ **You will be hospitalized in the ... ward**
U wordt hier opgenomen op de afdeling ...
ew wort heer **op**ghenoamen op de **af**dayling ...

◄ **You will be treated in the outpatients' department**
U wordt poliklinisch behandeld
ew wort poalee-**klee**-nees be**han**delt

◄ **You will probably have to stay for .. days**
U moet waarschijnlijk .. dagen blijven
ew moot wahr-**sghaiyn**lek .. **dah**ghen **blaiy**ven

◄ **You will be operated on ...**
U wordt ... geopereerd
ew wort ... ghe-oape**rayrt**

◄ **We will only run some tests on you**
U blijft alleen voor onderzoek
ew blaiyft a**layn** voar **on**derzook

◄ **You may leave the hospital on ...**
U mag ... het ziekenhuis weer verlaten
ew magh ... heht **zee**kenhœs wayr ver**lah**ten

◄ **You can be transported to England/America**
U mag naar Engeland/Amerika worden vervoerd
ew magh nahr **eng**elant/ah**may**reekah **wor**den ver**voort**

What time are visiting hours?
Wanneer is het bezoekuur?
wanayr is heht be**zook**ewr?

Can the children come along?
Mogen kinderen meekomen?
moaghen **kin**deren **may**koamen?

◄ **The patient is not allowed to receive any visitors**
De patiënt mag geen bezoek ontvangen
de pah**syehnt** magh ghayn be**zook** ont**vang**en

114

at the bank

Where can I find a bank?
Waar kan ik een bank vinden?
wahr kan ik en bank **vin**den?

Could you change these pounds/dollars for me?
Wilt u deze ponden/dollars voor mij wisselen?
wilt ew dayze **pon**den/"dollars" voar maiy **wis**-e-len?

What's the exchange rate?
Wat is de wisselkoers?
wat is de **wis**-el-koors?

How many euros do I get for twenty pounds?
Hoeveel euro krijg ik voor twintig pond?
hoovayl **uh**ro kraiygh ik voar **twin**tegh pond?

Do you also take coins?
Neemt u ook munten aan?
naymt ew oak **mun**ten ahn?

Could you cash this cheque?
Kunt u deze cheque verzilveren?
kunt ew **day**ze shekh ver**zil**veren?

I'd like to have three 100 euro notes, five 50 euro notes ...
Graag 3 biljetten van 100 euro, 5 van 50 ...
ghrahgh dree bil**yeh**ten van **hon**dert **uh**ro, vaiyf van **vaiyf**tegh ...

... and the balance in small change
... en de rest in kleingeld
... ehn de rehst in **klaiyn**ghelt

I prefer money of small denominations
Het liefst in kleine coupures
heht leefst in **klaiy**ne koo**pew**res

◄ **May I see your passport/banker's card?**
Mag ik uw paspoort/betaalpas zien?
magh ik eww **pas**poart/be**tahl**pas zeen?

◄ **Would you sign here, please?**
Wilt u hier tekenen?
wilt ew heer **tay**kenen?

Where do I sign?
Waar moet ik tekenen?
wahr moot ik **tay**kenen?

◄ **You can collect the money from the cashier**
U kunt het geld krijgen bij de kas
ew kunt heht ghelt **kraiy**ghen baiy de kas

I'd like to transfer this amount of money (by wire/telephone) to ...
Ik wil dit bedrag (telegrafisch/telefonisch) overmaken naar ...
ik wil dit be**dragh** (tayle**ghrah**fees/tayle**foa**nees) **oa**vermahken nahr ...

Has there any money been transferred to me?
Is er geld voor mij overgemaakt?
is ehr ghelt voar maiy **oa**verghemahkt?

115

American dollars	Amerikaanse dollars	ahmayree**kahn**se "dollars"
amount, sum	bedrag *n*	be**dragh**
bank(er's) card	pinpas/betaalpas	**pin**pahs/be**tahl**pahs
banker's commission	bankprovisie	**bank**proaveesee
bank notes	bankbiljetten	**bank**-bil-yeh-ten
bank order	bankopdracht	**bank**-op-draght
bill of exchange	wisselbriefje *n*	**wis**-el-breef-ye
British/Irish pounds*	Britse/Ierse ponden	**brit**se/**eer**se **pon**den
cash	contant geld *n*	kontant ghehlt
cash dispenser (ATM)	geldautomaat	**gheld**owtomaht
coins	munten	**mun**ten
counter	loket *n*	loa**keht**
credit card	creditcard	"creditcard"
current account	rekening-courant	**ray**kening-koo**rant**
current rate, today's rate (of exchange)	dagkoers	**dagh**koors
to deposit	storten	**stor**ten
exchange rate	wisselkoers	**wis**-el-koors
foreign currency	deviezen	de**vee**zen
form	formulier *n*	formew**leer**
identity papers	legitimatie(bewijs)	lay-gheetee-**mah**see(be-waiys)
opening hours	openingstijden	**oa**pe-nings-taiy-den
receipt	kasbewijs *n*, kwitantie	**kas**bewaiys, kwee**tan**see
savings account	spaarrekening	**spahr**-ray-ke-ning
small change	kleingeld *n*	**klaiyn**ghehlt
using the PIN code	pinnen	**pin**nen
stock	effecten	eh**fehk**ten
to transfer	overmaken	**oa**vermahken
transfer form	overschrijvingsformulier *n*	**oa**-ver-sghraiy-vings-for-mew-leer
traveller's cheques	reischeques	**raiys**-shehks
to withdraw	opnemen	**op**naymen

notices

GELD WISSELEN	CHANGE
(HOOFD)KAS	(HEAD)CASHIER'S DESK
INLICHTINGEN	INFORMATION
KREDIETEN	LOANS
SPAARBANK	SAVINGS BANK
UITBETALINGEN	PAY-COUNTER

Where is the nearest post office?
Waar is het dichtstbijzijnde postkantoor?
wahr is heht **dightst**-baiy-zaiyn-de **post**kantoar?

Where can I find a letter box?
Waar is een brievenbus?
wahr is en **bree**venbus?

How much is a stamp for a letter/postcard to England/America?
Hoeveel moet er op een brief/ansichtkaart naar Engeland/Amerika?
hoovayl moot ehr op en breef/**an**sightkahrt nahr **engel**and/ah**may**reekah?

Do you have any special stamps?
Heeft u ook bijzondere postzegels?
hayft ew oak bee**zon**dere **post**-zay-ghels?

I'd like to have this series
Ik wil graag deze serie
ik wil ghrahgh **day**ze **say**ree

Three stamps of ... cents, please
Drie postzegels van … cent alstublieft
dree pohst**zay**ghels vahn … cent ahl**stew**bleeft

addressee	geadresseerde	ghe-ah-dreh-**sayr**-de
air mail	luchtpost	**lught**post
collection	lichting	**ligh**ting
express post	exprespost	"express"-post
letter	brief	breef
letter box, postbox	brievenbus	**bree**venbus

Addressing letters

In the Netherlands you frequently use the recipient's initials rather than writing out the first names in full. The name is preceded by **Dhr.** (de Heer = Mr) or **Mevr.** (Mevrouw = Mrs, Ms). Usage is rather more flexible in Belgium, where people also often write their surname first. Postcodes consist of four digits (two for the place, two for the postal district), in Holland followed by two letters (denoting the part of the street).

Dhr. J.H. van Vliet
Nassaukade 102
1054 SH AMSTERDAM
Nederland

Mevr. Verbiest Jeanne
Oude Steenweg 42
2000 ANTWERPEN
België

Some house numbers also have an additional **II** (or **"**), meaning "second floor", or **hs** (huis - "house", meaning ground floor and originally used to indicate flats in the same building as a shop).

ALLE LOKETHANDELINGEN	ALL SERVICES
(HOOFD)KAS	(HEAD) CASHIER
POSTBANK	GIRO BANK
INLICHTINGEN	INFORMATION
POSTPAKKETTEN	PARCEL POST
UITBETALINGEN	PAYMENTS
FILATELIE	PHILATELY
AANGETEKENDE STUKKEN	REGISTERED MAIL
ZEGELVERKOOP	STAMPS
TELEFOON	TELEPHONE

opening hours	openingstijden	**oa**-pe-nings-tay-den
parcel	pakket *n*	pa**keht**
parcel post	pakketpost	pa**keht**post
PO box	postbus	**post**bus
postage paid by addressee	kosten ontvanger	**kos**ten ont**vang**er
postal code	postcode	**post**koade
postcard	briefkaart	**breef**kahrt
(picture) postcard	ansichtkaart	**an**sightkahrt
printed matter	drukwerk *n*	**druk**wehrk
recorded mail	post met ontvangst- bevestiging	post meht ont-**vangst**- be-vehs-te-ghing
registered	aangetekend	**ahn**-ghe-tay-kent
sample	monster *n* zonder waarde	**monster zon**der **wahr**de
sender	afzender	**af**zehnder
stamp	postzegel	**post**zayghel
stamp(-vending) machine	postzegelautomaat	**post**zayghel-outoamaht

Where can I find a telephone booth?
Waar is een telefooncel?
wahr is en tayle**foan**sehl?

Where can I make a phone call?
Waar kan ik telefoneren?
wahr kan ik taylefoa**nay**ren?

Can I phone with a credit card?
Kan ik hier bellen met een creditcard?:
kahn ik heer **bel**len met en "**cre**ditcard"

I'd like to make a phone call to Britain/America
Ik wil graag een gesprek met Engeland/Amerika voeren
ik wil ghrahgh en ghe**sprehk** meht **ehng**elant/ah**may**reeka **voo**ren

Do you know the international access code/international dialing code/dialing code?
Weet u het internationaal toegangsnummer/landnummer/netnummer?
wayt ew heht **in**ter-na-syoa-nahl **too**ghangs-nu-mer/**lant**nu-mer/**net**numer?

◄ **You can dial the number yourself**
U kunt zelf het nummer draaien
ew kunt zehlf heht **nu**mer **drah**yen

How much is the call per minute?
Hoeveel kost het gesprek per minuut?
hoovayl kost heht ghe**sprehk** pehr mee**newt**?

How much do I owe you?
Hoeveel ben ik u schuldig?
hoovayl behn ik ew **sghul**degh?

I can't get through
Ik krijg geen verbinding
ik kraiygh ghayn ver**bin**ding

The line is engaged
De lijn is bezet
de laiyn is be**zeht**

There's no reply
Ik krijg geen gehoor
ik kraiygh ghayn ghe**hoar**

◄ **Hold on please**
Blijft u aan de lijn
blaiyft ew ahn de laiyn

The line is bad/has been disconnected
De verbinding is slecht/verbroken
de ver**bin**ding is slehght/ver**broa**ken

◄ **One moment please**
Een moment alstublieft
en moa**meht** alstew**bleeft**

Could I speak to Mr/Mrs Jansma?
Kan ik met de heer/mevrouw Jansma spreken?
kan ik meht de hayr/me**vrou jan**smah **spray**ken?

◄ **I'll put you through**
Ik verbind u door
ik ver**bint** ew doar

◄ **He/She is not in**
Hij/Zij is niet aanwezig
haiy/zaiy is neet ahn**way**zegh

Can he/she call me back?
Kan hij/zij mij terugbellen?
kahn haiy/zaiy maiy te**rugh**behlen?

busy, engaged	bezet	be**zeht**
call	gesprek *n*	ghe**sprehk**
to call	opbellen	**op**behlen
cell phone	mobiele telefoon	mow**bee**le tele**foan**
coins	munten	**mun**ten
collect call	collectcall	"col**lect**call"
dialling code	netnummer *n*	**net**numer
direct	automatisch	outoa**mah**tees
insert	inwerpen	**in**wehrpen
international	internationaal	**in**ter-nah-syoa-nahl

local	lokaal	loa**kahl**
out of order	defect	de**fehkt**
provider	provider	"pro**vi**der"
refund	teruggave	te**rugh**-ghahve
send an text message, to	sms'en	es-em-**es**sen
subscriber's number	abonneenummer *n*	a-bo-**nay**-nu-mer
telephone booth	telefooncel	tayle**foan**sehl
telephone directory	telefoonboek *n*	tayle**foan**book
telephone exchange	centrale	sehn**trahle**
trunk, long-distance	interlokaal	interloa**kahl**
upgrade, to	opwaarderen	**op**wahrdehren
telephone card	telefoonkaart	tele**foan**kahrt
WAP-ing	wappen	**wahp**pen

internet

Where can I find an Internet point?
Waar vind ik een internetcafé?
wahr vind ik en **in**ternet-ka**fay**

How much will it cost?
Hoeveel kost het?
hoovayl kost het

◄ **Using the Internet will cost ... euros per (half) hour**
Internetten kost ... euro per (half) uur
internetten kost ... **uh**roh per (hahlf) ewr

There is no sound
Het geluid doet het niet
het ghe**lœd** doot het neet

I cannot log in
Het lukt niet om in te loggen
het lukt neet om in te **logh**ghen

I would like to print a few pages
Ik wil graag een paar pagina's uitprinten
ik will grahgh en pahr **pah**gheenahs **œt**printen

The PC is stuck
De PC is vastgelopen
de pay-**say** is **vahst**ghelohpen

I think there is a virus in the computer
Ik denk dat er een virus in deze computer zit
ik denk daht er en **vee**rus in **day**ze "com**pu**ter" zit

◄ **You are not allowed to download here**
Je mag hier niets downloaden
ye magh heer neets "**down**load"-en

Can I burn a CD here?
Kan ik hier een cd branden?
kahn ik heer en say-**day brahn**den

chatting	chatten	"**chat**"-ten
sending an e-mail message	e-mailen	"**e**-mail"-en
user's name	gebruikersnaam	ghe**brœ**kersnahm
homepage	homepage	"**home**page"
password	wachtwoord	**waght**twoard
website	website	"**web**site"

on the beach/in the swimming pool

How far is it to the beach/swimming pool?
Hoe ver is het naar het strand/zwembad?
hoo vehr is heht nahr heht strant/**zwehm**bat?

Is swimming allowed here?
Mag hier worden gezwommen?
magh heer **wor**den ghe**zwo**men?

◄ **You're not allowed to swim here**
U mag hier niet zwemmen
ew magh heer neet **zweh**men

Is there a dangerous current?
Is er een gevaarlijke stroming?
is ehr en ghe**vahr**leke **stroa**ming?

What's the temperature of the water?
Hoe warm is het water?
hoo warm is heht **wah**ter?

Is it dangerous here for children?
Is het hier gevaarlijk voor kinderen?
is heht heer ghe**vahr**lek voar **kin**deren?

Is there any supervision?
Is er toezicht?
is ehr **too**zight?

The sea is calm/turbulent
De zee is kalm/woelig
de zay is kalm/**woo**legh

The waves are high
Er zijn hoge golven
ehr zaiyn **hoa**ghe **ghol**ven

There is a storm coming up
Er komt storm
ehr komt storm

Are dogs allowed here?
Mogen hier honden komen?
moaghen heer **hon**den **koa**men?

I find the water too cold
Het water is mij te koud
heht **wah**ter is maiy te kout

I can't swim
Ik kan niet zwemmen
ik kahn neet **zweh**men

How much is the entrance fee for two adults and one child?
Hoeveel is de entree voor twee volwassenen en een kind?
hoovayl is de ehn**tray** voar tway vol**wa**senen ehn en kint?

Two tickets please
Twee kaartjes alstublieft
tway **kahr**tyes alstew**bleeft**

One child's ticket please
Een kinderkaartje alstublieft
en **kin**derkahrtye alstew**bleeft**

Is there a children's pool here?
Is hier een kinderbadje?
is heer en **kin**derbatye?

Is it an indoor/open-air/heated pool?
Is het zwembad overdekt/onoverdekt/verwarmd?
is heht **zwehm**bat oaver**dehkt/on**oaverdehkt/ver**warmt**?

bather	badgast	**bat**ghast
bathing cap	badmuts	**bat**muts
bathing towel	badhanddoek	**bat**handook

bathing/swimming trunks	zwembroek	**zwehm**brook
bikini	bikini	bee**kee**nee
changing cubicles	omkleedcabines	**om**klayt-kah-bee-nes
chute	waterglijbaan	**wah**ter-glaiy-bahn
fine sand	fijn zand *n*	faiyn zant
high tide	vloed	vlood
jellyfish	kwal	quahl
lifeguards	reddingsbrigade	**reh**dings-bree-ghah-de
low tide	eb	eb
open-air swimming pool	openluchtbad *n*	oapen**lught**bat
shells	schelpen	**sghehl**pen
showers	douches	**doo**syes
surf	branding	**bran**ding
swimming pool attendant	badmeester	**bat**mayster
swimsuit	(eendelig) badpak *n*	(**ayn**daylegh) **bat**pak
walk along the beach	strandwandeling	**strant**wan-de-ling
water temperature	watertemperatuur	**wah**ter-tehm-pay-rah-tewr

I'd like to rent ...
Ik wil graag ... huren
ik wil ghrahgh ... **hew**ren

an air mattress	een luchtbed	en **lught**bet
a deck chair	een ligstoel	en **ligh**stool
a pedal boat	een waterfiets	en **wah**terfeets
a sunshade	een parasol	en pahrah**sol**
swimwear	badkleding	**bat**klayding

water sports

boardsailing, windsurfing	(wind)surfen	(**wint**)surfen
canoeing	kanovaren	**kah**noavahren
canyoning	wildwatervaren	willd**wah**tervahren
diving	duiken	**dœ**ken
kite surfing	kitesurfen	"**kite**surf"-en
motor boat sailing	motorbootvaren	**moa**tor-boat-vah-ren
parasailing	parasailen	"**para**sail"-en
rowing	roeien	**roo**yen
sailing	zeilen	**zaiy**len
snorkling	snorkelen	**snor**kelen
surfriding	brandingsurfen	**bran**ding-surfen
water scooter	waterscooter	**wah**ter-"scooter"
waterskiing	waterskiën	**wah**ter-skee-yen

notices

STRAND	BEACH
VRIJ TOEGANKELIJK	OPEN TO THE PUBLIC
ZWEMMEN VERBODEN	NO SWIMMING
GEVAARLIJKE STROMING	DANGEROUS CURRENT
(OPENLUCHT)ZWEMBAD	(OPEN-AIR) SWIMMING POOL
BADMEESTER	SWIMMING POOL ATTENDANT
OMKLEEDCABINES	CHANGING CUBICLES
TOILETTEN	TOILETS
DOUCHES	SHOWERS
DAMES	LADIES
HEREN	GENTS
HONDEN NIET TOEGELATEN	NO DOGS ALLOWED
KINDERBAD	CHILDREN'S POOL
NATURISTENSTRAND	NUDIST BEACH

Is there a marina nearby?
Is hier een jachthaven in de buurt?
is heer en **yacht**hahven in de bewrt?

Where is the harbour master's office?
Waar is het havenkantoor?
wahr is heht **hah**venkantoar?

How much for a berth?
Wat kost hier een ligplaats?
wat kost heer en **ligh**plahts?

Can I rent ...?
Kan ik ... huren?
kan ik ... **hew**ren?

diving gear	duikspullen	**dœk**spu-len
a motor boat	een motorboot	en **moa**torboat
a rowing boat	een roeiboot	en **rooy**boat
a sailing boat, yacht	een zeilboot	en **zaiyl**boat
a surfboard	een surfplank	en **surf**plank
water skis	waterski's	**wah**terskees

Is diving allowed here?
Mag hier gedoken worden?
magh heer ghe**doa**ken **wor**den?

Is a permit required?
Is daar een vergunning voor nodig?
is dahr en ver-**ghu**-ning voar **noa**degh?

123

Is there a sailing school here?
Is hier een zeilschool?
is heer en **zaiyl**sghoal

How much for a lesson?
Wat kost een les?
wat kost en lehs?

berth	ligplaats	**ligh**plahts
buoy	boei	booy
catamaran	catamaran	kata**mah**ran"
decompression chamber	decompressiekamer	daykom**preh**seekahmer
diving mask	duikbril	**dœk**bril
flippers	flippers	"**flip**pers"
harbour master	havenmeester	**hah**venmayster
jetty, mole	havenhoofd, steiger	**hah**venhoaft, **staiy**gher
lifebuoy	reddingsboei	**reh**dingsbooy
life jacket	zwemvest *n*	**zwehm**vehst
oars	roeiriemen	**rooy**reemen
outboard motor	buitenboordmotor	**bœten**boartmoator
paddles	peddels	**peh**dels
rowing boat	roeiboot	**rooy**boat
sailing boat, yacht	zeilboot, jacht *n*	**zaiyl**boat, yaght
snorkel	snorkel	**snor**kel
speedboat	speedboat	"speedboat"
oxygen cylinder	zuurstofles	**zewr**stof-flehs

horse riding

Is there a riding school around?
Is hier een manege/rijschool?
is heer en mah**nay**zhe/**raiy**sghoal?

Can I rent a horse/pony?
Kan ik een paard/pony huren?
kan ik en pahrt/**pon**nee **hew**ren?

Are there lessons for children?
Kunnen kinderen hier les krijgen?
ku-nen **kin**deren heer lehs **kraiy**ghen?

How much is the rent/a lesson per hour?
Wat kost de huur/een les per uur?
wat kost de hewr/en lehs pehr ewr?

I can't ride yet
Ik kan nog niet paardrijden
ik kan nogh neet **pahrt**raiyden

This horse is too wild for me
Het paard is mij te wild
heht pahrt is maiy te wilt

Where can I rent a bike?
Waar kan ik een fiets huren?
wahr kan ik en feets **hew**ren?

How much is it a day/an hour?
Wat kost dit per dag/uur?
wat kost dit pehr dagh/ewr?

◄ **You must pay a deposit**
U moet een borgsom betalen
ew moot en **borgh**som be**tah**len

◄ **Do you have any identification?**
Kunt u zich legitimeren?
kunt ew zigh lay-ghee-tee-**may**-ren?

I want a three-speed bike
Ik wil een fiets met drie versnellingen
ik will en feets met dree ver**snel**lingen

Could you adjust the saddle for me?
Wilt u het zadel voor mij afstellen?
wilt ew heht **zah**del voar maiy **af**stellen?

It's too high/too low
Het staat te hoog/te laag
heht staht te hoagh/te lahgh

Do you have a cyclists' map?
Heeft u een fietskaart?
hayft ew en **feets**kahrt?

Do you have any information on cycle routes?
Heeft u informatie over fietsroutes?
hayft ew infor**mah**tsee **oa**ver **feets**rootes?

bicycle lock	fietsslot n	**feets**-slot
bicycle pump	fietspomp	**feets**pomp
children's bicycle	kinderfiets	**kin**derfeets
child's seat	kinderzitje n	**kin**derzitye
combination lock	ringslot n	**ring**slot
crash helmet	fietshelm	**feets**helm
cross-country bike	crossfiets	"**cross**"-feets
gent's bike/bicycle	herenfiets	**hay**renfeets
lady's bike	damesfiets	**dah**mesfeets
mountain-bike	mountainbike	"**moun**tainbike"
rent-a-bike	fietsverhuur	**feets**verhewr
tandem	tandem	"tandem"

(see also "Bicycle parts" on page 61)

roping down	abseilen	ab**zaiy**len
guide	gids	ghids
hill	heuvel	**hø**vel
marking	markering	mahr**keh**ring
climbing hall	klimhal	**klim**hahl
climbing	klimmen	**klim**men
ascending	stijgen	**staiy**ghen
route	route	**roo**te
rucksack	rugzak	**rugh**zahk
view point	uitzichtpunt	**œt**zightpunt
foot path	wandelpad	**wahn**delpahd
walking shoes	wandelschoenen	**wahn**delsghoonen

golf

buggy	buggy	"**bug**gy"
club	club/golfstok	"club"/**g(h)olf**stock
golf course	golfbaan	**g(h)olf**bahn
green fee	green fee	"green fee"
handicap	handicap	"**han**dicap"
holes	holes	"holes"
track	parcours	pahr**koor(s)**
trolley	trolley/wagentje	"**trol**ley"/**wah**ghentye

football (soccer)

Is there an interesting match today?
Is er vandaag een leuke wedstrijd?
is ehr van**dahgh** en **lø**ke **weht**straiyt?

What time does it start?
Hoe laat begint het?
hoo laht be**ghint** heht?

One seat/terrace please
Een zitplaats/staanplaats alstublieft
en **zit**plahts/**stahn**plahts alstew**bleeft**

The English/Scottish team plays better/worse
Engeland/Schotland speelt beter/slechter
ehngelant/**sghot**lant spaylt **bay**ter/**slehgh**ter

The referee is just awful!
Wat een slechte scheidsrechter!
wat en **slehgh**te **sghaiyts**rehghter!

break	pauze, rust	**pou**ze, rust
corner	hoekschop, corner	**hook**sghop, "corner"
defeat	nederlaag, verlies n	**nay**derlahgh, ver**lees**
defence	verdediging, achterhoede	ver-**day**-de-ghing, **agh**ter-hoo-**de**
draw, tie	gelijkspel n	ghe-laiyk-**spehl**
extra time	verlenging	ver**lehng**ing
forward line	aanval, spits	**ahn**-val, spits
free kick	vrije schop	**vraiy**-e sghop
game, match	wedstrijd	**wet**straiyt
goal (area)	doel	dool
goal (point scored)	doelpunt, goal	**dool**punt, "goal"
goal keeper	keeper	"keeper"
half	(speel)helft	**(spayl)**-hehlft
half-time	rust	rust
linesman	grensrechter	**ghrehns**rehghter
midfield player	middenveldspeler	**mi**-den-vehlt-spay-ler
offside	buitenspel	bœten**spehl**
penalty (kick)	strafschop, penalty	**straf**sghop, "penalty"
red card	rode kaart	**roa**de kahrt
referee, umpire	scheidsrechter	**sghaiyts**-rehghter
victory	overwinning, winst	oaver**wi**ning, winst
yellow card	gele kaart	**ghay**le kahrt

other sports

Where is the ...?
Waar is de/het ...?
wahr is de/heht ...?

circuit	circuit	sir**quee**
climbing hall	klimhal	**klim**hahl
golf course/links	golfbaan	**gholf**bahn
race track	draf- en renbaan	draf- ehn **rehn**bahn
(artificial) skating rink	(kunst)ijsbaan	**(kunst)**aiysbahn
(artificial) skiing slope	(kunst)skibaan	**(kunst)**skeebahn
soccer stadium	voetbalstadion n	**voot**bal-stah-dee-yon
sports hall/centre	sporthal	**sport**hal
sports park	sportpark n	**sport**park
tennis court	tennisbaan	"tennis"-bahn
aerobics	aerobics	"ae**ro**bics"
athletics	atletiek	atle**teek**
badminton	badminton	"badminton"

baseball	honkbal	**honk**bal
basketball	basketbal	**bas**ketbal
bicycle racing	wielrennen	**weel**rehnen
billiards	biljarten	bil**yar**ten
(tenpin) bowling	bowling	"bowling"
boxing	boksen	**box**en
bungy jumping	bungyjumpen	"**bun**gyjump"-en
chess	schaken	**sghah**ken
cricket	cricket	"cricket"
fencing	schermen	**sghehr**men
fitness training	fitness (training)	"**fit**ness (**trai**ning)"
football	voetbal	**voot**bal
golf	golf	gholf
handball	handbal	**hant**bal
hockey	hockey	"hockey"
(ice) hockey	(ijs)hockey	(**ice**)-"hockey"
horse racing	draf- en rensport	draf- ehn **rehn**sport
in-line skating	inline skaten	**in**line skate"-en
jogging	joggen	"jog"-en
judo	judo	**yew**doa
karate	karate	kah**rah**te
motor sports	autosport, motorsport	**ou**toasport, **moa**torsport
mountaineering	bergklimmen	**bergh**-kli-men
riding	paardrijden	**pahrt**raiyden
rowing	roeien	**roo**-yen
rugby league	rugby (13-tallen)	**rugh**bee (**dehr**teen-ta-len)
rugby union	rugby (15-tallen)	**rugh**bee (**vaiyf**teen-ta-len)
soccer	voetbal	**voot**bal
swimming	zwemmen	**zweh**men
table tennis	tafeltennis	**tah**fel-"tennis"
tennis	tennis	"tennis"
volleyball	volleybal	"volley"-bal

relaxing

massage	massage	mas**sa**zhe
sauna	sauna	**sow**nah
solarium	zonnebank	**zon**nebahnk
Turkish bath	Turks bad	turks bahd
jacuzzi	bubbelbad	**bub**belbahd
public baths	badhuis	**bad**hœs

Where do I find a shopping street/supermarket/shopping centre?
Waar vind ik hier een winkelstraat/supermarkt/winkelcentrum?
wahr vint ik heer en **win**kelstraht/**su**permarkt/**win**kelsehntrum?

What time do the shops open/close?
Hoe laat gaan de winkels hier open/dicht?
hoo laht ghahn de **win**kels heer **oa**pen/dight?

Where do I find a market/flee market?
Waar vind ik een markt/vlooienmarkt?
wahr vint ik en markt/**vloa**yenmarkt?

Do they close for lunch/are they open at night?
Is er een middagpauze/koopavond?
is ehr en **mi**daghpouze/**koap**ahvont?

Is there a shop which is open on sundays/at night?
Is er een winkel die op zondag/'s avonds open is?
is ehr en **win**kel dee op **zon**dagh/**sah**vonts **oa**pen is?

conversations with shop assistants

◄ **Can I help you?**
Kan ik u ergens mee helpen?
kan ik ew **ehr**ghens may **hehl**pen?

I am only browsing
Ik kijk zo maar wat rond
ik kaiyk zoa mahr wat ront

Do you have a ... for me?
Heeft u voor mij een ...?
hayft ew voar maiy en ...?

Do you also sell ...?
Heeft u ook ...?
hayft ew oak ...?

◄ **No, we don't sell that/I'm afraid it's sold out**
Nee, dat hebben we niet/dat is helaas uitverkocht
nay, dat **heh**ben we neet/dat is hay**lahs œt**verkoght

Do you have another ...?
Heeft u een andere ...?
hayft ew en **an**dere ...?

How much is this one?
Wat kost dit/deze?
wat kost dit/**day**ze?

That's too expensive for me
Dat is mij te duur
dat is maiy te dewr

AANBIEDING	SPECIAL OFFER
ANTIEK	ANTIQUES
APOTHEEK	DISPENSING CHEMIST'S
BAKKERIJ	BAKERY
BANKET	CONFECTIONARY
BIJOUX	JEWELS
BLOEMEN	FLOWERS
BOEKEN	BOOKS
BOEKHANDEL	BOOKSHOP
BROOD	BREAD
CADEAUARTIKELEN	GIFTS
CHEMISCH REINIGEN	DRY-CLEANER
CURIOSA	BRIC-A-BRAC
DAMESKAPPER	LADIES' HAIRDRESSER
DAMESKLEDING	LADIES' WEAR
DEKENS	BLANKETS
DELICATESSENHANDEL	DELICATESSEN
FRUIT	FRUIT
GEOPEND	OPEN
GESLOTEN	CLOSED
GLAS	GLASSWARE
GOUD(SMID)	GOLD(SMITH)
GROENTEHANDEL	GREENGROCER'S
HANDWERK	HANDICRAFT
HERENKAPPER	BARBER
HERENKLEDING	MEN'S WEAR
HORLOGER	WATCHMAKER
INGANG	ENTRANCE
JUWELEN	JEWELRY
KANTOORBOEKHANDEL	STATIONER
KAPPER	HAIRDRESSER
KINDERKLEDING	CHILDREN'S WEAR
KLEERMAKER	TAILOR
KUNSTNIJVERHEID	ARTS AND CRAFTS
LEDERWAREN	LEATHER GOODS
MELKHANDEL	DAIRY
MEUBELS	FURNITURE
MUNTEN	COINS
OPTICIEN	OPTICIAN

OVERHEMDEN	(MEN'S) SHIRTS
PAPIERWAREN	STATIONERY
PORSELEIN	CHINA
POSTZEGELS	STAMPS
REISARTIKELEN	TRAVEL SUPPLIES
REISBUREAU	TRAVEL AGENCY
ROOKWAREN	TOBACCO
SCHOENEN	SHOES
SCHOENMAKER	COBBLER
SCHOONHEIDSSALON	BEAUTY PARLOUR
SLAGER	BUTCHER
SLIJTERIJ	OFF-LICENCE
SPEELGOED	TOYS
STOMERIJ	DRY-CLEANER'S
TWEEDEHANDS ARTIKELEN	SECOND HAND GOODS
TIJDSCHRIFTEN	MAGAZINES
UITGANG	EXIT
UITVERKOCHT	SOLD OUT
UITVERKOOP	SALE
VISHANDEL	FISHMONGER'S
VLEESWAREN	COLD MEATS
WARENHUIS	DEPARMENT STORE
WASSERETTE	LAUNDERETTE
WERKDAGEN	WEEKDAYS
WONINGINRICHTING	HOME FURNISHINGS
WIJNHANDEL	WINE SHOP
IJZERWAREN	HARDWARE
ZON- EN FEESTDAGEN	SUNDAYS AND PUBLIC HOLIDAYS

English-Dutch

ANTIQUES	ANTIEK
ARTS AND CRAFTS	KUNSTNIJVERHEID
BAKERY	BAKKERIJ
BARBER	HERENKAPPER
BEAUTY PARLOUR	SCHOONHEIDSSALON

BLANKETS	DEKENS
BOOKS	BOEKEN
BOOKSHOP	BOEKHANDEL
BREAD	BROOD
BRIC-A-BRAC	CURIOSA
CHILDREN'S WEAR	KINDERKLEDING
CHINA	PORSELEIN
CLOSED	GESLOTEN
COBBLER	SCHOENMAKER
COINS	MUNTEN
COLD MEATS	VLEESWAREN
CONFECTIONARY	BANKET
DAIRY	MELKHANDEL
DELICATESSEN	DELICATESSENHANDEL
DEPARTMENT STORE	WARENHUIS
DISPENSING CHEMIST'S	APOTHEEK
DRY-CLEANER'S	STOMERIJ
DRY-CLEANING	CHEMISCH REINIGEN
ENTRANCE	INGANG
EXIT	UITGANG
FISHMONGER'S	VISHANDEL
FLOWERS	BLOEMEN
FRUIT	FRUIT
FURNITURE	MEUBELS
GIFTS	CADEAUARTIKELEN
GLASSWARE	GLAS
GOLD(SMITH)	GOUD(SMID)
GREENGROCER'S	GROENTEHANDEL
HAIRDRESSER	KAPPER
HANDICRAFT	HANDWERK
HARDWARE	IJZERWAREN
HOME FURNISHINGS	WONINGINRICHTING
JEWELRY	JUWELEN
JEWELS	BIJOUX
LADIES' HAIRDRESSER	DAMESKAPPER
LADIES' WEAR	DAMESKLEDING
LAUNDERETTE	WASSERETTE
LEATHER GOODS	LEDERWAREN
MAGAZINES	TIJDSCHRIFTEN

MEN'S SHIRTS	OVERHEMDEN
MEN'S WEAR	HERENKLEDING
OFF-LICENCE	SLIJTERIJ
OPEN	OPEN
OPTICIAN	OPTICIEN
SALE	UITVERKOOP
SECOND HAND GOODS	TWEEDEHANDS ARTIKELEN
SHIRTS	OVERHEMDEN
SHOES	SCHOENEN
SOLD OUT	UITVERKOCHT
SPECIAL OFFER	AANBIEDING
STAMPS	POSTZEGELS
STATIONER	KANTOORBOEKHANDEL
STATIONERY	PAPIERWAREN
SUNDAYS AND PUBLIC HOLIDAYS	ZON- EN FEESTDAGEN
TAILOR	KLEERMAKER
TOBACCO	ROOKWAREN
TOYS	SPEELGOED
TRAVEL AGENCY	REISBUREAU
TRAVEL SUPPLIES	REISARTIKELEN
WATCHMAKER	HORLOGER
WEEKDAYS	WERKDAGEN
WINE SHOP	WIJNHANDEL

Do you have anything cheaper?
Heeft u iets goedkopers?
hayft ew eets ghoot**koa**pers?

I'll take this one
Dit/deze neem ik
dit/**day**ze naym ik

This one doesn't fit
Dit/deze past mij niet
dit/**day**ze past maiy neet

It's too ...
Hij/Het is te ...
haiy/heht is te ...

long	lang	lang
loose	wijd	waiyt
narrow	smal	smal
short	kort	kort
small	klein	klaiyn
tight	nauw	nou
wide	breed	brayt

Could this be sent directly to Britain/America?
Kan dit rechtstreeks naar Engeland/Amerika worden gestuurd?
kan dit **rehght**strayks nahr **eng**elant/ah**may**reekah **wor**den ghe**stewrt**?

This is the address
Dit is het adres
dit is heht ah**drehs**

Could you wrap it for me?
Wilt u het voor me inpakken?
wilt ew heht voar me **in**pak-en?

◄ **Do you want anything else?**
Nog iets van uw dienst?
nogh eets van eww deenst?

No thank you, that will be all
Nee dank u, dat was het
nay dank ew, dat was heht

◄ **You can pay at the cash register**
U kunt betalen aan de kassa
ew kunt be**tah**len ahn de **kas**ah

◄ **You can change it within 8 days**
U kunt het binnen 8 dagen ruilen
ew kunt heht **bin**en aght **dah**ghen **rœ**len

Can I pay with a credit card?
Kan ik betalen met een creditcard?
kan ik be**tah**len meht en "creditcard"?

◄ **Do you have an account here?**
Hebt u hier een rekening (lopen)?
hehpt ew heer en **ray**kening (**loa**pen)?

I'd like to exchange this
Ik wil dit graag ruilen
ik wil dit ghrahgh **rœ**len

Here is the receipt
Hier is de kassabon
heer is de **kas**ahbon

◄ **You can exchange this at the customer service**
U kunt dit ruilen bij de klantenservice
ew kunt dit **rœ**len baiy de **klan**ten"service"

Could I have a refund?
Kan ik het geld terugkrijgen?
kan ik heht ghehlt te**rugh**kraiyghen?

◄ **No, you will receive a credit note**
Nee, u krijgt een tegoedbon
nay, ew kraiyght en te**ghoot**bon

colors, patterns, fabrics

See the list under "Clothes and shoes".

weights, measures, quantities

a box	een doos	en doas
a tin, can	een blik *n*	en blik
a packet	een pak *n*	en pak

one piece	één stuk *n*	ayn stuk
a pair	een paar *n*	en pahr
a set	een set	en seht
a bottle	een fles	en flehs
a roll	een rol	en rol
a tube	een tube	en **tew**be
a bag	een zak	en zak

foodstuffs, vegetables, fruit, etc.

(See also the chapter on "Food and drink")

apples	appels	**a**pels
apricots	abrikozen	ahbree**koa**zen
bananas	bananen	bah**nah**nen
beer	bier *n*	beer
biscuits	koekjes	**kook**yes
bread	brood *n*	broat
butter	boter	**boa**ter
cake	koek	kook
candy	snoep *n*	snoop
cash register	kassa	**kas**ah
cheese	kaas	kahs
cherries	kersen	**kehr**sen
chicken	kip *f*, haantje *n*	kip, **hahn**tye
chocolate	chocolade	shoakoa**lah**de
coffee	koffie	**kof**ee
instant coffee	oploskoffie	**op**loskofee
filter coffee	filterkoffie	**fil**terkofee
coffee filter	koffiefilter	**kof**feefilter
cold meats	vleeswaren	**vlays**wahren
cottage cheese	kwark	kwark
cream	room	roam
sour cream	zure room	**zew**re roam
whipped cream	slagroom	**slagh**roam
dairy products	zuivelprodukten	**zœ**velproadukten
eggs	eieren	**aiy**-ye-ren
flower	meel *n*	mayl
fruit juice	vruchtensap *n*	**vrugh**te(n)-sap
grapes	druiven	**drœ**ven
ham	ham	ham

hamburger	hamburger	**ham**burgher
herbs	kruiden	**krœ**den
ice cream	ijs *n*	aiys
lettuce	sla	slah
matches	lucifers	**lew**seefehrs
mayonnaise	mayonaise	mah-yoa-**nay**-se
melon	meloen	me**loon**
honeydew melon	suikermeloen	**sœ**kermeloon
water melon	watermeloen	**wah**termeloon
(whole) milk	(volle) melk	(**vol**-e) mehlk
buttermilk	karnemelk	**kar**ne-mehlk
low-fat milk	halfvolle melk	**half**vol-e mehlk
mineral water	mineraalwater *n*	meene**rahl**wahter
mustard	mosterd	**mos**tert
spicy/mild	scherp/mild	sghehrp/milt
napkins	servetten	sehr**veh**ten
oil	olie	**oh**lee
oranges	sinaasappels	**see**nahs-ap-els
pasta	pasta	**pahs**ta
pastry	gebak *n*	ghe**bak**
peach	perzik	**pehr**zik
pears	peren	**pay**ren
pickles	augurken	ou**ghur**ken
plastic bag	plastic zak	"plastic" zak
potatoes	aardappelen	**ahrt**ap-e-len
raspberies	frambozen	fram**boa**zen
rolls	broodjes	**broat**yes
salad	salade	sah**lah**de
soft drinks	frisdranken	**fris**dranken
tinned food	conserven	kon**sehr**ven
salt	zout *n*	zout
soup	soep	soop
sugar	suiker	**sœ**ker
tea	thee	tay
tea bags	theezakjes	**tay**zakyes
tomatoes	tomaten	toa**mah**ten
trolley	winkelwagentje *n*	**win**kel-wah-ghen-tye
vinegar	azijn	a**zaiyn**
wine	wijn	waiyn
yoghurt	yoghurt	**yo**ghurt

(See also "At the hairdresser", "In the beauty parlour" and "At the dispensing chemist's".)

Do you have a remedy against ...?
Heeft u een middel tegen ... ?
hayft ew en **mid**el **tay**ghen ...?

burns	brandwonden	**brant**wonden
carsickness	wagenziekte	**wah**ghenzeekte
a cold	verkoudheid	ver**kout**haiyt
coughing	hoest	hoost
diarrhoea	diarree	dee-yah-**ray**
earache	oorpijn	**oar**paiyn
fever	koorts	koarts
the flue	griep	ghreep
gastrointestinal disorders	maag- en darmstoornissen	mahgh ehn **darm**stoar-nis-en
a hangover	een kater	en **kah**ter
hay fever	hooikoorts	**hooy**koarts
headache	hoofdpijn	**hoaft**paiyn
insect bites	insectenbeten	in**sehk**tenbayten
a sore throat	keelpijn	**kayl**paiyn
sunburn	zonnebrand	**zon**-e-brant
wound infection	wondinfectie	**wont**infehksee

◄ **This is only available at the dispensing chemist's/on prescription**
Dat is alleen verkrijgbaar bij een apotheek/op recept
dat is a**layn** ver**kraiygh**bahr baiy en ahpoa**tayk**/op re**sehpt**

◄ **You'd better first consult a doctor**
U kunt beter eerst een arts raadplegen
ew kunt **bay**ter ayrst en arts **raht**playghen

◄ **This may not be sold to children**
Dit mag niet aan kinderen verkocht worden
dit magh neet ahn **kin**deren ver**koght wor**den

◄ **This medicine affects one's ability to drive**
Dit middel beïnvloedt de rijvaardigheid
dit **mid**-el be-**in**-vloot de raiy-**vahr**-degh-haiyt

◄ **This is toxic/inflammable/dangerous to children**
Dit is giftig/brandbaar/gevaarlijk voor kinderen
dit is **ghif**tegh/**brant**bahr/ghe**vahr**lek voar **kin**deren

SHOPPING

aftershave (lotion)	after shave	"after shave"
brush	borstel	**bor**stel
clinical thermometer	koortsthermometer	**koarts**-tehr-moa-may-ter
comb	kam	kam
condom	condoom	con**dohm**
contraceptive	voorbehoedsmiddel	**voar**be-hoots-mid-el
cotton wool	watten	**wat**-en
cough drops	keelpastilles	**kayl**-pas-tee-yes
cough mixture	hoestdrank	**hoost**drank
deodorant	deodorant	day-yoa-doa-**rant**
disposable nappies	wegwerpluiers	**wehgh**wehrp-lœ-yers
dummy	(fop)speen	(**fop**)spayn
eardrops	oordruppels	**oar**drup-els
earplugs	oorwatjes	**oar**watyes
eau de Cologne	eau de cologne	oa de koa**lon**ye
elastic bandage	rekverband *n*	**rehk**verbant
eye shadow	oogschaduw	**oagh**-sghah-dew
feeding bottle	zuigfles	**zœgh**flehs
first-aid kit	verbandtrommel	ver**bant**-trom-el
gauze	verbandgaas *n*	ver**bant**ghahs
hairbrush	haarborstel	**hahr**borstel
healing ointment/salve	wondzalf	**wont**zalf
insect repellent (lotion/stick)	muggenolie/muggenstick	**mu**ghen-oalee/**mu**ghen-"stick"
iodine	jodium	**yoa**deeyum
laxative	laxeermiddel *n*	la-**xayr**-mid-el
lip balm	lippenzalf	**lip**-en-zalf
lipstick	lippenstift	**lip**-en-stift
nail brush	nagelborstel	**nah**ghel-borstel
nailfile	nagelvijl	**nah**ghel-vaiyl
nail polish/varnish	nagellak	**nah**ghel-lak
nose drops	neusdruppels	**nøs**drup-els
painkiller	pijnstiller	**paiyn**stil-er
perfume	parfum *n*	**par**fum
razor blades	scheermesjes	**sghayr**mehsyes
sanitary towels	maandverband *n*	**mahnt**verbant
scissors	schaar	sghahr
sedative	kalmeringsmiddel *n*	kal-**may**-rings-mid-el
shampoo	shampoo	sham**poa**
shaving brush	scheerkwast	**sghayr**kwast
shaving soap	scheerzeep	**sghayr**zayp
skin cream	huidcrème	**hœt**krehm
sleeping pills	slaaptabletten	**slahp**tahblehten

soap	zeep	zayp
sponge	spons	spons
spot/stain remover	vlekkenwater *n*	**vleh**kenwahter
sticking plaster	pleisters	**plaiy**sters
sun(tan) oil	zonnebrandolie	**zon**-e-brant-oa-lee
tampons	tampons	tam**pons**
tissues	papieren zakdoekjes	pah**pee**ren **zak**dookyes
toilet paper	toiletpapier *n*	twah**leht**pahpeer
tooth brush	tandenborstel	**tan**denborstel
tooth paste	tandpasta	**tant**pastah
vitamine pills	vitaminepillen	vee-tah-**mee**-ne-pil-en

clothes and shoes

I prefer something ...
Ik heb het liefst iets in het ...
ik hehp heht leefst eets in heht ...

beige	beige	**beh**zhe
black	zwart	zwart
blue	blauw	blou
brown	bruin	brœn
green	groen	ghroon
grey	grijs	ghraiys
orange	oranje	oa**ran**ye
pink	roze	**ro**ze
red	rood	roat
white	wit	wit
yellow	geel	ghayl
multicoloured	bont	bont
deep/pale blue	donkerblauw/lichtblauw	**don**kerblou/**light**blou

I prefer ...
Ik geef de voorkeur aan ...
ik ghayf de **voar**kør ahn ...

a floral pattern	een bloemmotief	en **bloom**-moa-teef
unpatterned	effen	**eh**fen
checked	geruit	ghe**rœt**
large check	geblokt	ghe**blokt**
dotted	gestippeld	ghe-**stip**-elt
striped	gestreept	ghe**straypt**

Is this made of ...?
Is dit gemaakt van ...?
is dit ghe**mahkt** van ...?

corduroy	ribfluweel	**rip**flew-wayl
cotton	katoen	kah**toon**
felt	vilt	vilt
flannel	flanel	flah**nehl**
imitation leather	kunstleer	**kunst**layr
lace	kant	kant
leather (cowskin)	(rund)leer	**(runt)**layr
linnen	linnen	**lin**-en
new wool	scheerwol	**sghayr**wol
nylon	nylon	**nai**ylon
rayon	kunstzijde	**kunst**zaiyde
silk	zijde	**zaiy**de
stretchy material	stretch	"stretch"
synthetic fibre	kunstvezel	**kunst**vayzel
synthetic material	kunststof	**kunst**stof
velvet	fluweel	flew-**wayl**
worsted	kamgaren	**kam**ghahren

Can this be ironed/Is this machine-washable?
Kan dit worden gestreken/in de machine worden gewassen?
kan dit **wor**den ghe**stray**ken/in de mah**shee**ne **wor**den ghe**was**-en?

Is this colourfast/non-shrinkable?
Is dit kleurecht/krimpvrij?
is dit klør**ehght**/krimp**vraiy**?

I take (a) size ...
Mijn maat is ...
maiyn maht is ...

This is too big/small for me
Dit is mij te groot/klein
dit is maiy te ghroat/klaiyn

It's too tight/loose
Hij valt te nauw/wijd
haiy valt te nou/waiyt

The shoes pinch here
De schoenen knellen hier
de **sghoo**nen **kneh**len heer

Do you have a larger/smaller size?
Heeft u een maatje groter/kleiner?
hayft ew en **mah**tye **ghroa**ter/**klaiy**ner?

Can it be altered?
Kan het vermaakt worden?
kan heht ver**mahkt wor**den?

When will it be ready?
Wanneer is het klaar?
wa**nayr** is heht klahr?

May I try it on?
Mag ik het passen?
magh ik heht **pa**-sen?

Where is the fitting room?
Waar is de paskamer?
wahr is de **pas**kahmer?

Where can I find a mirror?
Waar is een spiegel?
wahr is en **spee**ghel?

Can these shoes/this shoe be repaired?
Kunnen deze schoenen/kan deze schoen worden gerepareerd?
kunen **day**ze **sghoo**nen/kan **day**ze sghoon **wor**den geraypah**rayrt**?

Where is the nearest cobbler's?
Waar is een schoenmaker?
wahr is en **sghoon**mahker?

I'd like to have new soles/heels
Ik wil nieuwe zolen/hakken
ik wil **neeoo**e **zoa**len/**hak**-en

belt (for men)	broekriem	**broek**reem
belt (for women)	ceintuur	saiyn**tewr**
blouse	blouse	bloos
boots	laarzen	**lahr**zen
brassiere, bra	beha	bay**hah**
buttons	knopen	**knoa**pen
cardigan	vest *n*	vehst
children's clothes	kinderkleding	**kin**derklayding
coat	mantel	**man**tel
denim jacket	spijkerjasje *n*	**spaiy**ker-yasye
dress	jurk	yurk
dressing gown, robe	kamerjas	**kah**meryas
fur coat	bontjas	**bont**yas
gloves	handschoenen	**hant**sghoonen
handkerchief	zakdoek	**zak**dook
hat	muts	muts
headscarf	hoofddoek	**hoaft**dook
jacket (for gentlemen)	colbert	kol**bair**
jeans	spijkerbroek	**spaiy**kerbrook
knee socks	kniekousen	**knee**kousen
knitting wool	breiwol	**braiy**wol
ladies' wear	damesconfectie	**dah**meskonfehksee
men's wear	herenconfectie	**hay**renkonfehksee
nightdress, nightgown	nachtpon	**naght**pon
(under)pants/panties	onderbroek, slipje *n*	**on**derbrook, **slip**ye
pyjamas	pyjama	pee**yah**mah
rain/trench coat	regenjas	**ray**ghenyas
sandals	sandalen	san**dah**len
shirt	overhemd *n*	**oa**verhehmt
sleeve	mouw	maow

shoehorn	schoenlepel	**sghoon**laypel
shoe laces	schoenveters	**sghoon**vayters
shoe polish	schoensmeer	**sghoon**smayr
shoes	schoenen	**sghoo**nen
shorts	short *n*	"short"
skirt	rok	rok
slippers	slippers	"**slip**pers"
socks	sokken	**sok**en
sole	zool	zoal
sports wear	sportkleding	**sport**klayding
string	string	"string"
suit	kostuum *n*	kos**tewm**
sweater	trui	trœ
T-shirt	T-shirt	"t-shirt"
thread	garen	**ghah**ren
tie	das	das
tights	panty	**pehn**tee
tracksuit	trainingspak	"**trai**nings"-pak
trouser-leg	broekspijp	**brooks**paiyp
trousers	pantalon, lange broek	**pan**tahlon, **lang**e brook
umbrella	paraplu	pahrah**plew**
underwear	ondergoed *n*	**on**derghoot
vest	(onder)hemd *n*	(**on**der)hehmt
waist slip	onderrok	**on**der-rok
women's suit	mantelpak *n*	**man**telpak
zip	ritssluiting	**rits**-slœting

photo, film and video equipment

I'd like to have a ...
Ik wil graag een ...
ik wil ghrahgh en ...

colour film	kleurenfilm	**klœ**renfilm
black-and-white film	zwartwitfilm	zwart**wit**film
cassette, cartridge	filmcassette	**film**ka-seh-te
slide film	diafilm	**dee**yah-film
100 ASA film	een film van 100 ASA	en film van **hon**dert **ah**sah
for 20/36 shots	voor 20/36 opnamen	voar **twin**tegh/ zehs-ehn-dehrtegh **op**nahmen
for outdoors	voor daglicht	voar **dagh**light
for indoors	voor kunstlicht	voar **kunst**light

I'd like to have a 8 millimeter/super 8 cassette/video cassette
Ik wil graag een 8 mm/super 8 filmcassette/videofilmcassette
ik wil ghrahgh en aght **mee**leemayter/**sew**per aght ka**seh**te/**vee**deeyoa-film-ka-seh-te

I'd like to have this film developed and printed
Kunt u deze film voor mij ontwikkelen en afdrukken?
kunt ew **day**ze film voar maiy ont**wik**e-len ehn **af**dru-ken?

mat	mat	mat
glossy	glanzend	**ghlan**zent
10 by 15 cm	10 x 15 cm	teen baiy **vaiyf**teen
		sehnteemayter

I'd like to have these slides framed
Ik wil de dia's ingeraamd hebben
ik wil de **dee**yahs **in**gherahmt **heh**ben

When will they be ready?
Wanneer zijn ze klaar?
wa**nayr** zaiyn ze klahr?

Could you make 4 passport photos?
Kunt u vier pasfoto's maken?
kunt ew veer **pas**foatoas **mah**ken?

Can this camera be repaired?
Kan deze camera worden gerepareerd?
kan **day**ze **kah**merah **wor**den gheraypah**rayrt**?

The ... is broken
Er is een defect aan de ...
ehr is en de**fehkt** ahn de ...

◀ **The camera will have to be sent to the manufacturer**
U moet de camera naar de fabriek sturen
ew moot de **kah**merah nahr de fah**breek stew**ren

◀ **It will be quite expensive**
Dit zal veel gaan kosten
dit zal vayl ghahn **kos**ten

APS	APS	ah-pay-**es**
battery	batterij	ba-te-**raiy**
camera	fototoestel *n*	**foa**toa-toostehl
cine film	smalfilm	**smal**film
digital camera	digitale camera	deeghee**tah**le **kah**mera
enlargement	vergroting	ver**ghroa**ting
exposure counter	opnameteller	**op**nahme-tehler
exposure meter	belichtingsmeter	be**ligh**tings-mayter
film camera	filmcamera	**film**kah-me-rah
film transport mechanism	filmtransport *n*	**film**transport
filter screen	filter *n*	**fil**ter

colour filter	kleurenfilter n	**klœ**renfilter
sun filter	UV-filter	ew-vay **fil**ter
flashbulbs	flitslampjes	**flits**lampyes
flashcubes	flitsblokjes	**flits**blokyes
flash gun, electronic flash	flitser	**flit**ser
flashlight	flitslicht n	**flits**light
high/low resolution	hoge/lage resolutie	**hoh**ghe/**lah**ghe rayso**lew**tsee
high-speed film	snelle film	**sneh**le film
lens	lens	lehns
lens cap	lenskap	**lehns**kap
lens hood	zonnekap	**zon**-e-kap
micro objective	micro-objectief n	**mee**kroa-op-yehk-teef
negative	negatief n	nay-ghah-**teef**
objective, object glass	objectief n	opyehk**teef**
35 mm	vijfendertig millimeter	**vaiyf**-ehn-dehrtegh **mee**leemayter
70 mm	zeventig millimeter	**zay**ventegh **mee**leemayter
135 mm	honderdvijfendertig millimeter	**hon**dert-**vaiyf**-ehn-dehrtegh **mee**leemayter
photo-CD	foto-cd	foto-say-**day**
pixels	pixels	"**pix**els"
rangefinder	afstandsmeter	**af**stantsmayter
shutter	sluiter	**slœ**ter
size	formaat n	for**maht**
slide	dia	**dee**yah
slide frames	diaraampjes	**dee**yah-rahmpyes
soundtrack	geluidsspoor n	ghel**œts**-spoar
tripod	statief n	stah**teef**
underwater camera	onderwatercamera	onder**wah**ter-kahmerah
video camera	videocamera	**vee**-dee-yoa-kah-me-rah
video cassette	videocassette	**vee**-dee-yoa-ka-seh-te
video cassette recorder	videorecorder	**vee**-dee-yoa-"recorder"
viewfinder	zoeker	**zoo**ker
wide-angle lens	groothoeklens	**ghroat**hooklens
zoom lens	zoomlens	**zoom**lehns

books, magazines, stationary

Where do I find a bookshop/stationer/newsstand?
Waar is een boekhandel/kantoorboekhandel/kiosk?
wahr is en **book**handel/kan**toar**bookhandel/kee**yosk**?

Do you have any books in English on ...?
Heeft u boeken in het Engels over ...?
hayft ew **boo**ken in heht **ehng**els **oa**ver ...?

the Netherlands	Nederland	**nay**derlant
Belgium	België	**behl**-ghee-ye
this area	deze streek	**day**ze strayk
this town	deze stad	**day**ze stat
the scenery	het natuurschoon	heht nah**tewr**sghoan
history	geschiedenis	ghe**sghee**denis
monuments	monumenten	moanew**mehn**ten
bicycle tours	fietstochten	**feets**toghten
walks	wandelingen	**wan**delingen
with lots of pictures	met veel foto's	meht vayl **foa**toas

Do you also have translated Dutch/Flemish literature?
Heeft u vertaalde Nederlandse/Vlaamse literatuur?
hayft ew ver**tahl**de **nay**derlantse/**vlahm**se leeterah**tewr**?

Do you sell British/American newspapers/magazines?
Heeft u Engelse/Amerikaanse kranten/tijdschriften?
hayft ew **ehng**else/ahmayree**kahn**se **kran**ten/**taiyt**sghriften?

art books	kunstboeken	**kunst**booken
atlas	atlas	**at**las
ball pen	balpen	**bal**pehn
book	boek *n*	book
calculator	calculator	kalkew**lah**tor
children's books	kinderboeken	**kin**derbooken
cookbook	kookboek *n*	**koak**book
crayons	kleurpotloden	**klør**potloaden
crime novel	detectiveroman	"detective"-roaman
dictionary	woordenboek *n*	**woar**denbook
Dutch-English	Nederlands-Engels	**nay**derlants-**eng**els
English-Dutch	Engels-Nederlands	**eng**els-**nay**derlants
drawing pins	punaises	pew**nay**ses
envelopes	enveloppen	ehn-ve-**lop**-en
airmail	voor luchtpost	voar **lught**post
eraser	vlakgom *n*	**vlak**ghom
exercise book	schrift *n*	sghrift
felt-tip pen	viltstift	**vilt**stift
foreign newspapers	buitenlandse kranten	**bœ**tenlantse **kran**ten
fountain pen	vulpen	**vul**pehn

glue	lijm	laiym
ink (cartridges)	inkt(patronen)	inkt(pah**troa**nen)
literature	literatuur	leeterah**tewr**
magazine	tijdschrift *n*	**taiyt**sghrift
map	landkaart	**lant**kahrt
(city) map, street plan	plattegrond	plat-e-**ghront**
road map	wegenkaart	**way**ghen-kahrt
topographical map	topografische kaart	toa-poa-**grah**-fee-se kahrt
walking/hiking map	wandelkaart	**wand**el-kahrt
monthly	maandblad *n*	**mahnt**blat
(daily) newspaper	dagblad *n*	**dagh**blat
newspaper	krant	krant
notepad, writing pad	schrijfblok *n*	**sghraiyf**blok
paper	papier *n*	pah**peer**
paperbacks	pockets	"pockets"
paperclips	paperclips	"paperclips"
pencil	potlood *n*	**pot**loat
pencil sharpener	puntenslijper	**pun**tenslaiyper
playing cards	speelkaarten	**spayl**kahrten
postcards	ansichtkaarten	**an**sightkahrten
rubber bands	elastiekjes	aylas**teek**yes
ruler	lineaal	leenee**yahl**
sale	opruiming, uitverkoop	**op**rœming, **œt**verkoap
sellotape, Scotch tape	plakband *n*	**plak**bant
travel guide	reisgids	**raiys**ghits
art guide	kunstreisgids	**kunst**-raiys-ghits
hiking guide	wandelgids	**wand**el-ghits
weekly	weekblad *n*	**wayk**blat
wrapping paper	pakpapier *n*	**pak**pahpeer

jewelry and watches

Can you fix this watch/bracelet/chain?
Kunt u dit horloge/deze armband/deze ketting repareren?
kunt ew dit hor**loa**zhe/**day**ze **arm**bant/**day**ze **keh**ting raypah**ray**ren?

Could you clean this?
Kunt u dit schoonmaken?
kunt ew dit **sghoan**mahken?

The watch is fast/slow
Het horloge loopt voor/achter
heht hor**loa**zhe loapt voar/**agh**ter

When will it be ready?
Wanneer is het klaar?
wanayr is heht klahr?

◄ This cannot be repared
Dit is onherstelbaar
dit is **on**hehrstehlbahr

◀ **The battery must be changed**
De batterij moet vervangen worden
de ba-te-**raiy** moot ver**vang**en **wor**den

How many carats is this?
Hoeveel karaat is dit?
hoovayl kah**raht** is dit?

◀ **14/18 carats**
14/18 karaat
vayrteen/**agh**teen kah**raht**

Can I have this name engraved in it?
Kan deze naam erin gegraveerd worden?
kan **day**ze nahm eh**rin** gheghrah**vayrt wor**den?

(travel) alarm clock	(reis)wekker	(**raiys**)wehker
amulet	amulet	ahmew**leht**
battery	batterij	ba-te-**raiy**
bracelet	armband	**arm**bant
brass	messing *n*	**meh**sing
brooch	broche	brosh
chain bracelet	schakelarmband	**sghah**kel-armbant
chrome	chroom *n*	ghroam
copper	(rood)koper *n*	(roat)**koa**per
crown	opwindknopje *n*	**op**wint-knopye
crystal	kristal *n*	kris**tal**
cut diamond, brilliant	briljant	bril**yant**
diamond	diamant	deeyah**mant**
earrings	oorbellen	**oar**behlen
emerald	smaragd	smah**ragt**
glass	glas *n*	ghlas
gold	goud *n*	ghout
gold leaf	bladgoud *n*	**blat**ghout
gold-plated	doublé	doo**blay**
jade	jade	**yah**de
jewel box/case	juwelenkistje *n*	yew-**way**-len-kis-ye
ladies' watch	dameshorloge *n*	**dah**mes-horloazhe
leather	leer *n*	layr
men's watch	herenhorloge *n*	**hay**ren-horloazhe
mother of pearl	parelmoer	**pah**relmoor
necklace	halsketting	**hals**kehting
pearl necklace	parelsnoer *n*	**pah**relsnoor
pewter	tin *n*	tin
pin	speld	spehlt
platinum	platina *n*	**plah**teenah
pocket watch	zakhorloge *n*	**zak**horloazhe
quartz watch	kwartshorloge *n*	**quarts**-horloazhe

ring	ring	ring
wedding ring	trouwring	**trou**ring
signet ring	zegelring	**zay**ghelring
ruby	robijn	roa**baiyn**
sapphire	saffier	sa**feer**
silver	zilver *n*	**zil**ver
silverware	tafelzilver *n*	**tah**felzilver
spring	veer	vayr
(stainless) steel	(roest)vrij staal *n*	**(roost)**vraiy stahl
tobacco box	tabaksdoos	tah**baks**doas
topaz	topaas	toa**pahs**
watch	horloge *n*	hor**loa**zhe
digital	digitaal	deeghee**tahl**
dial watch	met wijzers	meht **waiy**zers
watch chain	horlogeketting	hor**loa**zhe-kehting
watchstrap	horlogebandje *n*	hor**loa**zhe-bantye
white gold	witgoud *n*	**wit**ghout
wristwatch	polshorloge *n*	**pols**horloazhe

coins and stamps

annual collection	jaarcollectie	**yahr**-ko-lehk-see
block	blok *n*	blok
coin album	muntenalbum *n*	**mun**ten-album
commemorative coins	gelegenheidsmunten	ghe**lay**-ghenhaiyts-munten
commemorative stamps	gelegenheidspostzegels	ghe**lay**-ghenhaiyts-postzayghels
first day cover	eerstedagenveloppe	ayrste-**dagh**-ehnvelop
gold coins	gouden munten	**ghou**den **mun**ten
loose-leaf	losbladig	los**blah**degh
mint proof, specimen coin	muntproef	**munt**proof
not perforated	ongetand	**on**ghetant
ordinary stamps	gewone zegels	ghe**woa**ne **zay**ghels
perforated	getand	ghe**tant**
postmarked	gestempeld	ghe**stehm**pelt
series	serie	**say**ree
sheet	vel *n*	vehl
silver coins	zilveren munten	**zil**veren **mun**ten
special postmark	gelegenheidsstempel	ghe**lay**ghenhaiyts-stempel
stamp	postzegel	**post**zayghel
stamp album	postzegelalbum *n*	**post**zayghel-album
very beautiful	zeer fraai	zayr frahy

optician

Can these glasses be repaired?
Kan deze bril gerepareerd worden?
kan **day**ze bril gheraypah**rayrt wor**den?

Do you have a pair of sunglasses for me?
Heeft u voor mij een zonnebril?
hayft ew voar maiy en **zon**-e-bril?

contact lenses, contacts	contactlenzen	kon**takt**lenzen
fluid for contact lenses	vloeistof voor contactlenzen	**vlooy**stof voar kon**takt**lehnzen
hard lenses	harde lenzen	**har**de lenzen
soft lenses	zachte lenzen	**zagh**te lenzen
short-sighted	bijziend	**baiy**zeend
long-sighted	verziend	**vair**zeend
optician	opticiën	opti**shan**

I am wearing + 1.5
Ik heb + 1,5
ik heb plus ayn **kom**mah vaiyf

I am wearing − 2.25
Ik heb − 2,25
ik heb min tway **kom**mah vaiyfen**twin**tigh

tobacco shop

Do you sell foreign cigars/cigarettes?
Heeft u buitenlandse sigaren/sigaretten?
hayft ew **bœ**tenlantse see**gah**ren/seegah**reh**ten?

cigarette paper	vloei	vlooy
filter-tipped cigarettes	filtersigaretten	**fil**ter-seegah**reh**ten
lighter	aansteker	**ahn**stayker
matches	lucifers	**lew**seefehrs
pipe	pijp	paiyp
rolling tobacco	shag	shehk
tobacco	tabak	tah**bak**

laundrette and dry-cleaner's

Where can I find a laundrette?
Waar is een wasserette?
wahr is en was-e-**reh**-te?

Where can I have my clothes cleaned?
Waar kan ik kleding laten reinigen?
wahr kan ik **klay**ding **lah**ten **raiy**neghen?

Could I have this cleaned/dry-cleaned?
Kan dit voor mij gereinigd/gestoomd worden?
kan dit voar maiy ghe**raiy**neght/ghe**stoamt wor**den?

◄ **This needs special treatment**
Dit vraagt een speciale behandeling
dit vrahght en spayseeyahle behandeling

◄ **This stain won't come out**
Deze vlek krijgen wij er niet uit
dayze vlehk kraiyghen waiy ehr neet œt

English	Dutch	Pronunciation
crease-resistant	kreukvrij	**krøkvraiy**
detergent	zeeppoeder *n*	**zayp**-pooder
to dry-clean	stomen	**stoa**men
dry-cleaning	chemisch reinigen	**ghay**mees **raiy**neghen
dryer	droogtrommel	**droagh**trom-el
hand wash only	met de hand wassen	meht de hant **was**-en
to iron	strijken	**straiy**ken
main wash	hoofdwas	**hoaft**was
no ironing	niet strijken	neet **straiy**ken
prewash	voorwas	**voar**was
synthetic, artificial	synthetisch	sin**tay**tees
to wash	wassen	**was**-en
wash at 40 degrees	op 40 graden wassen	op **vayr**tegh **ghrah**den **was**-en
wash in lukewarm water	lauw wassen	lou **was**-en
washing machine	wasautomaat	**was**outoamaht
waterproof	waterdicht	**wah**terdight

at the hairdresser's

English	Dutch	Pronunciation
ladies' hairdresser	dameskapper	**dah**mes-kap-er
barber	herenkapper	**hay**ren-kap-er

Can I make an appointment?
Kan ik een afspraak maken?
kan ik en **af**sprahk **mah**ken?

How long will it take?
Hoe lang kan het duren?
hoo lang kan heht **dew**ren?

Do you also cut children's hair?
Knipt u ook kinderen?
knipt ew oak **kin**deren?

A shave and a haircut, please
Knippen en scheren alstublieft
knip-en ehn **sghay**ren alstew**bleeft**

Not so short
Niet te kort
neet te kort

A little shorter ...
Iets korter ...
eets **kor**ter ...

English	Dutch	Pronunciation
on top	bovenop	boaven**op**
at the back of the neck	in de nek	in de nehk
at the back	aan de achterkant	ahn de **agh**terkant
on the sides	aan de zijkanten	ahn de **zaiy**kanten

Just a trim, please
Wilt u alleen de punten bijknippen?
wilt ew a**layn** de **pun**ten **baiy**knip-en?

Washing and dying, please
Wassen en verven alstublieft
was-en ehn **vair**ven alstew**bleeft**

beard	baard	bahrt
bleached streaks	coupe soleil	koop soa**laiy**
to blow-dry	föhnen	**fø**nen
braid, plait	vlecht	vlehght
brilliantine	brillantine	brilyan**tee**ne
colour rinse	kleurspoeling	**klør**spooling
comb	kam	kam
to comb	kammen	**kam**-en
to cut	knippen	**knip**-en
dandruff	roos	roas
dry hair	droog haar n	droagh hahr
to dye	verven	**vehr**ven
greasy hair	vet haar n	veht hahr
hairdo	kapsel n	**kap**sel
hair dryer	droogkap	**droagh**kap
hair gel	gel	"gel"
hair spray	haarlak	**hahr**lak
long hair	lang haar n	lang hahr
loss of hair	haaruitval	**hahr**œtval
lotion	lotion	loa**syon**
manicure	manicure	mahnee**kew**re
moustache	snor	snor
perm	permanent n	pehrmah**nehnt**
ponytail	paardenstaart	**pahr**de(n)-stahrt
punk hairstyle	punkkapsel n	**punk**-kapsel
rinse	spoeling	**spoo**ling
setting-lotion	haarversteviger	**hahr**ver-stay-ve-ghing
shampoo	shampoo	**sham**poa
to style	opkammen	**op**kam-en
wave	watergolf	**wah**ter-gholf
to wave/curl/crimp	krullen	**krul**-en
whiskers	bakkebaard	**bak**-e-bahrt

Can I make an appointment?	**How long will it take?**
Kan ik een afspraak maken?	Hoe lang kan het duren?
kan ik en **af**sprahk **mah**ken?	hoo lang kan heht **dew**ren?

beauty parlour	schoonheidssalon	**sghoan**-haijts-sahlon
to depilate	ontharen	ont**hah**ren
face pack	gezichtsmasker *n*	ghe**zights**masker
a facial	gezichtsverzorging	ghe**zights**verzorghing
full treatment	volledige behandeling	vo-**lay**-de-ghe be**han**deling
manicure	manicure	mahnee**kew**re
mudpack	modderbehandeling	**mo**derbehandeling
pedicure	pedicure	paydee**kew**re
to shave	scheren	**sghay**ren

(see also the list under "Toiletries and medicines")

beach spoon	strandschepje	**strahnd**sghepye
lifebelt	zwemband	**zwem**bahnd
ball	bal	bahl
pack of cards	kaartspel	**kahrt**spel
dice	dobbelstenen	**dob**belstaynen
jig-saw puzzle	legpuzzle	**legh**puzzel
computer game	computerspelletje	"com**pu**ter"-**spel**letye
CD	cd	say-**day**
CD-player	cd-speler	say-**day**-spayler
portable record player	walkman	"**walk**man"
DVD-player	dvd-speler	day-vay-**day**-spayler
MP3-player	mp 3-speler	em-pay **dree**-spayler
Barbie doll	barbiepop	"**bar**bie"-pop
cuddly toy	knuffelbeest	**knuf**felbayst

tourist information office

Where is the tourist information?
Waar is het VVV-kantoor?
wahr is heht vay-vay-vay-kan**toar**?

Do you speak English?
Spreekt u Engels?
spraykt ew **ehng**els?

I'd like to have some information/a leaflet on ...
Ik wil graag inlichtingen/een folder hebben over ...
ik wil ghraagh **in**lichtingen-en/en **fol**der **heh**ben **oa**ver ...

bus services	busdiensten	**bus**deensten
camp sites	kampeerterreinen	kam**payr**teh-raiy-nen
car hire/rental	autoverhuur	**ou**toa-verhewr
city walks	stadswandelingen	**stats**wan-de-ling-en
.. day excursions	meerdaagse excursies	**mayr**dahgh-se ex**kur**sees
day trips	dagexcursies	**dagh**ehx-kur-sees
entertainment	uitgaansmogelijkheden	**œt**ghahns-moa-ghe-lek-hay-den
guest houses	pensions	pehn**syons**
holiday cottages/	vakantiehuisjes/	vah**kan**see-hœsyes/
bungalows	bungalows	'bungalows'
hotels	hotels	hoa**tehls**
museums	musea	mew-**say**-yah
public transport	openbaar vervoer	**oa**penbahr ver**voor**
rent-a-bike	fietsverhuur	**feets**verhewr
sightseeing cruises	rondvaarten	**ront**vahrten
youth hostels	jeugdherbergen	**yøgt**hehr-behr-ghen
fishing	vissen	**vis**-en
walks, hikes	wandelingen	**wan**de-ling-en

Do you have any leaflets in English?
Hebt u folders in het Engels?
hehbt ew **fol**ders in heht **ehng**els?

Do you have a map of the city/area?
Hebt u een stadsplattegrond/streekkaart?
hehpt ew en **stats**plat-e-ghront/**strayk**kahrt?

Do you have bicycle/hikers' maps?
Hebt u fietskaarten/wandelkaarten?
hehpt ew **feets**kahrten/**wan**delkahrten?

Could you draw the route?
Kunt u de route intekenen?
kunt ew de **roo**te **in**taykenen?

Where do I find the ...?
Waar vind ik de/het ...?
wahr vint ik de/heht ...?

aquarium	aquarium *n*	ah-**quah**-ree-yum
botanical garden	botanische tuin	boa**tah**neese tœn
castle	kasteel *n*	kas**tayl**
cathedral	kathedraal, dom	kate**drahl**, dom
chapel	kapel	kah**pehl**
church	kerk	kehrk
fortress	vesting	**vehs**ting
houses of parliament	parlementsgebouw *n*	par-le-**mehnts**-ghe-bou
market, market place	markt, marktplein *n*	markt, **markt**plaiyn
monastery, convent	klooster *n*	**kloas**ter
museum	museum *n*	mew-**say**-yum
observation point	uitzichtpunt *n*	œtzights-punt
opera (house)	opera	**oa**perah
palace	paleis *n*	pah**laiys**
park	park *n*	park
ruins	ruïne	rew-**ee**-ne
theatre	schouwburg	**sghou**burgh
town/city hall	raadhuis *n*	**raht**hœs
zoo	dierentuin	**dee**rentœn

Do they charge an entrance fee?
Moet er entree betaald worden?
moot ehr ehn**tray** be**tahlt wor**den?

Do you also sell guides/maps/street plans?
Verkoopt u ook gidsen/kaarten/plattegronden?
ver**koopt** ew oak **ghit**sen/**kahr**ten/plat-e-**ghron**-den?

Where do the buses leave?
(Van)waar vertrekken de bussen?
(van)**wahr** ver**trehk**ken de **bus**-en?

◄ **You will be picked up at your hotel**
U wordt bij uw hotel afgehaald
ew wordt baiy eww hoa**tel af**ghe-hahlt

visiting a museum

Where is the (museum of/for) ...?
Waar is het (museum van/voor) ...?
wahr is heht (mew-**say**-yum van/voar) ...?

applied arts	toegepaste kunst	**too**ghe-pas-te kunst
archaeology	oudheidkunde	**out**haiyt-kunde
arts and crafts	kunstnijverheid	kunst**naiy**verhaiyt
ceramics	keramiek	kayrah**meek**
ethnographical museum	volkenkundig museum	volken**kun**degh mew-**say**-yum
folk art	volkskunst	**volks**kunst

geology	geologie	ghay-oa-loa-**ghee**
history	historisch museum	his**to**-rees mew-**say**-yum
literature	letterkunde	**leh**terkunde
maritime museum	scheepvaartmuseum	**sghayp**-vahrt-mew-say-yum
military museum	legermuseum	**lay**gher-mew-say-yum
natural sciences	natuurwetenschappen	nah-**tewr**-way-ten-sghap-en
open-air museum	openluchtmuseum	oa-pen-**lught**-mew-say-yum
oriental art	oosterse kunst	**oas**terse kunst
prehistory	prehistorie	**pray**histoaree
railway museum	spoorwegmuseum	**spoar**wehgh-mew-say-yum
sculpture	beeldhouwkunst	**baylt**-hou-kunst
stamps	postzegelmuseum	**post**zayghel-mew-say-yum
technique	techniek	tehgh**neek**
textile industry	textielnijverheid	tex**teel**naiy-ver-haiyt
visual arts	beeldende kunst	**bayl**dende kunst

Is the museum open to the public?   ◄ **No, you have to take a guided tour**
Is het museum vrij toegankelijk?   Nee, alleen met een rondleiding
is heht mew-**say**-yum vraiy too**ghan**kelek?   nay, a**layn** meht en **ront**laiyding

How much is the entrance fee? ◄ **The entrance is free Two children's tickets**
Hoeveel bedraagt de entree?   De toegang is vrij   Twee kinderkaartjes
hoovayl be**drahgt** de ehn**tray**?   de **too**ghang is vraiy   tway **kin**derkahrtyes

Two adult tickets   **Is there a special exhibition?**
Twee kaartjes voor volwassenen   Is er een bijzondere tentoonstelling?
tway **kahr**tyes voar vol-**wa**-se-nen   is ehr en bee**zon**dere tehn**toan**stehling?

Do you have a map/guide/catalogue?   **Can I take pictures?**
Heeft u een plattegrond/gids/catalogus?   Mag ik fotograferen?
hayft ew en plat-e-**ghront**/ghits/kah**tah**loaghus?   magh ik foatoa-ghrah**fay**ren?

Is there a .../Where is the ...?
Is er een .../Waar is de/het ...?
is ehr en .../wahr is de/heht ...?

attendant	suppoost	su**poast**
cloakroom	garderobe	gharde**ro**be
exit	uitgang	**œt**ghang
lecture	lezing	**lay**zing
museum shop	museumwinkel	mew-**say**-yum-win-kel
restaurant	restaurant *n*	rehstoa**rant**
toilet	toilet *n*	twah**leht**

fortress	vesting	**vehs**ting
rampart	vestingwal	**vehs**tingwal
bastion	bastion *n*	bastee**yon**
roundel	rondeel *n*	ron**dayl**
ammunition room	munitiekamer	mew**nee**tsee-kahmer
dungeon	kerker	**kehr**ker
country estate	landgoed *n*	**lant**ghoot
castle	kasteel *n*	kas**tayl**
palace	paleis *n*	pah**laiys**
great hall	ridderzaal	**ri**-der-zahl
reception hall	ontvangsthal	ont**vangst**hal
monastery, convent	klooster *n*	**kloas**ter
abbey	abdij	ap**daiy**
cathedral	kathedraal, dom	kate**drahl**, dom
church	kerk	kehrk
nave	schip *n*	sghip
choir	koor *n*	koar
altar	altaar *n*	**al**tahr
vault	gewelf *n*	ghe**wehlf**
treasure room	schatkamer	**sghat**kahmer
Benedictines	benedictijnen	bay-ne-dik-**taiy**-nen
Cistercians	cisterciënzers	sis-ter-see-**yehn**-sers
Dominicans	dominicanen	doa-mee-nee-**kah**-nen
Franciscans	franciscanen	fran-sis-**kah**-nen
prehistoric	prehistorisch	prayhis**toa**rees
Roman	Romeins	roa**maiyns**
Medieval	middeleeuws	mi-del-**ayoos**
Pre-Romanesque	preromaans	prayroa**mahns**
Romanesque	romaans	roa**mahns**
Gothic	gotisch	**ghoa**tees
Renaissance	renaissance	re-nay-**san**-se
Baroque	barok	bah**rok**
Rococo	rococo	ro-ko-**koa**
classicistic	classicistisch	klas-see-**sis**-tees
Neo-Gothic	neogotisch	nay-oa-**ghoa**tees
modernistic	modernistisch	moa-dehr-**nis**-tees
modern	modern	moa**dehrn**
Art Nouveau	Jugendstil (Neths. only)	**yoo**-gent-shteel
contemporary	eigentijds, hedendaags	aiy-ghent**aiyts**, **hay**den-dahghs
16th century	16de-eeuws	zehsteende-**ayoos**

In this list you will find in the second colomn sometimes the abreviations *v* (= verb), *n* (= noun), *a* (= adjective) and *adv* (= adverb). In the third colomn you will find the pronunciation.

A

abandon	opgeven	**op**ghayven
able, to be	in staat zijn	in staht zaiyn
aboard	aan boord (van)	ahn board (vahn)
about	over, omstreeks	**o**ver, **om**strayks
above	boven	**boh**ven
abroad	(in/naar) het buitenland	(in/nahr) het **bœ**tenlahnd
absent	afwezig, ontbrekend	ahf**way**zigh
accelerate	versnellen	ver**snel**len
accept	aannemen	**ahn**naymen
accident	ongeluk, ongeval	**on**gheluk, **on**ghevahl
accompany	vergezellen	verghe**zel**len
account	rekening	**ray**kening
accurate	nauwkeurig	now**kuh**righ
ache	pijn doen	paiyn doon
acid	zuur	zewr
acquaintance	kennis, bekende, kennismaking	**ken**nis, be**ken**de, **ken**nismahking
across	over	**o**ver
adapt	aanpassen	**ahn**pahssen
add	toevoegen, optellen	**too**vooghen, **op**tellen
adhesive (tape)	plakband	**plahk**bahnd
adjust	verstellen, aanpassen	ver**stel**len, **ahn**pahssen
aerial	antenne	ahn**ten**ne
afraid	bang, angstig	bahng, **ahng**stigh
afternoon	(na)middag	(nah)**mid**dagh
afterwards	daarna, later	dahr**nah**, **lah**ter
again	weer, nogmaals	wehr, **nogh**mahls
against	tegen	**tay**ghen
agency	agentschap, bureau	ah**ghent**sghahp, bew**roh**
agent	vertegenwoordiger, agent	vehrtayghen**woar**digher

agree	afspreken, accoord gaan	ahfsprayken, ahkkoard-ghahn
agreeable	aangenaam	ahnghenahm
agreement	afspraak, overeenkomst	ahfsprahk
ahead	vooruit, verderop	voarœt, verderop
aid, (first)	(eerste) hulp	(ehrste) hulp
ailment	kwaal, ziekte	quahl, zeekte
aim	v mikken, doelen op;	mikken, doolen op;
	n doel(stelling)	dool(stelling)
air (mattress)	lucht(matras)	lught (mahtrahs)
aircraft	vliegtuig	vleeghtœgh
airmail, by	per luchtpost	per lughtpohst
airport	vliegveld	vleeghveld
airsick	luchtziek	lughtzeek
alarm clock	wekker	wekker
alien	vreemdeling	vraymdeling
all	alles, alle(n), allemaal	ahlles, ahlle(n), ahllemahl
all of a sudden	plotseling	plotseling
allow	toestaan	toostahn
all right	in orde	in orde
almost	bijna	baiyna
alone	alleen	ahllayn
also	ook, eveneens	oak, ayvenayns
alter	wijzigen	waiyzighen
always	altijd	ahltaiyd
amazed	verbaasd	verbahsd
among	onder, tussen, te midden van	onder, te midden vahn
amount	v bedragen; n bedrag,	bedrahghen; bedragh,
	hoeveelheid	hoovaylhaiyd
animal	dier, beest	deer, bayst
annexe	dependance, aanhangsel	daypendahns, ahnhahngsel
announcement	mededeling, aankondiging	maydedayling, ahnkondighing
annual(ly)	jaarlijks	yahrlaiyks
ant	mier	meer
anxious	benieuwd, [worried] ongerust	beneewd, ongherust
any	enig(e)	aynigh(e)
anybody/anyone	iemand	eemahnd
anything	iets	eets
answer	v antwoorden, n antwoord	ahntwoarden, ahntwoard
	[telephone] opnemen;	opnaymen;
antique dealer	antiquair	ahntikair
antiques	antiek	ahnteek
apartment (building)	flat(gebouw)	flat(ghebow)

apologize	zich verontschuldigen	zigh veront**sghul**dighen
apology	verontschuldiging	veront**sghul**dighing
appeal	*v* beroep doen op; *n* beroep	be**roop** doon op; be**roop**
apple (juice)	appel(sap)	**ahp**pel(sahp)
application (form)	aanvraag(formulier)	**ahn**vrahgh(formew**leer**)
apply	aanvragen, solliciteren	**ahn**vrahghen, sollici**teh**ren
appointment	afspraak	**ahf**sprahk
approximately	ongeveer	onghe**vehr**
area	gebied, streek	ghe**beed**, strayk
around	rond(om), ongeveer,	rond(**om**), onghe**vehr**,
	in de buurt van	in de bewrt vahn
arrange	afspreken	**ahf**sprayken
arrival (time)	aankomst(tijd)	**ahn**komst(taiyd)
arrive	aankomen	**ahn**kohmen
arrow	pijl	paiyl
artificial (respiration)	kunstmatig(e ademhaling)	kunst**mah**tigh(e **ah**demhahling)
art(ist)	kunst(enaar)	**kunst**(enahr)
as	(zo)als	(zoh)**ahls**
ash (tray)	as(bak)	**ahs**(bahk)
ask (for)	vragen (om/naar)	**vrah**ghen (om/nahr)
attention!	attentie! [mil.] geef acht!	aht**ten**tsee; ghayf aght
attention, draw/pay	aandacht trekken/schenken	**ahn**daght **trek**ken/**sghen**ken
attic	zolder	**zol**der
attract	aantrekken	**ahn**trekken
audience	gehoor, toehoorders,	ghe**hoar**, **too**hoarders,
	[theatre] publiek	pew**bleek**
authorization	[legal] machtiging,	**mahgh**tighing,
	[permission] toestemming	**too**stemming
autumn	herfst	hairfst
aviation	luchtvaart	**lught**vahrt
award	*v* belonen; *n* prijs, beloning	be**loa**nen; praiys, be**loa**ning
awful	afschuwelijk, erg	ahf**sghe**welik, airgh
awkward	lastig, naar	**lahs**tigh, nahr
axle	(wiel)as	(**weel**)ahs

B

bachelor	vrijgezel	vraiyghe**zel**
back	rug, terug, achterzijde	rugh, te**rugh**, **ahgh**terzaiyde
back, in the	achterin	**ahgh**terin
backwards	achteruit, terug	ahghter**œt**, te**rugh**
bacon	(ontbijt)spek	(ontb**aiyt**)spek
bad	slecht, [food] bedorven	sleght, be**doar**ven
bad luck	pech	pegh

ENGLISH - DUTCH

159

bag	zak, tas	zahk, tahs
bake	bakken	**bahk**ken
bakery	bakkerij	bahkke**raiy**
balcony	balkon	bahl**kon**
ball	bal, [cannon] kogel	bahl, **koa**ghel
balloon	ballon	bahl**lon**
ban	v verbieden, uitbannen; n verbod	ver**bee**den, **œt**bahnnen; ver**bod**
bandage	v verbinden; n verband	ver**bin**den; ver**bahnd**
bank	[office] bank, [river] oever	bahnk, **oo**ver
banknote	bankbiljet	**bahnk**bilyet
bar	v afsluiten; n [pub] bar, [barrier] slagboom, tralie, [chocolate] reep	**ahf**slœten; 'bar', **slahgh**boam, **trah**lee, rayp
barrier	[railway crossing] spoorboom, [fence] afrastering, hindernis	**spoar**boam, **ahf**rahstering, **hin**dernis
barrow	handkar	**hahnd**kahr
basket	mand	mahnd
bath (tub)	bad(kuip)	**bahd**(kœp)
bath, take a	baden	**bah**den
bath foam	badschuim	**bahd**sghœm
bath room	badkamer, toilet	**bahd**kahmer, twah**let**
bath towel	badhanddoek	**bahd**hahnddook
battery	batterij, [engine] accu	bahtte**raiy**, **ahk**kew
bay	baai	bye
beach	strand	strahnd
beans, haricot	witte bonen	**wit**te **boa**nen
beans, kidney	bruine bonen	**brœ**ne **boa**nen
bear	v dragen; n [animal] beer	**drah**ghen, behr
beard	baard	bahrd
beautiful	mooi	moay
because	omdat	om**daht**
because of	door(dat)	door(**daht**)
bee	bij	baiy
beef	rundvlees	**rund**vlays
beer	bier	beer
before	voor(dat)	voar(**daht**)
begin	beginnen	be**ghin**nen
beginning	begin	be**ghin**
behind	achter, achterop	**agh**ter, aghter**op**
belly	buik	bœk
below	beneden, onder	be**nay**den, **on**der

belt	gordel, riem	**ghoar**del, reem
bench	(zit)bank	(zit)bahnk
bend	v buigen; n bocht	**bœ**ghen, boght
berth	couchette, slaapplaats	koo**shet**, **slahp**plahts
best before ...	houdbaar tot ..., [on a label] THT	**howd**bahr tot
between	tussen	**tus**sen
beyond	voorbij, achter	voar**baiy**, **ahgh**ter
bicycle (track)	fiets(pad)	**feets**(pahd)
big	groot	ghroat
bile	gal	ghahl
bird	vogel	**voa**ghel
birthday	verjaardag	ver**yahr**dagh
bit	beetje	**bayt**ye
bite	v bijten; n [in food] hap, [animal] beet	**baiy**ten, hahp, bayt
black	zwart	zwahrt
blackboard	(school)bord	(**sghoal**)bord
blame	v kwalijk nemen, de schuld geven; n schuld	**quah**lik **nay**men, de sghuld **ghay**ven, sghuld
bland	flauw, slap	flaow, slahp
blanket	deken	**day**ken
blinker	knipperlicht	**knip**perlihght
blister	blaar	blahr
blockage	verstopping	ver**stop**ping
blocked	(af)gesloten, geblokkeerd	(**ahf**)ghe**sloa**ten, gheblok**kehrd**
blood	bloed	bloohd
blue	blauw	blaow
blunt	bot	bot
blush	v blozen; n blos	**bloa**zen; bloss
board	v aan boord gaan; n [wood] plank, [leaders] bestuur, [boat] boord	ahn board ghahn; plahnk, be**stewr**, board
body	lichaam, [corpse] lijk, [car] carrosserie	**lih**ghahm, laiyk, kahrrosse**ree**
boil	v koken; n puist	koaken; pœst
bond	[tie] band, verbondenheid, [stock exchange] obligatie	bahnd, ver**bon**denhaiyd, oablee**ghah**tsee
bone	bot	bot
bonnet	[wool] muts, [felt] hoedje, [car] motorkap	muts, **hood**ye, **mo**torkahp
book	v boeken, reserveren; n boek	**boo**ken, **ray**servehren; book

bookshop	boekhandel	**book**hahndel
boot	[high] laars, [low] schoen,	lahrs, sghoon,
	[car] bagageruimte, kofferbak	bah**gha**zhe-**rœm**te, **kof**ferbahk
border	v begrenzen;	be**ghren**zen;
	n [frontier, limit] grens,	ghrens.
	[edge] rand	rahnd
born	geboren	ghe**boa**ren
borrow (from)	lenen (van)	**lay**nen (vahn)
both	beide(n), allebei	**baiy**de(n), ahlle**baiy**
both ... and ...	zowel ... als ...	zo**well** ... ahls ...
bother	lastigvallen, storen	**lah**stighvahllen, **stoa**ren
bottle	v bottelen; n fles	**bot**telen; fless
bottom	bodem, grond, onderkant	**boa**dem, ghrond, **on**derkahnt
boulder	rotsblok	**rots**blok
bowl	vaas, schaal, pot	vahs, sghahl, pot
box	doos, [wooden] kist	doas, kist
boy	jongen	**yong**en
bracelet	armband	**ahrm**bahnd
brake	rem	rem
branch	[tree] tak,	tahk,
	[department] (onder)afdeling,	(**on**der)af**day**ling,
	[business] filiaal	feelee**yahl**
brass	(geel) koper	(ghayl) **koa**per
brass band	fanfare	fahn**fah**re
bread	brood	broahd
breadth	breedte	**brayd**te
break	v breken; n [interval] pauze,	**bray**ken; **pow**zeh,
	onderbreking	onder**bray**king
breakdown	[technical] pech,	pegh,
	[nervous] inzinking	**in**zinking
breakdown van	kraanwagen	**krahn**wahghen
breakfast	ontbijt	ont**baiyt**
breast	borst	bohrst
breath(less)	adem(loos)	**ah**dem(loas)
bridge	v overbruggen; n brug	over**brugh**ghen; brugh
brief	kort, beknopt, vluchtig	kort, be**knopt**, **vlugh**tigh
bright	helder, licht	**hel**der, lihght
bring	(mee)brengen	(**may**)brengen
broken	gebroken, kapot	ghe**broa**ken, kah**pot**
brother	broer	broor
brother-in-law	zwager	**zwah**gher
brown	bruin	brœn

bruise	blauwe plek	**bla**owe plek
brush	v poetsen, borstelen; n borstel	**poot**sen, **bors**telen; **bors**tel
bucket	emmer	**em**mer
buckle	gesp	ghesp
build	bouwen	**ba**owen
building	gebouw	ghe**ba**ow
burden	last , gewicht	lasst, ghe**wight**
burn	v branden; n brandwond	**brahn**den; **brahnd**wond
burnt	[destroyed] verbrand, [food] aangebrand	ver**brahnd**, **ahn**ghebrahnd
bus (stop)	bus(halte)	**bus**(hahlte)
bush	[low] struik, [high] geboomte	strœk, ghe**boam**te
busy	druk, bezig, bezet	druk, **bay**zigh, be**zet**
butcher	slager	**slah**gher
butter	v smeren; n boter	**smeh**ren; **boa**ter
buttermilk	karnemelk	**kahr**nemelk
button	[switch] knop, [clothes] knoop	knop, knoap
buy	kopen	**koa**pen
buyer	koper	**koa**per
byroad	binnenweggetje	**bin**nen-**wegh**ghetye

C

cabbage	kool	koal
cabin	[truck] cabine, [ship] stuurhut, [berth] hut	kah**bee**ne, **stewr**hut, hut
cabin cruiser	motorjacht	**mo**toryahght
cable	kabel, draad, telegram	**kah**bel, drahd, tele**ghrahm**
cake	[small] cake, gebakje, [large] koek, taart	'cake', ghe**bahk**ye, kook, tahrt
calf	[cow] kalf, [leg] kuit(been)	kahlf, **kœt**(bayn)
call	v (op)roepen, [phone] (op)bellen; n oproep, [phone] telefoongesprek	(**op**)**roo**pen, (**op**)bellen; **op**roop, tele**foan**ghesprek
camp fire	kampvuur	**kahmp**vewr
camp site	camping, kampeerplaats	'camping', kahm**pehr**plahts
can	v kunnen; n blik(je)	**kun**nen; blik(ye)
canal	kanaal	kah**nahl**
candle(light)	kaars(licht)	**kahrs**(liihght)
canned	ingeblikt	**in**gheblikt
canoe	kano	**kah**no
can opener	blikopener	**blik**opener
cancel	afzeggen, afgelasten, annuleren	**ahf**zegghen, **ahf**ghelahsten, ahnnew**leh**ren

cap	[headgeare] pet,	pet,
	[cover] deksel, dop, kap	**dek**sel, dop, kahp
caption	[illustration] onderschrift,	**on**dersghrift,
	bijschrift,	**baiy**sghrift,
	[sign, notice] opschrift	**op**sghrift
car	auto	**ow**to
cardigan	vest	vest
card	kaart	kahrt
cardboard	karton	kahr**ton**
care	zorg	zorgh
care about	geven om iets/iemand	**ghay**ven om eets/**ee**mand
careful	voorzichtig	voar**zigh**tigh
care of, take	zorgen voor	**zor**ghen voar
car park	parkeerterrein	pahr**kehr**terraiyn
carriage	rijtuig	**raiy**tœgh
carrot	wortel, peen	**wor**tel, payn
carry	dragen	**drah**ghen
carsick	wagenziek	**wah**ghenzeek
cart	kar	kar
case	[affair] zaak, geval,	zahk, ghe**vahl**,
	[wooden] kist,	kist,
	[cardboard] doos	doas
case of, in	in geval van	in ghe**vahl** vahn
cash	v [bill] incasseren, [change	inkahs**seh**ren,
	into money] verzilveren;	ver**zil**veren;
	n contant geld	kon**tahnt** gheld
cashier	[person] kassier, [till] kassa	kahs**seer**, **kahs**sa
cash register	kassa	**kahs**sa
castle	kasteel	kahs**tayl**
casualty	slachtoffer	**slagh**toffer
cat	kat	kaht
catch	v vangen, pakken; n vangst	**vahng**en, **pahk**ken; vahngst
catching	[emotion] aangrijpend,	ahn**ghraiy**pend,
	[disease] besmettelijk	be**smet**telik
cattle (grid)	vee(rooster)	**vay**(rooster)
cave	grot	ghrot
celebrate	vieren	**vee**ren
celebration	feest	fayst
cellar	kelder	**kel**der
cemetery	begraafplaats	be**ghrahf**plahts
central heating	centrale verwarming	sen**trah**le ver**wahr**ming
centre	centrum, middelpunt	**sen**trum, **mid**delpunt

century	eeuw	ayw
certain	zeker	**zay**ker
certificate	bewijs, [study] diploma	be**waiys**, dee**plo**ma
chain	v ketenen; n ketting, keten	**kay**tenen; **ket**ting, **kay**ten
chair	stoel	stool
chairman	voorzitter	**voar**zitter
chambermaid	kamermeisje	**kah**mer-**maiys**ye
chamber of commerce	kamer van koophandel	**kah**mer vahn **koap**hahndel
chamois	zeem	zaym
chance	kans, gelegenheid	kahns, ghe**lay**ghenhaiyd
chance, by	toevallig	too**vahl**ligh
change	v [alter] veranderen, [money] wisselen, [transport] overstappen, [clothes] omkleden; n verandering, [money] wisselgeld	ver**ahn**deren, **wis**selen, **o**verstahppen, **om**klayden; ver**ahn**dering, **wis**selgheld
change, small	kleingeld	**klaiyn**gheld
channel	(t.v.-)/kanaal	(tay-**vay**-)ka**nahl**
charcoal	houtskool	**howts**koal
charge	belasten, in rekening brengen	be**lahs**ten, in **ray**kening **breng**en
charge of, be in	belast zijn met, de leiding hebben	be**lahst** zaiyn met, de **laiy**ding **heb**ben
cheap	goedkoop	ghood**koap**
cheat	v bedriegen, [financially] oplichten; n bedrog	be**dree**ghen, **op**lighten; be**drogh**
check	v controleren; n controle	kontro**leh**ren; kon**troh**le
cheek	wang	wahng
cheer	juichen	**yœ**ghen
cheerful	blij	blaiy
cheers!	proost!	proast
cheese	kaas	kahs
chess	schaken	**sghah**ken
chew	kauwen	**kow**en
chewing gum	kauwgom	**kow**ghom
chicken	[animal] kip, [meat] kippenvlees	kip, **kip**penvlays
chief	hoofd	hoafd
child	kind	kihnd
chilly	kil, koud, fris	kil, kowd, friss
chin	kin	kin
chippings	steenslag	**stayn**slagh

ENGLISH – DUTCH

choice	keuze	**kø**ze
choose	kiezen	**kee**zen
chop	hakken	**hahk**ken
Christian name	voornaam	**voar**nahm
church(yard)	kerk(hof)	**kairk**(hof)
cinema	bioscoop	beeyo**skoap**
city	stad	stahd
civil servant	ambtenaar	**ahmbt**enahr
clean	v [tidy] schoonmaken,	**sghoan**mahken,
	[mess] opruimen; n schoon	op**rœ**men; sghoan
clear	[transparant] helder,	**hel**der,
	[understandable] duidelijk	**dœ**delik
cliff	klip, rots(punt)	klip, **rots**punt
cloakroom	garderobe	gharde**rohb**e
clock	klok	klok
clock, two o'	2 uur	tway ewr
cloister	kloostergang	**kloas**terghahng
close	v [door] sluiten,	**slœ**ten,
	[lock, end] afsluiten; n dichtbij	**ahf**slœten; dight**baiy**
close to	dicht bij	dight baiy
closed	[door] gesloten,	ghe**sloa**ten,
	[locked, ended] afgesloten	**ahf**ghesloaten
closet	(kleren)kast	(**klehr**en)kahst
closing time	sluitingstijd	**slœ**tingstaiyd
cloth	stof, lap, (zeil)doek, kleed	stof, lahp, (**zaiyl**)dook, klayd
clothes	kleding, kleren	**klay**ding, **klehr**en
cloud/cloudy	wolk/bewolkt	wohlk/be**wohlkt**
clutch	v vastpakken; n [car] koppeling	**vahst**pahkken; **kop**peling
coach	(reis)bus, [horsedrawn] koets	(**raiys**)bus, koots
coachwork	carrosserie	karrosse**ree**
coast (guard)	kust(wacht)	**kust**(wahght)
coat	jas, [ladies'] mantel	yahs, **mahn**tel
coat hanger	klerenhanger	**klehr**en-**hahng**er
cobbler	schoenmaker	**sghoon**mahker
cockroach	kakkerlak	**kahk**kerlahk
coffee	koffie	**kof**fee
coin	munt	munt
cold	a koud; n [temperature] kou,	kowd; kow,
	[disease] verkoudheid	ver**kowd**haiyd
collar	kraag	kragh
collection	[stamps etc.] verzameling,	ver**zah**meling,
	[mail] buslichting	**bus**lihghting

collector	verzamelaar	ver**zah**melahr
collector, ticket	controleur	kontroh**luhr**
collision	botsing, [ships] aanvaring	**bot**sing, **ahn**vahring
colour	v kleuren; n kleur	**kluh**ren; kluhr
column	[building] pilaar, zuil, printing] kolom, [press] column	pee**lahr**, zœl, koh**lom**, 'column'
comb	v kammen; n kam	**kahm**men; kahm
come	komen	**koa**men
comfortable	[pleasant] gemakkelijk, [at ease] op zijn gemak	ghe**mahk**kelik, op zaiyn ghe**mahk**
compartment	(trein)coupé	(traiyn)koo**pay**
complain	klagen	**klah**ghen
complaint	klacht	klaght
compulsory	verplicht	ver**plihght**
concerning	betreffende, in verband met	be**treff**ende, in ver**bahnd** met
concussion	hersenschudding	**hair**sen-**sghud**ding
condition	[situation] toestand, [restriction] voorwaarde	**too**stahnd, **voar**wahrde
conditional	voorwaardelijk	voar**wahr**delik
confectionary	snoep(goed)	**snoop**(ghood)
congratulate	feliciteren	fayleesee**teh**ren
congratulations!	gefeliciteerd!	ghefayleesee**tehrd**
congregation	(kerk)gemeente	(kairk)ghe**mayn**te
connection	verband, verbinding	ver**bahnd**, ver**bin**ding
constable	(politie)agent	(po**leet**see)ah**ghent**
contageous	besmettelijk	be**smet**telik
continue	voortzetten, voortduren, vervolgen	**voart**zetten, **voart**dewren, ver**vol**ghen
contraceptive	voorbehoedsmiddel	**voar**behoods-**mid**del
convent	klooster	**kloas**ter
cook	v koken; n [male] kok, [female] kokkin	**koh**ken; kok, kok**kin**
cooked	gekookt	ghe**koakt**
cool	v koelen; n koel	**koo**len; kool
cooled	gekoeld	ghe**koold**
copper	(rood)koper	(road)**koh**per
cork(screw)	kurk(entrekker)	**kuhr**ken-**trek**ker
corner	hoek	hook
corridor	gang	ghahng
costume	costuum	kos**tewm**
cosy	gezellig, aangenaam	ghe**zell**igh, **ahn**ghenahm

cot	kinderbedje	**kin**derbedye
cotton	katoen	kah**toon**
cotton wool	watje	**waht**ye
couch	zitbank, divan	**zit**bahnk, **dee**vahn
cough	v hoesten; n hoest	**hoo**sten; hoost
council	[general] raad,	rahd,
	[city] gemeenteraad	ghe**mayn**te-rahd
counter	[apparatus] teller,	**tel**ler,
	[shop] toonbank, [office] loket	**toan**bahnk, lo**ket**
country	[state] land,	lahnd,
	[rural area] platteland	plahtte**lahnd**
country house	buitenhuis	**bœ**tenhœs
countryside, in the	op het platteland	op het plahtte**lahnd**
couple	[some, two] paar, [duo] koppel	pahr, **kop**pel
couple of, a	een paar, een stuk of wat	en pahr, en stuk of waht
course	[river, road] loop,	loap,
	[race, direction] koers,	koors,
	[running] gang	ghahng
course, of	natuurlijk	nah**tewr**lik
court	v het hof maken; n [royal or	het hof **mah**ken;
	juridical institution] hof,	hof,
	[court of law] gerecht,	ghe**reght**,
	rechtbank	**reght**bahnk
court(yard)	binnenplaats	**bin**nenplahts
cousin	[male] neef, [female] nicht	nayf, nihght
crack	v barsten; n barst	**bahrs**ten; bahrst
cradle	[baby] wieg, [origin] bakermat	weegh, **bah**kermaht
crash	v [vehicle, ship] botsen,	**bot**sen,
	[plane] neerstorten,	**nehr**storten,
	[object] (neer)vallen ;	(**nehr**)vahllen;
	n [vehicle] botsing, aanrijding,	**bot**sing, **ahn**raiyding,
	[ship] aanvaring	**ahn**vahring
crate	[closed] kist, [open] krat	kist , kraht
cream, (whipped)	(slag)room	(**slahgh**)roam
crevice	kloof	kloaf
crooked	[dispositioned] scheef,	sghayf,
	[evil] kwaadaardig	kwahd**ahr**digh
cross	v kruisen, [road] oversteken;	**krœ**sen, **o**verstayken;
	n [shape] kruis	krœs
crossing	[two roads] kruispunt,	**krœs**punt,
	[pedestrians'] oversteekplaats	**o**verstaykplahts

168

cry	v [tears] huilen,	hœlen,
	[shout] schreeuwen,	**sghray**wen,
	[call] roepen; n (ge)roep,	**roo**pen; (ghe)**roop**,
	(ge)schreeuw	(ghe)**sghrayw**
cub	[lion, tiger] welp, [general] jong	welp, yong
cup	[low] kop(je), [high, prize] beker	kop(ye), **bay**ker
cupboard	(wand)kast	(**wahnd**)kahst
current	[course] stroom,	stroam,
	[river] stroming,	**stroa**ming,
	[actual] huidig,	**hœ**digh,
	[running] lopend	**loa**pend
curtain	gordijn	ghor**daiyn**
curve	bocht	boght
custom	gewoonte, traditie	ghe**woan**te, trah**dee**tsee
customs	[border] douane	doo**wah**ne
cut	snee	snay
cut	[knife] snijden,	**snaiy**den,
	[scissors] knippen	**knip**pen
cut off	afsnijden, afknippen,	**ahf**snaiyden, **ahf**knippen,
	afbreken	**ahf**brayken
cutlery	bestek	be**stek**

D

damage	v beschadigen; n schade,	be**sghah**dighen; **sghah**de,
	[slightly] beschadiging	be**sghah**dighing
damp	vochtig	**vogh**tihgh
dampproof	vochtwerend	**vogh**twehrend
dance	v dansen; n dans	**dahn**sen; dahns
dandruff	roos	roas
danger(ous)	gevaar(lijk)	ghe**vahr**(lik)
dare	durven, wagen	**dur**ven, **wah**ghen
date	v dateren; n [calendar]datum,	dah**teh**ren; **dah**tum,
	[informal meeting] afspraakje	ahf**sprahk**ye
daughter	dochter	**dogh**ter
day	dag	dahgh
day after tomorrow, the	overmorgen	**o**vermorghen
dazzle	verblinden	ver**blin**den
dead	dood	doad
dead-end street	doodlopende straat	**doad**loapende straht
deaf (and dumb)	doof(stom)	doaf(**stom**)
debt	schuld	sghuld
deckchair	ligstoel	**ligh**stool

ENGLISH – DUTCH

decoration	[party, addition] versiering, [medal] onderscheiding, [painting] schilderwerk	ver**see**ring, onder**sghai**ding, **sghil**derwairk
decrease	verminderen, afnemen	ver**min**deren, **ahf**naymen
deep	diep	deep
degree	graad	ghrahd
dehydrated	(uit)gedroogd	(œt)ghe**droaghd**
delay	v vertragen; n vertraging	ver**trah**ghen; ver**trah**ghing
deliver	bezorgen, afleveren	be**zor**ghen, **ahf**layveren
dentist	tandarts	**tahnd**arts
dentures	kunstgebit	**kunst**ghebit
department	afdeling	**ahf**dayling
department store	warenhuis	**wah**renhœs
departure	vertrek, [ship] afvaart	ver**trek**, **ahf**vahrt
depiction	voorstelling, afbeelding	**voar**stelling, **ahf**baylding
deposit	[bank] storting, [bottles] statiegeld	**stor**ting, **stah**tseegheld
depth	diepte	**deep**te
descend	afdalen, naar beneden gaan	**ahf**dahlen, nahr be**nay**den ghahn
desire	v wensen, verlangen; n wens, verlangen	**wen**sen, ver**lahn**gen; wens, ver**lahn**gen
desk	[furniture] bureau, [reception] balie	be**wroh**, **bah**lee
desolate	verlaten, afgelegen	ver**lah**ten, ahfghe**lay**ghen
destination	bestemming	be**stem**ming
detain	in hechtenis houden	in **hegh**tenis **how**den
detergent	wasmiddel	**wahs**middel
detour	omweg, [road works] omleiding	**om**wegh, **om**laiyding
develop	ontwikkelen	ont**wik**kelen
deviate	afwijken	**ahf**waiyken
diet (food)	dieet(voeding)	dee**ayt**(vooding)
different	verschillend, anders	ver**sghil**lend, **ahn**ders
difficult	moeilijk	**mooy**lik
dig	graven	**ghrah**ven
digestion	spijsvertering	**spaiys**vertehring
dinner	avondeten, [formal] diner	**ah**vond-**ay**ten, dee**nay**
direction	richting	**rih**ghting
directions (for use)	(gebruiks)aanwijzing	(ghe**brœks-**)ahn**waiy**zing
dirty	vies, vuil, smerig	vees, vœl, **smeh**righ
disabled	gehandicapt	ghe**han**dicapt
discharge	[sack, release] ontslaan, [load] lossen	ont**slahn**, **los**sen

discount	korting	**kor**ting
discover	ontdekken	ont**dek**ken
discuss	bespreken	be**spray**ken
dish	[plate, menu] schotel, [menu] gerecht	**sghoa**tel, ghe**reght**
dishes, do the	afwassen	**ahf**wahssen
dishonest	oneerlijk	on**ehr**lik
disinfectant	ontsmettingsmiddel	ont**smet**tings-**mid**del
dispatch	verzending	ver**zen**ding
dispensing chemist	apotheek	ahpo**tayk**
distance	afstand	**ahf**stahnd
distant	[far away] ver(af), [behaviour] afstandelijk	vair(ahf), ahf**stahn**delik
distress	nood	noad
ditch	sloot	sloat
dive	v duiken; n duik	**dœ**ken; dœk
diversion	wegomlegging	**wegh**omleghghing
division	[section] afdeling, [partition] indeling	**ahf**dayling, **in**dayling
divorce	v scheiden; n (echt)scheiding	**sghaiy**den; (**eght**)sghaiyding
dizzy(ness)	duizelig(heid)	**dœ**zeligh(haiyd)
dog	hond	hond
doll	pop	pop
domestic	binnenlands	**bin**nenlahnds
domestic animal	huisdier	**hœs**deer
done	gedaan, [finished] afgelopen, [cooking] gaar	ghe**dahn**, **ahf**gheloapen, ghahr
donkey	ezel	**ay**zel
door(knob)	deur(knop)	**duhr**(knop)
doorkeeper/doorman	portier	por**teer**
double	v verdubbelen; n dubbel, [bed] tweepersoons	ver**dub**belen; **dub**bel, **tway**persoans
down	(naar) beneden, omlaag	(nahr) be**nay**den, om**lahgh**
downhill	bergafwaarts	bairg**ahf**wahrts
downstairs	(naar) beneden	(nahr) be**nay**den
draught	[beer] tapbier, [wind] tocht	**tahp**beer, toght
draw	v [design] tekenen, [pull] trekken; n [sport] gelijkspel	**tay**kenen, **trek**ken; ghelaiyk**spel**
drawback	nadeel	**nah**dayl

dress	v [clothes] (aan)kleden, [bandage] verbinden; n [ladies'] jurk, [gentlemen's] kostuum, [traditional] dracht	(**ahn**)klayden, ver**bin**den; yurk, kos**tewm**, drahght
drive	v [car] rijden, [steering] (be)sturen, [engine] voortstuwen; n rit	**raiy**den, (be)**stew**ren, voart**stew**wen; rit
driving license	rijbewijs	**raiy**bewaiys
drum	trommel, [oil] vat	**trom**mel, vaht
dry	v drogen; n droog	**droa**ghen; droagh
dry cleaner's	stomerij	stoame**raiy**
dull	saai, flets	sigh, flets
duration	duur	dewr
during	gedurende, [at the same time] tijdens	ghe**dew**rende, **taiy**dens
dust	stof, vuil	stof, vœl
dust bin	[small] prullenbak, [large] vuilnisbak	**prul**lenbahk, **vœl**nisbahk
Dutch	Nederlands	**nay**derlahnds

E

each	elk, elke, ieder(e)	elk, **el**ke, **ee**der(e)
ear	oor	oar
early	[time] vroeg, [date] aan het begin van	vroogh, ahn het be**ghin** vahn
earth	aarde	**ahr**de
earthenware	aardewerk	**ahr**dewairk
ease, at	op zijn gemak	op zaiyn ghe**mahk**
east	oosten	**oas**ten
easy	gemakkelijk, licht	ghe**mahk**kelik, lihght
eat	eten	**ay**ten
economical	zuinig	**zœ**nigh
edge	kant, rand	kahnt, rahnd
edible	eetbaar	**ayt**bahr
egg, (hard/soft boiled)	(hard-/zachtgekookt) ei	(**hahrd**-/**zaght**-ghekoakt) aiy
elbow	elleboog	**el**leboagh
elevator	lift	lift
else(where)	(ergens) anders	(**air**ghens) **ahn**ders
emergency	[problems] nood, alarm, [urgency] spoed	noad, ah**larm**, spoed
embark	inschepen, aan boord gaan	**in**sghaypen, ahn board ghahn
embassy	ambassade	ahmbas**sah**de
employee	werknemer	**wairk**naymer

172

employer	werkgever	**wairk**ghayver
empty	v leegmaken; n leeg	**laygh**mahken; laygh
encounter	ontmoeting	ont**moo**ting
end	v beëindigen; n einde, [edge] uiteinde	be-**aiyn**dighen; **aiyn**de, **œt**-aiynde
engagement	verbintenis, [to marry] verloving	verb**in**tenis, ver**loa**ving
engine	motor, machine	**mo**tor, mah**shee**ne
engine trouble	motorpech	**mo**torpegh
enjoy	genieten van, plezier hebben in/van	ghe**nee**ten vahn, ple**zeer hebb**en in/vahn
enlarge	vergroten	ver**ghroa**ten
enough	genoeg	ghe**noogh**
enroll	inschrijven, aanmelden	**in**sghraiyven, **ahn**melden
enter	[room] binnenkomen, [enroll] inschrijven	**bin**nenkohmen, **in**sghraiyven
entire(ly)	geheel, helemaal	ghe**hayl**, **hay**lemahl
entrails	ingewanden	**in**ghewahnden
entrance	ingang	**in**ghahng
environment	[surroundings] omgeving, [nature] milieu	om**ghay**ving, meel**jø**
equal	gelijk	ghe**laiyk**
equipment	uitrusting	**œt**rusting
era	tijdperk	**tayid**paik
error	fout, [minor] vergissing	fowt, ver**ghis**sing
escalator	roltrap	**rohl**trahp
escape	v vluchten; n vlucht	**vlugh**ten; vlught
establish	vestigen	**ves**tighen
estate	onroerend goed, [large] landgoed	on**roo**rend ghood, **lahnd**ghood
estate agent	makelaar	**mah**kelahr
even	zelfs, [number] even	zelfs, **ay**ven
evening	avond	**ah**vond
every	elk, elke, ieder(e)	elk, **el**ke, **ee**der(e)
everybody/everyone	iedereen	eeder**ayn**
exact	precies, nauwkeurig	pre**seece**, now**kuh**righ
exact money	gepast geld	ghe**pahst** gheld
excellent	voortreffelijk	voar**tref**felik
except	v uitzonderen; adv behalve, uitgezonderd	**œt**zonderen; be**hahl**ve, **œt**gehzonderd
exchange	v uitwisselen; n [finance] beurs	**œt**wisselen; buhrs
exchange office	wisselkantoor	**wis**selkantohr
exhibition	tentoonstelling	ten**toan**stelling
exit	uitgang, [motorway] afrit	**œt**ghang, **ahf**rit

expect	verwachten	ver**wagh**ten
expenses	onkosten, uitgaven	**on**kosten, **œt**ghaven
expensive	duur	dewr
expire	[validity] verlopen, [end] aflopen	ver**loa**pen, **ahf**loapen
external	uitwendig, van buiten af, extern	**œt**wendigh, vahn **bœ**ten ahf, ex**tairn**
extinguish	blussen	**blus**sen
eye	oog	oagh
F		
fabric	stof, doek	stof, dook
face	v uitzien op; n gezicht	**œt**zeen op; ghe**zihght**
facing	tegenover	tayghen**over**
factory	fabriek	fah**breek**
faint	v flauwvallen; n [fainting] flauwte, [weak] zwak, flets	**flaow**vahllen; **flaow**te, z wahk, flets
fall	v vallen; n [going down] val, [season] herfst	**vahl**len; vahl, hairfst
family	[parents and children] gezin, [relatives] familie	ghe**zin**, fa**mee**lee
family name	achternaam	**agh**ternahm
famous	beroemd	beroemd
fancy	[like] zin hebben in, [imagine] zich inbeelden	zin **heb**ben in, zigh in**bayl**den
far	ver	vair
far from	allesbehalve	**ahl**les-be**hahl**ve
farm	boerderij	boorde**raiy**
farmer	boer	boor
fast	v vasten; n snel	**vahs**ten; snell
fasten	vastmaken	**vahst**mahken
fat	vet, [body] dik	vet, dik
father(-in-law)	(schoon)vader	(**sghoan**)vahder
faulty	defect	day**fekt**
favour(able)	gunst(ig)	ghunst(ihgh)
fear	v vrezen; n angst	**vray**zen; ahngst
feather	veer	vehr
feel	voelen	**voo**len
feeling	gevoel	ghe**vool**
felt	vilt	vilt
felt-tip pen	viltstift	**vilt**stift
fence	hek	hek
ferry	v overvaren; n (veer)pont	**o**vervahren; (**vehr**)pont
fetch	[bring] halen, [grab] pakken	**hah**len, **pahk**ken

174

English	Dutch	Pronunciation
fever	koorts	koarts
few	weinig	**waiy**nigh
few, a	enkele	**en**kele
fiancé(e)	verloofde	ver**loaf**de
field	[terrain] veld, [trade, profession] vak, vakgebied	veld, vahk, vahkghe**beed**
fierce	fel	fell
file	[documents] dossier, [tool] vijl	dos**shay**, vaiyl
fill (in)	(in)vullen	(in)vullen
filling station	tankstation	**tank**stahshon
find	[opinion] vinden, van mening zijn, [look for] (gaan) zoeken	**vin**den, vahn **may**ning zaiyn, (ghahn) **zoo**ken
fine	v bekeuren, boete geven; n boete; a fijn, goed, prettig	be**kuh**ren, **boo**teh **ghay**ven; **boo**teh; faiyn, ghood, **pret**tigh
finished	afgesloten, beëindigd, klaar	**ahf**ghesloaten, be-**aiyn**dighd, klahr
fire	v [bullet] vuren, [sack] ontslaan; n vuur, [accident] brand	**vew**ren, ont**slahn**; vewr, brahnd
fire brigade	brandweer	**brahnd**wehr
firm	n firma, bedrijf; a flink, stevig, vast	**fihr**ma, be**draiyf**; flink, **stay**vigh, vahst
first	eerst(e)	ehrst(e)
first-aid kit	verbandkist	ver**bahnd**kist
first name	voornaam	**voar**nahm
fish (bone)	vis(graat)	**vis**(ghraht)
fisherman	visser	**vis**ser
fit	passen	**pahs**sen
fitting room	paskamer	**pahs**kahmer
fix	[by appointment] afspreken, vastleggen, regelen, [repair] maken, [tie] vastmaken	**ahf**sprayken, **vahst**leghghen, **ray**ghelen, **mah**ken, **vahst**maken
fixed	[by appointment] afgesproken, [settled] vast	**ahf**gesprohken, vahst
flame	vlam	vlahm
Flanders	Vlaanderen	**vlahn**deren
flag (pole)	vlag(genmast)	**vlahgh**(ghemahst)
flask	veldfles	**veld**fless
flat	plat, vlak	plaht, vlahk
flea	vlo	vloh
Flemish	Vlaams	vlahms
flight	vlucht	vlught
floor	vloer, grond, [storey] etage	vloor, ghrond, ay**tah**zhe

ENGLISH - DUTCH

floppy	slap	slahp
flour	bloem	bloom
flow	v stromen, vloeien; n stroom, (toe)vloed	**stroa**men, **vloo**yen; stroam, (**too**)vlood
flower	bloem	bloom
flue	griep	ghreep
fluid	vloeistof	**vlooy**stof
flush	spoelen, [toilet] doorspoelen, [id. by chain] doortrekken	**spoo**len, **doar**spoolen, **doar**trekken
fly	v vliegen; n [insect] vlieg, [zipper] ritssluiting	**vlee**ghen; vleegh, **rits**slœting
flyover	viaduct	veeya**dukt**
fog	mist	mist
folk art	volkskunst	**volks**kunst
follow	volgen	**vol**ghen
food	voedsel, eten	**vood**sel, **ay**ten
foot	voet	voot
footwear	schoeisel	**sghooy**sel
force	kracht, macht, [violence] geweld	kraght, maght, ghe**weld**
foreign	buitenlands	**bœ**tenlahnds
foreigner	buitenlander	**bœ**tenlahnder
forest	[manmade] bos, [primaeval] woud	bos, wowd
forget	vergeten	ver**ghay**ten
fork	[tool, cutlery] vork, [road] splitsing	vork, **split**sing
for rent/sale	te huur/koop	te hewr/koap
fortresss	vesting, fort	**ves**ting, fort
fountain	fontein	fon**taiyn**
fountain pen	vulpen	**vul**pen
fowl	gevogelte	ghe**voa**ghelte
fracture	breuk	brøk
fragrant	geurig	**ghuh**righ
frame	kader, omlijsting, [painting] lijst, [spectacles] montuur, [car] chassis	**kah**der, om**laiy**sting, laiyst, mon**tewr**, shahs**see**
free	v bevrijden; a [freedom] vrij, [without cost] gratis	be**vraiy**den; vraiy, **ghrah**tis
fresh	[food, new] vers, [cool] fris	vehrs, friss
freshwater	zoetwater	**zoot**wah**ter
fridge	koelkast	**kool**kahst
fried	gebakken, gebraden	ghe**bahk**ken, ghe**brah**den
friend	[male] vriend, [female] vriendin	vreend, vreen**din**

friendly	vriendelijk, aardig, [game] vriendschappelijk	**vreen**delik, **ahr**digh, vreend-**sghahp**pelik
from	van, vanaf, vanuit	vahn, vahn**ahf**, vahn**œt**
front	voorzijde	**voar**zaiyde
front of, in	voor	voar
frost	vorst	vorst
fry	bakken, braden	**bahk**ken, **brah**den
fuel	brandstof	**brahnd**stof
fun	plezier	ple**zeer**
further	verder	**vair**der
fuse	stop, zekering	stop, **zay**kering

G

game	[informal] spel(letje), [sport] wedstrijd, [animals] wild	**spel**(letye), **wed**straiyd, willd
garbage	afval, vuilnis	**ahf**vahl, **vœl**nis
garden	tuin	tœn
garlic	knoflook	**knof**loak
gash	snee	snay
gate(way)	(toegangs)poort	(**too**ghangs)poart
gear	versnelling	ver**snel**ling
general	algemeen, [rank] generaal	ahlghe**mayn**, ghene**rahl**
general practitioner	huisarts	**hœs**arts
generate	ontwikkelen, in gang zetten	ont**wik**kelen, in ghang **zet**ten
gentleman (*mv* gentlemen)	heer	hehr
genuine	echt	eght
German	*a* Duits(e); *n* [language] Duits, [male] Duitser, [female] Duitse	**dœts**(e), dœts, **dœt**ser. **dœt**se
Germany	Duitsland	**dœts**lahnd
get	[receive] krijgen, [fetch] pakken, [arrive] komen	**kraiy**ghen, **pahk**ken, **koa**men
get lost	verdwalen	ver**dwah**len
get up	opstaan	**op**stahn
gift	cadeau, geschenk	ka**doh**, ghe**sghenk**
girl	meisje	**maiy**sye
give	geven	**ghay**ven
give (right of) way	voorrang verlenen	**voar**rahng ver**lay**nen
give way to	plaats maken voor	plahts **mah**ken voar
glad	blij	blaiy
gladly	met plezier, graag	met ple**zeer**, ghrahgh
glance	blik, oogopslag	blik, **oagh**opslagh
glass	glas	ghlahs
glasses	bril *sing.*	bril

glazy frost	ijzel	**aiy**zel
glue	*v* lijmen; *n* lijm	**laiy**men; laiym
go	gaan	ghahn
goat	geit	ghaiyt
gold	*a* gouden; *n* goud	**ghow**den; ghowd
gold-plated	verguld	ver**ghuld**
gone	weg, verdwenen	wegh, ver**dway**nen
good	goed	ghood
goodbye!	dag!	dahgh
good night!	welterusten!	wellte**rus**ten
goose	gans	ghahns
gradually	langzamerhand	lahngzamer**hahnd**
granddaughter/		
grandson	kleindochter/-zoon	**klaiyn**-doghter/-zoan
grandfather/		
grandmother	grootvader/-moeder	**ghroat**-vahder/-mooder
grandparents	grootouders	**ghroat**owders
grass	gras	ghrahs
gratitude	dank(baarheid)	**dahnk**(bahrhaiyd)
graveyard	begraafplaats	be**ghrahf**plahts
grease	*v* invetten, smeren; *n* vet, smeer	**in**vetten, **smeh**ren; vet, smehr
green	[colour] groen, [lawn] grasveld	ghroon, **ghrahs**veld
greengrocer	groentenboer	**ghroon**tenboor
grey	grijs	ghraiys
grilled	geroosterd	ghe**roas**terd
grocer	kruidenier	krœde**neer**
ground floor	begane grond, parterre	be**ghah**ne ghrond, par**ter**re
grounds	terrein, veld	ter**raiyn**, veld
ground sheet	grondzeil	**ghrond**zaiyl
guarantee	garantie	ghara**hnt**see
guard	bewaker, wachter, [army] gardist	be**wah**ker, **wahgh**ter, ghar**dist**
guarded	bewaakt	be**wahkt**
guest	gast	ghahst
guesthouse	pension	pen**shon**
guide	gids	ghids
guilty	schuldig	**sghul**digh
H		
habit	gewoonte	ghe**woan**te
Hague, The	Den Haag	den hahgh
hail	hagel	**hah**ghel
hair (spray)	haar(lak)	**hahr**(lahk)
hairdresser	kapper	**kahp**per

hairpin (bend)	haarspeld(bocht)	**hahr**speld(boght)
hall	[interior] gang, [sport] hal,	ghahng, hahl,
	[auditorium] zaal,	zahl,
	[mansion] landhuis	**lahnd**hœs
hammer	hamer	**hah**mer
hand(bag)	hand(tas)	**hahnd**tahs
handbrake	handrem	**hahnd**rem
handicrafts	handwerk	**hahnd**wairk
handkerchief	zakdoek	**zahk**dook
handlebars	(fiets)stuur	(**feets**)stewr
hand over	overhandigen	over**hahn**dighen
hangover	kater	**kah**ter
harbour	haven	**hah**ven
hard	hard, [difficult] moeilijk	hard, **mooy**lik
hardly	nauwelijks	**now**eliks
hard of hearing	slechthorend	sleght**hoa**rend
harsh	ruw, hardhandig	rew, hahrd**hahn**digh
harvest	oogst	oaghst
happiness	blijdschap, vreugde, geluk	**blaiyd**sghahp, **vrøgh**de, ghe**luk**
hassle	lastigvallen	**lah**stigh-**vahl**len
hat	hoed	hood
have	hebben	**heb**ben
head	hoofd	hoafd
heading	opschrift	**op**sghrift
health	gezondheid	ghe**zond**haiyd
Health Service		
(National)	ziekenfonds	**zee**kenfonds
hear	horen	**hoa**ren
hearing aid	gehoorapparaat	ghe**hoar**-ahppa**raht**
heart	hart	hart
heartburn	maagzuur	**maogh**zewr
heat	hitte, warmte	**hit**te, **wahrm**te
heating	verwarming	ver**wahr**ming
heaven	hemel	**hay**mel
heavy	zwaar	zwahr
heel	[shoe] hak, [foot] hiel	hahk, heel
height	[object] hoogte, [person] lengte	**hoagh**te, **leng**te
helm	stuur	stewr
helmet	[army] helm, [traffic, sport] valhelm	helm, **vahl**helm
help	v helpen; n hulp	**help**en; hulp
herbs	kruiden	**krœ**den
here	hier	heer

here you are	alstublieft	ahlstew**bleeft**
hide	verstoppen	ver**stop**pen
high	hoog	ho**agh**
highchair	kinderstoel	**kin**derstool
hike/hiking	trekken, rondtrekken	**trek**ken, **rond**trekken
hill	heuvel	**hø**vel
hip	heup	høp
hire	huren	**hew**ren
hitchhiker	lifter	**lif**ter
hold	(vast-/tegen)houden	(**vahst**-/**tay**ghen)**how**den
hole	gat, [in sand] kuil	ghaht, køl
holiday	[public] feestdag,	**fayst**dagh,
	[vacation] vakantiereis	vah**kahn**tsee-raiys
holidays	[vacation] vakantie,	vah**kahn**tsee,
	[school] schoolvakantie,	**sghoal**vahkahntsee,
	[public] feestdagen	**fayst**dahghen
home	thuis, [direction] naar huis,	tœs, naor hœs,
	[car centre] tehuis	te**hœs**
homework	huiswerk	**hœs**wairk
honest	eerlijk	**ehr**lik
hook	haak	hahk
horn	[animal, instrument] hoorn,	hoarn,
	[animal] horen, [car] claxon	**hoa**ren, **klahk**son
horse	paard	pahrd
horse power	paardenkracht	**pahr**denkraght
hose	[flexible] slang,	slahng,
	[metal, plastic] buis	bœs
hospitable	gastvrij	ghahst**vraiy**
host	[male] gastheer,	**ghahst**thehr,
	[female] gastvrouw	**ghahst**vrow
hot	heet, warm	hayt, wahrm
hour	uur	ewr
house	huis	hœs
house agent	makelaar	**mah**kelahr
household appliances	huishoudelijke artikelen	hœs**how**delaiyke ahr**tee**kelen
housekeeping	huishouding	**hœs**howding
housewife	huisvrouw	**hœs**vrow
how	hoe	hoo
hungry	hongerig	**hong**erigh
hungry, be	honger hebben	**hong**er hebben
hunt	v jagen; n jacht	**yah**ghen; yahght
hurry	v zich haasten; n haast	zigh **hah**sten; hahst

hurt	v [hurt somebody, wound] pijn doen, [mentally] kwetsen; a [wound] gewond, [mentally] gekwetst	paiyn doon, **kwet**sen; ghe**wond**, ghe**kwetst**
husband	echtgenoot	**eght**ghenoat
ice	ijs	aiys
ice cream	ijsje	**aiys**ye
icecubes	ijsblokjes	**aiys**blokyes
identity card/ID	legitimatiebewijs	layghee**tee**mah**tsee-**be**waiys**
ignition	ontsteking	ont**stay**king
ill(ness)	ziek(te)	**zeek**(te)
image	beeld, afbeelding, voorstelling, [personality] imago	bayld, **ahf**baylding, **voar**stelling, ee**mah**gho
imitation	namaak	**nah**mahk
immediately	onmiddellijk, direct	on**mid**dellik, dee**rekt**
impassable	onberijdbaar	onbe**raiyd**bahr
impeccable	foutloos	**fowt**loas
implement	invoeren	**in**vooren
impolite	onbeleefd	onbe**layfd**
important	belangrijk	be**lahng**raiyk
impossible	onmogelijk	on**moah**ghelik
included	inbegrepen	inbe**ghray**pen
increase	toenemen	**too**naymen
increasingly	steeds meer	stayds mehr
indeed	inderdaad	inder**dahd**
indicate	aanwijzen, aangeven	**ahn**waiyzen, **ahn**gheven
indicator	[car] knipperlicht, [direction] aanwijsbord, wegwijzer	**knip**perlihght, **ahn**waiysboard, **wegh**whaiyzer
indigenous	[animals, people] inheems, [people] autochtoon	in**hayms**, owtogh**toan**
indoors	binnen	**bin**nen
infectious	besmettelijk	besmet**telik**
inflammation	ontsteking, zwelling	ont**stay**king, **zwel**ling
inflate	[pump] oppompen, [mouth] opblazen, [infection] zwellen	**op**pompen, **op**blahzen, **zwel**len
inform	mededelen	**may**de-**day**len
information	inlichtingen, informatie	**in**lightingen, infor**mah**tsee
ink	inkt	inkt
injury	verwonding, [sport] blessure	ver**won**ding, bles**sew**re

ENGLISH – DUTCH

inlet	inham	**in**hahm
innocent	onschuldig	on**sghul**digh
inoculate	inenten	**in**enten
inquire	navragen	**nah**vrahghen
insipid	flauw, zouteloos	flaow, **zow**teloas
insist	aandringen	**ahn**dringen
insufficient	onvoldoende	onvol**doon**de
insurance (policy)	verzekering(spolis)	ver**zay**kering(s-**po**lis)
intention	bedoeling, plan	be**doo**ling, plahn
interest	belangstelling, [finance] rente	be**lahng**stelling, **ren**te
intermission	pauze	**pow**ze
internal	inwendig	in**wen**digh
interpreter	tolk	tolk
interrupt	onderbreken	onder**bray**ken
interval	pauze, tussenpoos	**pow**ze, **tus**senpoas
intestine	darm	dahrm
introduce	[first time] invoeren,	**in**vooren,
	[person] voorstellen,	**voar**stellen,
	[text] inleiden	in**laiy**den
introduction	[as above] invoering, voorstelling,	**in**vooring, **voar**stelling,
	kennismaking, inleiding	**ken**nis-mahking, **in**laiyding
inside	binnen	**bin**nen
iodene	jodium	**yo**dium
iron	v strijken; n strijkijzer	**straiy**ken; **straiyk**aiyzer
island	eiland	**aiy**lahnd
itch	v jeuken; n itch	**yø**ken; yøk

J

jack	krik, [cards] boer	krik, boor
jacket	jasje	**yahs**ye
jar	pot, kruik	pot, krœk
jaw	kaak	kahk
jelly	pudding	**puhd**ding
jellyfish	kwal	quahl
jetty	pier, steiger	peer, **staiy**gher
jewel	juweel, sieraad	yew**wayl**, **see**rahd
jolly	leuk	løk
jot down	opschrijven, noteren	op**sghraiy**ven, no**teh**ren
judge	v oordelen; n rechter	**oar**daylen; **regh**ter
jug	kan, kruik	kahn, krœk
jump	v springen; n sprong	**spring**en; sprong
junction	kruising	**krœ**sing

just	[time] net, zojuist, [only] slechts, [justified] rechtvaardig	net, zo**yœst**, sleghts, reght**vahr**digh
justice	recht	reght

K

keep	v houden, bewaren; n [castle] (kasteel)toren	**how**den, be**wah**ren; (kahstayl)**toh**ren
key (hole)	sleutel(gat)	**slø**tel(ghaht)
kick	v schoppen, trappen; n schop, trap, [excitement] opwinding	**sghop**pen, **trahp**pen; sghop, trahp, **op**winding
kind	[character] aardig, vriendelijk, [type] soort	**ahr**digh, **vreen**delik, soart
king	koning	**ko**ning
kiss	v kussen, zoenen; n kus, zoen	**kus**sen, **zoo**nen; kuss, zoon
kitchen	keuken	**kø**ken
knee(cap)	knie(schijf)	**knee**(sghaiyf)
knickers	onderbroek, [ladies'] slipje	**on**derbrook, **slip**ye
knife	mes	mess
knob	knop	knop
knock	kloppen	**klop**pen
knot	knoop	knoap
know	weten, kennen	**way**ten, **ken**nen
knowledge	kennis	**ken**nis
known	bekend	be**kend**

L

lace	kant	kahnt
lack	ontbreken	ont**bra**yken
lady	dame	**dah**me
ladies' toilet	damestoilet	**dah**mes-twah**let**
lake	meer	mehr
lamb	[animal] lam, [meat] lamsvlees	lahm, **lahms**vlays
lame	mank	mahnk
lamppost	lantaarnpaal	lahn**tahrn**pahl
landscape	landschap	**lahnd**sghahp
lane	[countryside] laantje, pad, [motorway] rijstrook, rijbaan	**lahn**tye, pahd, **raiy**stroak, **raiy**bahn
language	taal	tahl
last	v duren; n laatst(e), vorig(e)	**dew**ren; **laht**st(e), **voa**righ(e)
late	laat, [overdue] te laat, [deceased] wijlen	laht, te laht, **waiy**len
later (on)	later, [soon] straks	**lah**ter, strahks
latest	laatste, jongste	**laht**ste, **yong**ste
laugh	lachen	**lah**ghen

laughter	gelach	ghe**lagh**
laundry	was(goed)	**wahs**(ghood)
lavatory	toilet	twa**let**
law	wet	wet
lawn	grasveld	**ghrahs**veld
lawyer	advocaat	ahdvo**kaht**
lay (down)	leggen, neerleggen	**legh**ghen, **nehr**leghghen
layer	laag(je)	lahgh(ye)
lazy	lui	lœ
leaf	blad	blahd
leak	lek	lek
lean	*v* leunen; *n* mager	**lø**nen; **mah**gher
learn	[been taught, experience] leren,	**leh**ren,
	[been informed] vernemen	ver**nay**men
lease	[from] huren, [to] verhuren	**hew**ren, ver**hew**ren
leather	[material] leer, leder,	lehr, **lay**der,
	[shop article] lederwaren	**lay**derwahren
leave	*v* laten, [depart] verlaten,	**lah**ten, ver**lah**ten,
	[departure] vertrekken; *n* verlof	ver**trek**ken; ver**lof**
left	[direction] links, [side] linker-,	links, **lin**ker-,
	[abandoned] achtergelaten	**ahgh**ter-ghe**lah**ten
leg	[body] been, [sport] ronde	bayn, **ron**de
lemon	citroen	see**troon**
lend	[book] uitlenen, [money] lenen	œt**lay**nen, **lay**nen
length	lengte, [piece of cloth] lap stof	**leng**te, lahp stof
lengthy	langdurig	lahng**dew**righ
less (than)	minder (dan)	**min**der (dahn)
lesser	[quantity, distance] minder,	**min**der,
	[level] lager, [lower quality]	**lah**gher,
	van een mindere kwaliteit	vahn en **min**dere qualee**taiyt**
lesson	les	less
let	*v* [allow] laten,	**lah**ten,
	[room, house] verhuren;	ver**hew**ren;
	a gelaten, verhuurd	ghe**lah**ten, ver**hewrd**
let, to	te huur	te hewr
lethal	dodelijk	**doa**delik
letter	[alphabet] letter, [written] brief	**let**ter, breef
lettuce	(krop)sla	(**krop**)slah
level	niveau, [terrain] vlak	nee**voh**, vlahk
level crossing	gelijkvloerse kruising/overweg	ghe**laiyk-vloor**se **krœ**sing/**o**ver-
wegh		
license	vergunning	ver**ghun**ning

lick	likken	**lik**ken
lie	v [position] liggen, [not telling the truth] liegen; n leugen	**ligh**ghen, **lee**ghen; **løgh**en
life	leven	**laiy**ven
life boat/life jacket	reddingboot/reddingsvest	**red**dingboat/**red**dingsvest
lift	v optillen; n [elevator] lift	**op**tillen; lift
light	v verlichten, [fire, candle] aansteken; n licht	ver**lihgh**ten, **ahn**stayken; lihght
lighter	aansteker	**ahn**stayker
lightning	bliksem	**blik**sem
like	v houden van, [taste]lusten, [person, occupation] leuk vinden; adj zoals, net als	**how**den vahn, **lus**ten, løk **vin**den; zo**ahls**, net ahls
limp	slap, [lame] mank	slahp, mahnk
line	lijn, streep	laiyn, strayp
linen	linnen(goed)	**lin**nen(ghood)
liquid	n vloeistof, vocht; a vloeibaar	**vlooy**stof, voght; **vlooy**bahr
listen	luisteren	**løs**teren
litter	v afval weggooien; n afval	**ahf**vahl **wegh**ghoayen; **ahf**vahl
little		
liitle, a	[size] klein, [quantity] weinig, een beetje	klaiyn, **waiy**nigh, en **bayt**ye
live	leven, [dwell] wonen	**laiy**ven, **woh**nen
load	v laden; n [burden] last, [weight] gewicht, [cargo] lading	**lah**den; lahst, ghe**wight**, **lah**ding
lobby	hal	hahl
lobster	(zee)kreeft	**zay**krayft
local	plaatselijk	**plaht**selik
locals	plaatselijke bevolking	**plaht**selaiyke be**vol**king
location	plaats, plek	plahts, plek
lock/lock up	v afsluiten, op slot doen; n slot, [canal] sluis / opsluiten	**ahf**slœten, op slot doon; slot, slœs / **op**slœten
look	v kijken; n [opinion] kijk, [glance] blik, [appearance] aanblik	**kaiy**ken; kaiyk, blik, **ahn**blik
look after	zorgen voor	**zor**ghen voar
look at	kijken naar	**kaiy**ken nahr
look for	zoeken naar	**zoo**ken nahr
look like	[similar] lijken op, [appearance] er uitzien als	**laiy**ken op, ehr **œt**zeen ahls
look out	uitkijken	**œt**kaiyken

loose	*v* losmaken; *a* [not tied] los, [not tight] wijd	**loss**mahken; loss, waiyd
lose	verliezen	ver**lee**zen
loss	verlies	ver**lees**
lost	[missing] verloren, kwijt, [defeated] verloren, [lost one's way] verdwaald	ver**loa**ren, kwaiyt, ver**loa**ren, v er**dwahld**
lost and found	gevonden voorwerpen	ghe**von**den **voar**werpen
lot	[quantity] hoeveelheid, [estate] kavel	hoo**vayl**haiyd, **kah**vel
lot of, a	een heleboel, veel	en **hayl**ebool, vehl
loud	luid, [noisy] hard, [speaking] hardop	læd, hard, hard**op**
louse	luis	læs
love	*v* [person, like, appreciate] houden van, [person only] houden van, liefhebben; *n* [feeling] liefde, [beloved one] geliefde	**how**den vahn, **how**den vahn, **leef**hebben; **leef**de, ghe**leef**de
lovely	heerlijk	**hehr**lik
low	[deep, down] laag, [gently, slightly] zachtjes	lahgh, **zaght**yes
lower	*v* [from downstairs] omlaaghalen, [from above] laten zakken; *a* lager	om**lahgh**-hahlen, **lah**ten **zahk**ken; **lah**gher
low-fat	mager, vetarm	**mah**gher, **vet**arm
low-salt	zoutarm	**zowt**arm
lubricant	smeermiddel	**smehr**middel
luggage (rack)	bagage(rek)	bah**ghahz**he(rek)
lukewarm	lauw	laow
lump	klontje	**klont**ye
lung	long	long
M		
magazine	tijdschrift	**taiyd**sghrift
magnificent	prachtig	**prahgh**tigh
mail	post	posst
main	hoofd…, voornaamste	hoafd…, voar**nahm**ste
mainland	vasteland	vahste**lahnd**
make	[produce, do] maken, [give order to] laten (doen)	**mah**ken, **lah**ten (doon)
male	mannelijk	**mahn**nelik

man	[male person] man, [mankind] de mens	mahn, de mens
manual	a handmatig, met de hand; n handleiding	hahnd**mah**tigh, met de hahnd; **hahnd**laiyding
many	veel, vele	vayl, **vay**le
many a	menig(e), heel wat	**may**nigh(e), hayl waht_
map	kaart	kahrt
marble	[material] marmer, [toy] knikker	**mahr**mer, **knik**ker
marina	jachthaven	**yaght**hahven
marine	[army] marinier	maree**neer**
marine life	zeefauna	**zay**fowna
marriage	huwelijk	**hew**welaiyk
married	gehuwd	ghe**hewd**
marry	trouwen	**trow**en
match	v passen (bij); n [game] wedstrijd, [lighter] lucifer	**pahs**sen (baiy); **wed**straiyd, **lew**seefair
matchbox	lucifersdoosje	**lew**seefairs-**doas**ye
materney ward	kraamkliniek/-afdeling	**krahm**-kleeneek/-ahfdayling
mattress	matras	mah**trahs**
may	[possibility] (zou) kunnen, [permission] mogen	(zow) **kun**nen, **moa**ghen
maybe	misschien	mis**ggheen**
mayor	burgemeester	burghe**mays**ter
meal	maaltijd	**mahl**taiyd
mean	v [meaning] betekenen, [intention (to say)] bedoelen; a [nasty, cruel] gemeen	be**tay**kenen, be**doo**len; ghe**mayn**
meaning	betekenis, bedoelen, [use] zin	be**tay**kenis, be**doo**ling, zin
mechanic	monteur, technicus	mon**tuhr**, **tegh**neekus
medicine	geneesmiddel, [doctor] arts	ghe**nays**middel, arts
meet	ontmoeten, tegenkomen, [making acquaintance] kennismaken met, [get together] vergaderen, bijeenkomen	ont**moo**ten, **tay**ghenkohmen, **ken**nismahken met, ver**ghah**deren, baiy-**ayn**kohmen
meeting	vergadering, bijeenkomst	ver**ghah**dering, baiy-**ayn**komst
melon	meloen	me**loon**
mend	herstellen, repareren	hair**stel**len, raypa**reh**ren
message	boodschap, bericht	**boad**sghahp, be**rihght**
midnight	middernacht	midder**nahght**
milk	melk	melk
mill	molen, [factory] fabriek	**moa**len, fa**breek**

minced meat	gehakt	ghe**hahkt**
mirror	spiegel	**spee**ghel
missing	[not present] ontbrekend, [person] vermist	ont**bray**kend, ver**mist**
mistake	fout, vergissing	fowt, ver**ghis**sing
misunderstanding	misverstand	**mis**verstahnd
mixed	gemengd, vermengd	ghe**mengd**, ver**mengd**
mixed up	verward, in de war	ver**wahrd**, in de wahr
moan	klagen, [loudly] jammeren	**klah**ghen, **yahm**meren
moist(ure)	vocht	voght
monastery	klooster	**kloas**ter
money	geld	gheld
monk	monnik	**mon**nik
monkey	aap	ahp
month	maand	mahnd
moped	bromfiets, [< 20 km/h] snorfiets	**brom**feets, **snoar**feets
more (than)	meer (dan)	mehr (dahn)
morning	ochtend	**ogh**tend
morning, in the	's morgens	**smorg**hens
mosquito	mug	mugh
mother(-in-law)	(schoon)moeder	(sghoan)**moo**der
motorcar	auto	**ow**to
motorway	autosnelweg, [dual carriageway] autoweg	owto**snel**wegh, **ow**towegh
mountain (range)	berg(keten)	**bairgh**(kayten)
mountaineering	bergsport	**bairgh**sport
mouse	muis	mœs
moustache	snor	snohr
mouth	mond, [river] monding	mond, **mon**ding
move	[movement] beweging, [removal] verhuizen, [hurry] voortmaken	be**way**ghing, ver**hœ**zen, **voart**mahken
much	veel	vail
mud	modder	**mod**der
muscle	spier	speer
mushroom	paddestoel	**pahd**destool
music	muziek	mew**zeek**
must	moeten	**moo**ten
mustard	mosterd	**mos**terd
N		
nail	[finger] nagel, [iron] spijker	**nah**ghel, **spaiy**ker
nail polish	nagellak	**nah**ghel-lahk

naked	naakt, bloot	nahkt, bloat
name	v [mention, call] noemen, [give a name/function] benoemen; n naam	**noo**men, be**noo**men; nahm
napkin/nappy	[baby's] luier, [paper] servet	lœyer, sair**vet**
narrow	smal	smahl
nation	[country] land, [people] natie, volk	lahnd, **nah**tsee, volk
native	autochtoon, inheems	owtogh**toan**, in**haims**
nauseous	misselijk	**miss**elik
navy	marine	ma**ree**ne
near	(na)bij, in de buurt van	(nah)**baiy**, in de bewrt vahn
nearby	dichtbij	**dight**baiy
nearly	bijna	**baiy**nah
neat	[tidy] netjes, [pleasant, goodlooking] leuk	**net**yes, løk
neck	[back] nek, [front] hals	nek, hahls
necessary	nodig, noodzakelijk	**noa**digh, **noad**zahkelik
need	v [have to] moeten, [require] nodig hebben; behoefte	**moo**ten, **noa**digh **heb**ben; be**hoof**te
needle	naald	nahld
needlework	handwerk	**hahnd**wairk
neighbour	[male] buurman, [female] buurvrouw	**bewr**mahn, **bewr**vrow
nephew	neef(je)	**nayf**(ye)
never	nooit, [not even] zelfs niet	noayt, zelfs neet
newspaper	krant	krahnt
newsstand	krantenkiosk	**krahn**tenkiosk
next	volgend(e)	**vol**ghend(e)
nice	leuk, aardig, mooi	løk, **ahr**digh, moay
niece	nicht(je)	**nihght**(ye)
night	[after midnight] nacht, [late in the evening] late avond	naght, **lah**te ahvond
night, at	's nachts	snaghts
nobody/no one	niemand	**nee**mahnd
noise	lawaai, herrie	lah**waiy**, **her**ree
none	geen, [nothing] niets	ghayn, neets
north	noord(en)	noard(en)
nose	neus	nøs

note	*v* noteren; *n* [short letter] briefje,	no**teh**ren; **breef**ye,
	[bank note] biljet,	bil**yet**,
	[music] (muziek)noot,	(mew**zeek**)noat,
	[take a note] notitie	no**tee**tsee
note pad	schrijfblok	**sghraiyf**blok
nothing	niets	neets
now	nu	new
number	[order] nummer, [maths] cijfer,	**num**mer, **saiy**fer,
	getal, [quantity] aantal	ghe**tal**, **ahn**tahl
nun	non	non
nurse	[male] verpleger,	ver**play**gher,
	[female] verpleegster	ver**playgh**ster
nut	[part] moer, [fruit] noot(je)	moor, noat(ye)

O

oars	(roei)riemen	(rooy)**ree**men
objection	bezwaar, protest	be**zwahr**, pro**test**
obligatory	verplicht	ver**plight**
occupation	beroep, bezigheid	be**roop**, **bay**zigh-haiyd
odd	[number] oneven,	on**ay**ven,
	[unusual] vreemd	vraymd
odour	geur	ghuhr
off	[away] weg van,	wegh vahn,
	[near] ter hoogte van,	ter **hoagh**te vahn,
	[rotten] bedorven,	be**dohr**ven,
	[cancelled] afgelast	**ahf**ghelahst
offer	*v* bieden, [present] aanbieden;	**bee**den, **ahn**beeden;
	n [special price] aanbieding,	**ahn**beeding,
	[money/business] bod, offerte	bod, of**fair**te
office	kantoor	kahn**toar**
officer	[rank] officier, [police] agent,	offee**seer**, ah**ghent**,
	[civil servant] beambte	be-**ahmb**te
often	vaak, dikwijls	vahk, **dik**waiyls
oil	olie	**oa**lee
ointment	zalf	zahlf
old	oud	owd
once	[some time] eens,	ayns,
	[one time] een keer,	
	[as soon as] zodra	ayn kehr, zoa**drah**
once, at	ineens, direct, dadelijk	in**ayns**, dee**rekt**, **dah**delik
one	[number] één,	ayn,
	[unspecified person] men	men
oneself	zich, zichzelf	zihgh, zihgh**zelf**

one-way street	straat met eenrichtingverkeer	straht met ayn**rihgh**ting-ver**kehr**
one-way ticket	enkele reis	**en**kele raiys
onion	ui	œ
only	[just] alleen, slechts, pas, [only one] enige	ahl**layn**, sleghts, pahs, **ay**nighe
opponent	tegenstander	**tay**ghenstahnder
opposite	[facing] tegenover, [contrary] tegengesteld	tayghen**o**ver, **tay**ghen-ghe**steld**
oral	[by speaking] mondeling, [through the mouth] met/door de mond, [medicine] oraal	**mon**deling, met/daor de mond, oa**rahl**
orange	[colour] oranje, [fruit] sinaasappel	o**rahn**ye, **see**nahs-appel
orchard	boomgaard	**boam**ghahrd
order	v [placing an order] bestellen, [mil. command] bevelen; n bestelling, bevel, [alphabetical] volgorde	be**stel**len, be**vay**len; be**stel**ling, be**vel**, **volgh**orde
order, out of	buiten werking, defect	**bœ**ten **wair**king, day**fekt**
other	ander(e)	**ahn**der(e)
outdoor(s), outside	buiten	**bœ**ten
over here	hier	heer
overtake	inhalen	**in**hahlen
over there	daar(ginds)	dahr(**ghinds**)
owe	verschuldigd zijn	ver**sghul**dighd zaiyn
own	v bezitten; a eigen	be**zit**ten; **aiy**ghen
owner	eigenaar	**aiy**ghenahr
P		
pain(less)	pijn(loos)	**paiyn**(loas)
painstaking	moeizaam	**mooy**zahm
paint	v [general] schilderen, [non-artistic] verven; n verf	**sghil**deren, **vair**ven; vairf
painting	schilderij	**sghil**deraiy
pale	bleek	blake
pan(cake)	pan(nenkoek)	**pahn**(nenkook)
paper	papier, [newspaper] krant	pa**peer**, krahnt
paralysed	verlamd	ver**lahmd**
parcel	pakket, pakje	pahk**ket**, **pahk**ye
parents	ouders	**ow**ders
parking disc/meter	parkeerschijf/-meter	par**kehr**-sghaiyf/-**may**ter
part	[piece] stuk, deel, [spare part] onderdeel, [play] rol	stuk, dayl, **on**derdayl, rol

party	v feestvieren; n [political] partij, [festivity] feest, [people] groep	**fayst**veeren; pahr**taiy**, fayst, ghroop
pass	v [overtake] voorbijgaan, [present] overhandigen, [transfer] doorgeven; n [mountain] pas	voar**baiy**ghahn, over**hahn**dighen, **doar**gheven; pahs
passage	[between objects] doorgang, [sea voyage] overtocht	**doar**ghahng, **o**vertoght
past	n [time] verleden, a/adv [finished] voorbij	ver**lay**den, voar**baiy**
past, in the	vroeger, in het verleden	**vroo**gher, in het ver**lay**den
pastime	liefhebberij	leefhebbe**raiy**
pastry	gebakje	ghe**bahk**ye
path	pad	pahd
patience	geduld	ghe**duld**
pavement	stoep	stoop
pay	betalen, [restaurant] afrekenen	be**tah**len, **ahf**raykenen
pearl	parel	**pah**rel
peasant	boer	boor
peg	[clothes] klerenhanger, [tent] tentharing	**kleh**ren-**hahn**ger, **tent**hahring
pencil	potlood	**pot**load
people	mensen pl, [nation] volk	**men**sen, vohlk
pepper	peper	**pay**per
performance	voorstelling, opvoering, optreden den	**voar**stelling, **op**vooring, **op**tray-den
perfume	parfum	pahr**fum**
permit	v toestaan; n toestemming, [official] vergunning	**too**stahn; **too**stemming, ver**ghun**ning
pet	huisdier	**hœs**deer
pet shop	dierenwinkel	**dee**renwinkel
petrol	benzine	ben**zee**ne
petrol station	tankstation	**tank**stashon
phone	v bellen, opbellen; n telefoon	**bel**len, **op**bellen; tayle**foan**
physical	lichamelijk/[formal]	lih**ghah**melik
physical education	lichamelijke opvoeding. [pop.] gymnastiek	lih**ghah**melaiyke **op**vooding, ghimnahs**teek**
picture	foto, afbeelding, [painting] schilderij	**fo**to, **ahf**baylding, sghilde**raiy**
pie	pastei	pahs**taiy**
piece	stuk	stuk

pillow	kussen	**kus**sen
pin	v vastprikken; n speld	**vahst**prikken; speld
pipe	[smoking] pijp, [tube] pijp, buis	paiyp, bœs
plain	n vlakte; a [surface] vlak	**vlahk**te; vlahk
plant	[biology] plant, [factory] fabriek	plahnt, fah**breek**
plaster	pleister	**plaiys**ter
plate	bord	bord
play	v spelen; n [game] spel, [theatre] toneelstuk	**spay**len; spel, toa**nayl**stuk
pleasant	plezierig, aangenaam	ple**zee**righ, **ahn**ghenahm
please	v een plezier doen; adv alstublieft	en ple**zeer** doon; ahlstew**bleeft**
pleased	blij, [to meet you] aangenaam	blaiy, **ahn**ghenahm
pleasure	plezier, genoegen	ple**zeer**, ghe**noo**ghen
plug	stekker, [bath, sink] afvoerstop	**stek**ker, **ahf**voor-stop
point	v wijzen; n punt, plek	**waiy**zen; punt, plek
point out	aanwijzen, [make clear] duidelijk maken	**ahn**waiyzen, **dœ**delik **mah**ken
poison	vergif	ver**ghif**
pole	paal, stok	pahl, stock
polish	v poetsen; n [furniture, metal] poetsmiddel, [shoes] schoensmeer	**poot**sen; **poots**middel, **sghoon**smehr
police(man)	politie(agent)	poa**leet**see(ah**ghent**)
police station	politiebureau	poa**leet**see
poor	[financial, pityful] arm, [shabby] armzalig, [quality] slecht	ahrm, a hrm**zah**lig, sleght
population	bevolking	be**vol**king
pocket	(broek-/jas)zak	(**brook**-/**yahs**)zahk
pocket knife	zakmes	**zahk**mess
pork	[animal] varken, [meat] varkensvle	**vahr**ken, **vahr**kensvlays
port	[dock] haven, [city] havenstad	**hah**ven, **hah**venstahd
possible	mogelijk	**moa**ghelik
post	[stake] paal, [mail] post	pahl, posst
postcard	ansichtkaart	**ahn**sight-kahrt
potato	aardappel	**ahrd**ahppel
poultry	gevogelte	ghe**voa**ghelte
pour	inschenken	**in**sghenken
powder	poeder, [gun] kruit	**poo**der, krœt
power	macht, sterkte	maght, **stairk**te
pram	kinderwagen	**kin**der-**wah**ghen

prefer	liever hebben, de voorkeur geven aan	**lee**ver **heb**ben, de **voar**kuhr **ghay**ven ahn
pregnant	zwanger	**zwahng**er
prescription	voorschrift, [doctor] recept	**voars**ghrift, re**sept**
present	v aanbieden, [introduce] voorstellen; n [gift] cadeau, [actual] huidig, [presence] aanwezig	**ahn**beeden, **voar**stellen; kah**doh**, **hœ**digh, ahn**way**zigh
present, at	tegenwoordig	tayghen**woar**digh
press	v drukken, [squeeze] persen; n [news] pers, [publisher] uitgeverij	**druk**ken, **pair**sen; pehrs, œtghayve**raiy**
pressure	druk	druk
price	(kost)prijs	**(kohst)**praiys
print	v drukken; n afdruk	**druk**ken; **ahf**druk
prize	prijs	praiys
proceed	verdergaan, doorgaan	**vair**derghahn, **doar**ghahn
profession	beroep	be**roop**
prohibited	verboden	ver**bo**den
prolongation	verlenging	ver**leng**ing
promise	v beloven; n belofte	be**lo**ven; be**lof**te
proof	[evidence] bewijs, [resistant] bestand tegen	be**waiys**, be**stahnd tay**ghen
property	eigendom	**aiy**ghendom
propose	voorstellen	**voar**stellen
prove	bewijzen, [to be] blijken	be**wai**yzen, **blaiy**ken
pull	trekken	**trek**ken
pump	v pompen; n pomp	**pom**pen; pomp
puncture	lekke band	**lek**ke bahnd
pure	zuiver	**zœ**ver
purse	portemonnee	poarte-mon**nay**
put	leggen, zetten, doen	**legh**ghen, **zet**ten, doon

Q

quality	kwaliteit, [function] hoedanigheid	qualeе**taiyt**, hoo**dah**nighhaiyd
quarrel	v ruziemaken; n ruzie	**rew**zee-**mah**ken; **rew**zee
quarry	groeve	**ghroo**veh
quarter	[1/4] kwart, [15 min.] kwartier, [neighborhood] wijk	quahrt, quahr**teer**, waiyk
quay	kade	**kah**de
queen	koningin	koning**in**
quench	blussen	**blus**sen

x

question	vraag	vrahgh
quick	snel, vlug	snell, vlughh
quiet	a stil, rustig; n stilte	still, **rus**tigh; **still**te

R

rabies	hondsdolheid	honds**doll**haiyd
rag	doek, lapje	dook, **lahp**ye
rags	vodden	**vod**den
railway	spoorweg	**spoar**wegh
railway ticket	spoorkaartje, treinkaartje	**spoar**kahrtye, **traiyn**kahrtye
rain (coat)	regen(jas)	**ray**ghen(yahs)
rampart	vestingwal	**ves**tingwahl
rare	zeldzaam, [roasted] licht gebakken	**zeld**zahm, lihght ghe**bahk**ken
rate	[exchange] koers, [fare] tarief, [term] termijn	koors, tah**reef**, ter**maiyn**
raw	[meat] rauw, [conduct] ruw	rohw, rew
raw material	grondstof	**ghrond**stoff
razor blade	scheermesje	**sghehr**messye
read	lezen, [university] studeren	**lay**zen, **stew**dehren
ready	klaar, gereed	klahr, ghe**rayd**
real	echt	eght
real estate	onroerend goed	on**roo**rend ghood
rear (side)	achter(kant)	**agh**ter(kahnt)
reason	[mind] rede, [cause] reden	**ray**de, **ray**den
receipt	ontvangstbewijs, kwitantie	ont**vahngst**-be**waiys**, queet**ah**ntsee
receive	ontvangen	ont**vahng**en
recipe	recept	re**sept**
recently	onlangs, recent	on**lahngs**, re**sent**
recommend	aanbevelen	**ahn**bevaylen
record	v [on tape etc.] opnemen, [in writing] verslag doen; n [sport etc.] record, [report] verslag, [music] (grammofoon)plaat	**op**naymen, ver**slahgh** doon; re**koar**, ver**slahgh**, (grahmmo**foan**)plaht
recover	herstellen, beter worden	hair**stell**en, **bay**ter **wor**den
red	rood	road
reduce	verminderen, afnemen	ver**min**deren, **ahf**naymen
reel	spoel, klos	spool, kloss
refrigerator	koelkast	**kool**kahst
refuge	v weigeren; n schuilplaats, [mountain]schuilhut	**waiy**gheren; **sghœl**plahts, **sghœl**hut
refugee	vluchteling	**vlughh**teling

refund	teruggave, restitutie	te**rugh**-ghahve, restee**tewt**see

register	*v* inschrijven, [mail] aantekenen;
	   n [record] register, [cash] kassa
		insghraiyven, **ahn**taykenen;
		   ray**ghis**ter, **kahs**sa

related to	familie van	fa**mee**lee vahn

release	[let go] loslaten,
	   [product] op de markt brengen
		losslahten,
		   op de mahrkt **bren**gen

reliable	betrouwbaar	be**trow**bahr

relief	[reuction] vermindering,
	   [feeling] opluchting
		ver**min**dering,
		   op**lugh**ting

relieve	verlichten, ontlasten	ver**lihgh**ten, ont**lahs**ten

remote	[isolated] achteraf, afgelegen,
	   [from a distance] op afstand
		aghter**ahf**, **ahf**ghelayghen,
		   op **ahf**stahnd

rent	*v* [to] verhuren, [from] huren;
	   n huur
		ver**hew**ren, **hew**ren;
		   hewr

rented car	huurauto	**hewr**-owto
repair	herstellen, repareren	hair**stel**len, raypa**reh**ren
repeat	herhalen	hair**hah**len

represent	[agent] vertegenwoordigen,
	   [image] voorstellen
		vertayghen-**woar**dighen,
		   voarstellen

request	*v* verzoeken; *n* verzoek	ver**zoo**ken; ver**zook**
require	vereisen, nodig hebben	ver**aiy**sen, **noa**digh **heb**ben
research	*v* onderzoeken; *n* onderzoek	onder**zoo**ken; **on**derzook

residence	verblijf(plaats),
	   [permanently] woonplaats
		ver**blaiyf**(plahts),
		   woanplahts

responsible	verantwoordelijk	verahnt**woar**delik

rest	*v* (uit)rusten, [remain] resteren;
	   n rust, [remainder] restant
		(**œt**)rusten, res**teh**ren;
		   rust, res**tahnt**

return	*v* [from absence] terugkeren,
	   [give back] teruggeven;
	   n terugkeer, teruggave
		te**rugh**kehren,
		   te**rugh**-ghayven,
		   te**rugh**kehr, te**rugh**-ghahve

return ticket	retour	re**toor**
ribbon	lint	lint
rice	rijst	raiyst
rich	rijk	raiyk
ride	*v* rijden; *n* rit	**raiy**den; rit
ride, give a	een lift geven	en lift **ghay**ven

right	juist, [legal] recht,
	   [direction] rechts,
	   [position] rechter-
		yœst, reght,
		   reghts,
		   reghter-

right, to be	gelijk hebben	ghe**laiyk heb**ben
right of way	voorrang	**voar**rangh
right on	nu meteen	new met**ayn**

rim	rand	rahnd
ring	v [bell, phone] bellen, [phone] (op)bellen; n [jewel, round object] ring, [pople] kring, [geometry] cirkel	**bell**en, (**op**)bellen; ring, kring, **sihr**kel
rip	v scheuren; n scheur	**sghuhr**en; sghuhr
ripe	rijp	raiyp
rise	[on your feet] opstaan, [appear] opkomen	**op**stahn, **op**kohmen
risk	v riskeren; n risico	ris**keh**ren; **ree**seeko
river	rivier	ree**veer**
road	weg	wegh
road patrol	wegenwacht	**way**ghenwaght
roadside	berm	bairm
roast	braden, roosteren	**brah**den, **roas**teren
rob	bestelen	be**stay**len
robber	dief	deef
rock	v schudden; n rots, [boulder] rotsblok	**sghud**den; rots, **rots**blok
roll	v rollen; n rol, [bread] broodje	**roll**en; rohl, **broad**ye
room	[building] kamer, [space] ruimte	**kah**mer, **rœm**te
root	[plant] wortel, [origin] oorsprong	**wohr**tel, **oar**sprong
rope	touw, lijn	tow, laiyn
rose	roos	roas
rotten	rot	rot
rough	ruw, [violent] hardhandig	rew, hard**hahn**digh
round	rond(om), [lap, tour] ronde	rond(**om**), **ron**de
row	v roeien; n rij	**roo**yen; raiy
rub	wrijven	**wraiy**ven
rucksack	rugzak	**rugh**zahk
rudder	roer	roor
rude	onbeleefd, ongemanierd	onbe**layfd**, onghemah**neerd**
run	[walk, proceed] lopen, [fast] rennen, [liquid] stromen, [river] loop, [term] termijn	**loa**pen, **ren**nen, **stroh**men, loap, ter**maiyn**
rural	landelijk	**lahn**delik
rust	v roesten; n roest	**roos**ten; roost

S

saddle	zadel	**zah**del
safe	a veilig; n brandkast	**vaiy**lihgh; **brahnd**kahst
safety	veiligheid	**vaiy**lihgh-haiyd

safety belt	[car] autogordel, veiligheidsgordel	**ow**to-**ghor**del, **vaiy**lihgh-haiyds-**ghor**del
sail	v [any vessel] varen, [sailing boat] zeilen; n zeil	**vah**ren, **zaiy**len; zaiyl
sale	verkoop, [discount] opruiming	**vair**koap, **op**rœming
salt	zout	zowt
same	zelfde	**zelf**de
sand	zand	zahnd
sandwich	boterham	**boa**terhahm
sanitary towel	maandverband	**mahnd**verbahnd
satisfaction	tevredenheid, bevrediging, [compensation] genoegdoening	te**vray**denhaiyd, be**vray**dighing, ghe**noogh**-dooning
sauce	saus	sows
sausage	worst	wohrst
save	[money] sparen, [pay less] besparen, [keep] bewaren, [rescue] redden	**spah**ren, be**spah**ren, be**wah**ren, **red**den
savoury	hartig	**hahr**tigh
say	zeggen	**zegh**ghen
scarf	sjaal	shahl
schedule	schema, plan, [timetable] dienstregeling	**sghay**ma, plahn, **deenst-**raygheling
scissors, (pair of)	schaar sing	sghahr
scoop	schep	sghep
screw	v (vast)schroeven; n schroef	(vahst)**sghroo**ven; sghroof
screw driver	schroevendraaier	**sghroo**ven-**drah**yer
sea(sick)	zee(ziek)	**zay**(zeek)
seal	[wax] zegel, [rubber] stempel, [animal] zeehond	**zay**ghel, **stem**pel, **zay**hond
search	[look for] zoeken, [visitation] fouilleren	**zoo**ken, foo**yeh**ren
seat	stoel, [theatre] (zit)plaats, [high official/administration] zetel	stool, (**zit**)plahts, **zay**tel
second	[time] seconde, [order] tweede	se**kon**de, **tway**de
security	beveiliging, bewaking, [safety] veiligheid	be**vaiy**lighing, be**wah**king, **vaiy**ligh-haiyd
see	v zien; n zetel	zeen; **zay**tel
seed	zaad	zahd
seldom	zelden	**zel**den
sell	verkopen	ver**koh**pen
send	zenden, (ver)sturen	**zen**den, (ver)**stew**ren

sender	afzender	**ahf**zender
sense	[use] zin, [body] zintuig	zin, **zin**tœgh
sense, make	logisch zijn, zin hebben	**low**ghees zaiyn, zin **heb**ben
sensible	verstandig	ver**stahn**digh
sensitive	gevoelig	ghe**voo**ligh
sentence	*v* veroordelen; *n* [grammar] zin, [court] vonnis	ver**oar**daylen; zin, **von**nis
serve	bedienen, serveren	be**dee**nen, ser**veh**ren
service	dienst, [restaurant etc.] bediening, service, [technical] service, nazorg	deenst, be**dee**ning, '**ser**vice', **nah**zorgh
settled	[situated] gevestigd, [deal] afgesproken	ghe**ves**tighd, **ahf**ghesproaken
sewer	riolering	rio**leh**ring
shack	hut, gebouwtje	hut, ghe**baow**tye
shadow	schaduw	**sghah**dew
shallow	ondiep	on**deep**
shape	*v* vormen; *n* vorm	**vor**men; vorm
share	v delen; n (aan)deel	dayl; (**ahn**)dayl
shark	haai	haiy
sharp	scherp, fel	sghairp, fel
shave	scheren	**sgheh**ren
sheep	schaap	sghahp
sheet	[paper] vel, blad, [bed] laken	vel, blahd, **lah**ken
shelf	plank	plahnk
shell	schelp	sghelp
shelter	schuilplaats	**sghœl**plahts
shine	[cast light] schijnen, [shoes] poetsen	**sghaiy**nen, **poot**sen
ship	*v* versturen, [by ship] verschepen; *n* schip	ver**stew**ren, ver**sghay**pen; sghip
shirt	overhemd	**o**verhemd
shoe(string)	schoen(veter)	**sghoen**(vayter)
shop	*v* winkelen; *n* winkel	**win**kelen; **win**kel
shopping, go	boodschappen doen	**boad**sghahppen doon
short	kort	kort
shortage	tekort	te**kort**
short circuit	kortsluiting	**kort**slœting
short-cut	kortere route	**kor**tere **roo**te
short of, be	tekort komen	te**kort koh**men
shorts	korte broek *sing*	**kor**te brook
shoulder	[body] schouder, [roadside] berm	**sghow**der, bairm

199

E N G L I S H - D U T C H

show	*v* tonen, laten zien; *n* [theater] voorstelling, [promotional/exhib.] vertoning	tohnen, **lah**ten zeen; **voar**stelling, ver**toh**ning
shower	[bathroom] douche, [weather] regenbui	doosh, `ray`ghenbœ
sick	misselijk, ziek	**mis**selik, zeek
side	kant, zijde, [sport] elftal	kahnt, **zaiy**de, **elf**tahl
sieve	*v* zeven; *n* zeef	**zaiy**ven; zayf
sigh	*v* zuchten; *n* zucht	**zugh**ten; zught
sign	*v* ondertekenen; *n* teken, [notice board] bord(je)	onder**tay**kenen; tayken, board(ye)
significant	belangrijk, zinvol	be**lahng**raiyk, **zin**vol
signature	handtekening	**hahnd**-taykening
signpost(ed)	(be)wegwijzer(d)	(be)**wegh**waiyzer(d)
sight	[ability to see] gezichtsvermogen, [glance] het zien van	ghe**zights**-ver**moa**ghen, het zeen vahn
sights	bezienswaardigheden	bezeens**wahr**digh-hayden
silk	*n* zijde; *a* zijden	**zaiy**de; **zaiy**den
silver	*n* zilver; *a* zilveren	**zil**ver; **zil**veren
similar	gelijk, identiek, zelfde	ghe**laiyk**, eeden**teek**, **zelf**de
simple	eenvoudig	ayn**vow**digh
simultaneously	gelijktijdig	ghelaiyk-**taiy**digh
since	vanaf, sinds	vahn**ahf**, sinds
single	enkel, [unmarried] ongehuwd	**en**kel, onghe**hewd**
single room	eenpersoonskamer	**ayn**persoans-**kah**mer
singlet	onderhemd	**on**derhemd
sister(-in-law)	(schoon)zuster	(**sghoan**)zuster
sit	zitten	**zit**ten
size	grootte, maat, formaat	**ghroat**te, maht, for**maht**
skid	slippen	**slip**pen
skilful	handig, bekwaam	**hahn**digh, be**quahm**
skin	huid, vel	hœd, vel
skirt	rok	rok
sky	hemel, lucht	**hay**mel, lught
slaughter	[animal] slachten, [people] afslachten	**slagh**ten, **ahf**slaghten
sleep	*v* slapen; *n* slaap	**slah**pen; slahp
sleeping bag	slaapzak	**slahp**zahk
sleeve	[costume] mouw, [book] omslag	maow, **om**slagh
slice	plakje, sneetje	**plak**ye, **snay**tye
slide	*v* glijden; *n* dia	**ghlaiy**den; **dee**a
slightly	licht, enigszins	lihght, **ay**nighs-zins

slim	slank	slahnk
slippery	glad	ghlahd
slope	helling	**hel**ling
slow	langzaam	**lahng**zahm
slow down	afremmen, vaart minderen	**ahf**remmen, vahrt **min**deren
slow train	stoptrein	**stop**traiyn
small	klein	klaiyn
smell	v geuren, ruiken, [stink] stinken;	**ghuh**ren, **ræ**ken, **stin**ken;
	n geur, reuk, stank	ghuhr, røk, stahnk
smoke	v roken; n rook	**roa**ken; roak
smooth	[surface] glad, zacht,	ghlahd, zaght,
	[easy] probleemloos,	pro**blaym**loas
snail	slak	slahk
snake	slang	slahng
sneeze	niezen	**nee**zen
snow	v sneeuwen; n sneeuw	**snay**wen; snayw
soap	zeep	zayp
sock	sok	sok
socket	stopcontact, contactdoos	**stop**kontahkt, kon**tahkt**doas
soft	zacht, zwak	zaght, zwahk
soft drink	frisdrank	**fris**drahnk
soil	aarde, grond, bodem	**ahr**de, ghrond, **boa**dem
sole	[only] enige, [shoe] zool	**ay**nighe, zoal
solid	massief	mahs**seef**
sour	zuur	zewr
some	enige, enkele, sommige	**ay**nighe, **en**kele, **som**mighe
somebody/someone	iemand	**ee**mahnd
sometimes	soms	soms
somewhat	enigszins, iets	**ay**nighs-zins, eets
somewhere (else)	ergens (anders)	**air**ghens (**ahn**ders)
son(-in-law)	(schoon)zoon	(s**ghoan**)zoan
soon	gauw, binnenkort, spoedig	ghaow, binnen**kort**, **spoo**digh
sore	zeer, pijnlijk	zehr, **paiyn**lik
sound	v klinken; n [audible] geluid,	**klin**ken;
	[strait] zeestraat,	ghe**lœd**,
	a [healthy] gezond	**zay**straht, ghe**zond**
soup	soep	soop
south	zuid(en)	**zœd**(en)
spare parts	reserveonderdelen	re**sair**ve-**on**derdaylen
spark	vonk	vonk
speed	snelheid	**snel**haiyd
spell	v spellen; n betovering	**spel**len; be**to**vering

spicy	pittig, hartig, gekruid	**pit**tig, **hahr**tigh, ghe**krœd**
spider	spin	spin
spire	(toren)spits	(**toh**ren)spits
spit	spuwen, spugen	**spew**wen, **spew**ghen
splendid	prachtig	**pragh**tigh
sponge	spons	spons
spoon	lepel	**lay**pel
spot	[place] plek, [pimple] puist, [stain] vlek	plek, pœst, vlek
spray	v [from a can] spuiten, [from a hose] sproeien; n spuitmiddel, spray	**spœ**ten, **sproo**yen; **spœt**middel, 'spray'
spring(time)	lente	**len**te
square	[street] plein, [geometry] vierkant, [boaring] saai	plaiyn, **veer**kahnt, sigh
stable	n stal; a stabiel	stahl; sta**beel**
stage	[theatre] toneel, [phase] fase	to**nayl**, **fah**ze
stain	vlek	vlek
stairs, (flight of)	trap sing	trahp
stamp	v stempelen, [mail] frankeren; n stempel, [mail] (post)zegel	**stem**pelen, frahn**keh**ren; **stem**pel, (posst)**zay**ghel
stand	v staan; n [market] kraam(pje), [stadium] tribune, staanplaats	stahn; krahm(pye), tree**bew**ne, **stahn**plahts
stationary	schrijfwaren, kantoorbehoeften	**sghraiyf**wahren, kahn**toar**behooften
statue	standbeeld	**stahnd**bayld
stay	v blijven, [reside] verblijven, [overnight] logeren; n verblijf	**blaiy**ven, ver**blaiy**ven, loh**zheh**ren; ver**blaiyf**
steal	stelen	**stay**len
steel	staal	stahl
steep	steil	staiyl
steeple	stompe toren	**stom**pe **toh**ren
steering wheel	stuur	stewr
stick	v plakken, kleven; n stok, [iron] staaf	**plahk**ken, **klay**ven; stok, stahf
stiff	stijf	staiyf
still	[continuing] nog steeds, [nevertheless] nochtans, toch	nogh stayds, n ogh**tahns**, togh
stockings	kousen	**kow**sen
stomach	maag	mahgh
stone	steen	stayn

store	v opslaan, stallen; n [shop] winkel, [storage room] opslagplaats, stalling	**op**slahn; **win**kel, **op**slagh-plahts, **stahl**ling
stove	kachel	**kah**ghel
strange	[foreign, unusual] vreemd, [astonishing] raar	vraymd, rahr
stranger	vreemdeling	**vraym**deling
street(lamp)	straat(lantaarn)	**straht**(lahntahrn)
straight (on)	recht(door)	reght(**doar**)
string	draad, snoer	drahd, snoor
striped	gestreept	ghe**straypt**
strong	sterk	stairk
study	v (be)studeren; n studeerkamer	(be)stew**deh**ren; stew**dehr**kahmer
stuffed	gevuld, [dead animal] opgezet	ghe**vuld**, **op**ghezet
stuffy	benauwd	be**nowd**
suddenly	plotseling	**plot**seling
suffer(ing)	lijden	**laiy**den
sugar	suiker	**sœ**ker
suggest	voorstellen	**voar**stellen
suit	v passen, van pas komen; n costuum	**pahs**sen, vahn pahs **koa**men; kos**tewm**
suitcase	koffer	**kof**fer
summer	zomer	**zoh**mer
summit	top	top
sun(bathing)	zon(nebaden)	**zon**(nebahden)
sunburn	zonnebrand	**zon**nebrahnd
sunglasses	zonnebril	**zon**nebril
suppose	veronderstellen, aannemen	veronder**stel**len, **ahn**naymen
surcharge	toeslag	**too**slahgh
sure	zeker	**zay**ker
surgery	[doctor's cabinet] spreekkamer, [operations] chirurgie	**sprayk**kahmer, sheeruhr**ghee**
surgery (hours)	spreekuur sing	**sprayk**ewr
surname	achternaam	**agh**ternahm
surprise	verrassing	ver**rahs**sing
surrender	zich overgeven	zigh over**ghay**ven
surroundings	omgeving	om**ghay**ving
suspense	spanning	**spahn**ning
swallow	[food] inslikken, [liquid] opslokken, [medicine] innemen	**in**slikken, **op**slokken, **in**naymen
swamp	moeras	moo**rahs**
sway	slingeren	**sling**eren

sweat	v zweten; n zweet	zwayten, zwayt
sweater	trui	trœ
sweep	vegen	vayghen
sweet	[taste] zoet, [character] lief	zoot, leef
sweetener	zoetstof	zootstof
sweets	snoep sing, zoetwaren	snoop, zootwahren
swim	zwemmen	zwemmen
swimsuit	badpak	bahdpahk
switch	v (over)schakelen; n knop, schakelaar	(over)sghahkelen; knop, sghahkelahr

T

table	[furniture] tafel, [list] tabel	tahfel, tahbel
table cloth	tafelkleed	tahfelklayd
tack	spijker	spaiyker
tag	kaartje	kahrtye
tail	staart	stahrt
tailback	file	feeleh
take	[swallow] innemen, [grab] nemen, pakken, [away] wegbrengen	innaymen, naymen, pahkken, weghbrengen
take care of	zorgen voor, [task] op zich nemen	zorghen voar, op zigh naymen
take notice	nota nemen	nota naymen
tall	[height] hoog, [person] lang, [big] groot	hoagh, lahng, ghroat
tame	v temmen; a tam, mak	temmen; tahm, mahk
tanned	bruin, gebruind	brœn, ghebrœnd
tap	kraan	krahn
taste	v smaken, [sample] proeven; n smaak	prooven, smahken; smahk
tasty	lekker, smakelijk	lekker, smahkelik
taxi rank	taxistandplaats	tahksee-stahndplahts
tea	thee	tay
teach	leren, onderwijzen	lehren, onderwaiyzen
teacher	leraar, onderwijzer	lehrahr, onderwaiyzer
tear	v scheuren, (uiteen)trekken; n [torn apart] scheur, [eyes] traan	sghuhren, ([oie]t-ayn)trekken; sghuhr, trahn
teaspoon	theelepeltje	taylaypeltye
telephone booth	telefooncel	telefoansell
telephone directory	telefoonboek	telefoanbook
temporary	tijdelijk	taiydelik
tension	spanning	spahnning
tent peg	tentharing	tenthahring

tepid	lauw	laow
terminus	eindpunt	**aiynd**punt
terrible	verschrikkelijk	ver**sghrikk**elik
thank	(be)danken	(be)**dahn**ken
that	dat, die	daht, dee
theft	diefstal	**deef**stahl
therefore	daarom	**dahr**om
these	deze	**day**ze
thick	dik	dik
thief	dief	deef
thin	dun	dun
thing	ding	ding
think	denken, [opinion] vinden	**den**ken, **vin**den
thirst	dorst	dorst
thirsty, be	dorst hebben	dorst **heb**ben
this	dit, deze	dit, **day**ze
those	die	dee
thought	gedachte	ghe**dagh**te
thread	draad, garen	drahd, **gah**ren
thrilling	spannend	**spahn**nend
throat	keel	kayl
through	door	doar
thunderstorm	onweersbui	**on**wehrs-bœ
ticket	kaartje, biljet, [police] bekeuring	**kahrt**ye, bil**yet**, be**kuh**ring
ticket collector	conducteur	konduk**tør**
tide	getij(de)	ghe**taiy**(de)
tidy	v opruimen; a netjes, schoon	**op**rœmen; **net**yes, sghoan
tie	v vastbinden; n [connection] band, [knotted tie] stropdas	**vahst**binden; bahnd, **strop**dahs
tight	strak	strahk
tights	panty, [woollen] maillot	'pan**ty**', ma**yoh**
tile	tegel	**tay**ghel
time	tijd	taiyd
timetable	dienstregeling, [railways] spoorboekje	**deenst**raygheling, **spoar**bookye
tin	blik, bus, trommel	blik, bus, **trom**mel
tip	[top end] puntje, [gratuity] fooi	**punt**ye, foay
tired	moe	moo
tired of, be	zat zijn, genoeg hebben van	zaht zaiyn, ghe**noogh heb**ben vahn
toadstool	paddestoel	**pahd**destool
tobacco(nist)	tabak(swinkel)	ta**bahk**(s)winkel

today	vandaag	vahn**dagh**
toe	teen	tayn
together	samen, bij elkaar	**sah**men, baiy el**kahr**
tomorrow	morgen	**mor**ghen
tongs	tang	tahng
tongue	tong	tong
tongue, mother	moedertaal	**moo**dertahl
too much	teveel	te**vayl**
tool(s)	gereedschap, hulpmiddel	ghe**rayd**sghahp, **hulp**middel
tooth	[front] tand, [molar] kies	tahnd, kees
toothache	kiespijn	**kees**paiyn
tooth brush	tandenborstel	**tahn**denborstel
tooth paste	tandpasta	**tahnd**pahsta
top	[upper side] bovenkant, [highest point] top, [lid] deksel	**bo**venkahnt, top, **dek**sel
top (of), on	boven op	**bo**ven op
torch	[electric] zaklantaarn, [flame] fakkel	**zahk**lahntahrn, **fahk**kel
touch	v aanraken; n aanraking, [feeling] gevoel, [slight] zweem	**ahn**rahken; **ahn**rahking, ghe**vool**, zwaym
touchdown	landing	**lahn**ding
tough	taai, sterk, [nasty] lastig	tigh, stairk, **lahs**tig
tour	v rondreizen; n rondrit, [sport] ronde	**rond**raiyzen; **rond**rit, **ron**de
tow	slepen	**slay**pen
tow away zone	wegsleepzone	**wegh**slayp-**zoh**ne
towel	handdoek	**hahnd**dook
tower	toren	**toa**ren
town (hall)	stad(huis)	stahd(**hœs**)
toxic	n gif, a giftig	ghif, **ghif**tig
toy(s)	speelgoed	**spayl**ghood
trade	[business] handel, [company] handelsonderneming, [field] vak	**hahn**del, **hahn**dels-onder**nay**ming, vahk
traffic	verkeer	ver**kehr**
traffic jam	opstopping	**op**stopping
traffic warden	parkeerpolitie	pahr**kehr**-po**lee**tsee
trailer	aanhangwagen, [combined with lorry] vracht- wagen met aanhanger	**ahn**hahng-**wa**ghen, **vraght**- waghen met **ahn**hahnger
train	trein	traiyn

transfer	v [change] overstappen, [move people] overplaatsen, [move things] verplaatsen, [money] overmaken; n overstap, overplaatsing, verplaatsing, overmaking	**o**verstahppen, **o**verplahtsen, ver**plaht**sen, **o**vermahken; **o**verstahp, **o**verplahtsing, ver**plaht**sing, **o**vermahking
translate	vertalen	ver**tah**len
trap	val	vahl
travel	reizen	**raiy**zen
travel agent	reisbureau	**raiys**bewroh
travel guide	reisgids	**raiys**ghids
treatment	behandeling	be**hahn**deling
tree	boom	boam
trial	[court] rechtszaak	**reghts**zahk
trip	reis	raiys
tripod	statief	stah**teef**
trolley	[luggage] bagagewagen, [supermarket] winkelwagentje	baga**hah**zhe-**wah**ghen, **win**kel-**wa**ghentye
trouble	v lastigvallen; n pech, probleem	**lahs**tighvahllen; pegh, pro**blaym**
trouble, be in	in de problemen zitten	in pro**blay**men zitten
trousers	(lange) broek	**(lahnge)** brook
true	waar, echt	wahr, eght
trunk call	interlokaal gesprek	interlo**kahl** ghe**sprek**
trunks	korte broek, [swimming] zwembroek *sing*	**kor**te brook, **zwem**brook
truth	waarheid	**wahr**haiyd
try	proberen, trachten, [taste] proeven	pro**beh**ren, **tragh**ten, **proo**ven
try on	passen	**pahs**sen
tube	buis, [bicycle] (fiets)band, [underground] metro	bœs, **(feets)**bahnd, **may**tro
tune	v (af)stemmen; n liedje	**(ahf)**stemmen; **leed**ye
turn	v draaien, keren; n draai, [go] beurt	**drah**yen, **keh**ren; drahy, buhrt
turn around	omdraaien	**om**drahyen
turn aside	uitwijken	**œt**waiyken
turn away	wegdraaien, weglopen	**wegh**drahyen, **wegh**loapen
twins	tweeling	**tway**ling
tyre	(auto)band	**(ow**to)bahnd

u

ugly	lelijk	**lay**lik
ulcer	zweer	zwehr
umbrella	paraplu	para**plew**

unattended	onbewaakt, [left alone] alleen gelaten	onbe**wahkt**, ahl**layn** ghe**lah**ten
unconscious	bewusteloos	be**wus**teloas
under	onder	**on**der
underground	*a* ondergronds, *n* ondergrondse	onder**ghronds**. onder**ghrond**se
underneath	onder	**on**der
underpants	onderbroek	**on**derbrook
underside	onderkant	**on**derkahnt
understand	[meaning] begrijpen, [hear, language] verstaan	be**ghraiy**pen, ver**stahn**
underwear	ondergoed	**on**derghood
unfair	oneerlijk, onsportief	on**ehr**lik, onspor**teef**
unfavourable	ongunstig	ong**hunst**igh
unguarded	onbewaakt	onbe**wahkt**
unhappy	ongelukkig	onghe**luk**kigh
United Kingdom	Verenigd Koninkrijk	ver**aynighd ko**ninkraiyk
unload	lossen, uitladen	**loss**en, **œt**lahden
unmarried	ongehuwd	onghe**hewd**
unsatisfactory	onbevredigend	onbe**vray**dighend
untie	losmaken	**loss**mahken
untied	los	loss
up	[move] omhoog, [position] boven	om**hoagh**, **bo**ven
upstairs	boven	**bo**ven
urgent	dringend	**dring**end
use	*v* gebruiken, benutten; *n* gebruik, [benefit, value] nut	ghe**brœ**ken, be**nut**ten; ghe**brœk**, nut
useful	handig, nuttig	**hahn**digh, **nut**tigh

V

valley	dal	dahl
valid	geldig	**ghel**digh
valuables	kostbaarheden	**kost**bahr-**hay**den
value	waarde	**wahr**de
valve	klep	klep
varnish	*v* lakken, vernissen; *n* lak, vernis	**lahk**ken, ver**nis**sen; lahk, ver**nis**
vase	vaas	vahs
vast	uitgestrekt	**œt**ghestrekt
veal	kalfsvlees	**kahlfs**vlays
vegetables	groente *sing*	**ghroon**te
verdict	uitspraak	**œt**sprahk
vermin	ongedierte	**on**ghedeerte
vertigo	hoogtevrees	**hoagh**tevrays
very	erg, zeer, heel	airgh, zehr, hayl

vessel	vaartuig	**vahr**tœgh
vest	vest	vest
view	uitzicht	**œt**zight
village	dorp	dorp
vinegar	azijn	ah**zaiyn**
vineyard	wijngaard	**waiyn**ghahrd
visible	zichtbaar	**zight**bahr
visibility	zicht	zight
visit	v bezoeken; n bezoek, [at home] visite	be**zoo**ken; be**zook**, vee**see**teh
voice	stem	stem
void	ongeldig	on**ghel**digh
vomit	braken, overgeven	**brah**ken, **o**verghayven
vote	v stemmen; n stem	**stem**men; stem
voucher	reserveringsbewijs, tegoedbon	rayser**veh**rings-be**waiys**, te**ghood**bon
voyage	zeereis	**zay**raiys

W

wait	wachten	**wagh**ten
waist	middel	**mid**del
waiter	ober	**o**ber
waiting room	wachtkamer	**wagh**tkahmer
waitress	serveerster	sair**vehr**ster
wake	waken	**wah**ken
wake up	ontwaken, wakker worden	ont**wah**ken, **wahk**ker **wor**den
walk	v lopen, wandelen, [dog] uitlaten; n wahndeling, [way of walking] loop, tred	**loa**pen, **wahn**delen, **œt**lahten; **wahn**deling, loop, tred
wall	muur, [fortification] wal, [inside] wand	mewr, wahl, wahnd
wallet	portefeuille	porte**fœ**ye
want	willen	**wil**len
ward	ziekenzaal	**zee**kenzahl
warden	opzichter	**o**pzighter
wardrobe	klerenkast	**kleh**renkahst
warn	waarschuwen	**wahr**sghewwen
warning	waarschuwing	**wahr**sghewwing
washstand	wastafel	**wahs**tahfel
wasp	wesp	wesp
waste	v verspillen, verknoeien; n verspilling, [litter] afval	ver**spil**len, ver**knoo**yen; ver**spil**ling, **ahf**vahl

watch	v kijken, toekijken, [keep an eye on] in de gaten houden, [pay attention] opletten; n [timepiece] horloge, [guard] waker	kaiyken, tookaiyken, in de **ghah**ten **how**den, obletten; horlo**zhe**, **wah**ker
water	v water geven, [with a hose] sproeien; n water	**wah**ter **ghay**ven, **sproo**yen; **wah**ter
wave	golf	gholf
way	[way of acting] manier, [road] weg, [itinerary] route	ma**neer**, wegh, **roo**te
way, this	deze kant op, hierheen	**day**ze kahnt op, **heer**hayn
way out	uitgang, [motorway] afrit	**œt**ghahng
way through	doorgang	**doar**ghahng
weak	zwak	zwahk
wear	[clothes] dragen, [put on] aantrekken	**dra**ghen, **ahn**trekken
weather (forecast)	weer(svoorspelling)	wehr(svoar**spel**ling)
wedding	bruiloft	**brœ**loft
weigh	wegen	**way**ghen
weight	gewicht	ghe**wihgh**t
weight, gain/lose	aankomen/afvallen	**ahn**koamen/**ahf**vallen
weld	lassen	**lahs**sen
well	adv goed, welnu; n [natural] bron, [manmade] waterput	ghood, well**new**; bron, **wah**terputt
wet	v nat maken; a nat	naht **mah**ken; naht
wheel	wiel, [steering] stuur	weel, stewr
wheel chair	rolstoel	**roll**stool
where	waar	wahr
which	welk(e), wat	welk(e), waht
while	terwijl	ter**waiyl**
while, a	eventjes, een ogenblik	**ay**ventyes, en **oa**ghenblik
whistle	v fluiten; n fluit	**flœ**ten; flœt
who	wie, die	wee, dee
whole	(ge)heel	(ghe)**hayl**
why	waarom	wahr**om**
wide	breed, wijd	brayd, waiyd
width	breedte	**brayd**te
wife	echtgenote, vrouw	**eght**ghenoate, vrow
winding	bochtig, kronkelend	**bogh**tigh, **kron**kelend
window	venster, raam, [shop] etalage, [office] loket	**ven**ster, rahm, ayta**la**zhe, lo**ket**

windscreen	windscherm	**wind**sghairm
wine (list)	wijn(kaart)	waiyn(kahrt)
wire	draad	drahd
wish	*v* wensen; *n* wens	**wen**sen; wens
within	binnen	**bin**nen
witness	getuige	ghe**tœ**ghe
woman	vrouw	vrow
wood	[forest] bos, [material] hout	boss, howt
wool	wol	woll
word	woord	woard
work	*v* werken; *n* werk	**wair**ken; waik
works	[plant] fabriek *sing*,	fah**breek**,
	[activities] werkzaamheden	**wairk**zahmhayden
world	wereld	**weh**reld
worn out	versleten, afgedragen	ver**slay**ten, **ahf**ghedrahghen
worried	bezorgd, ongerust	be**zorghd**, onghe**rust**
worry	zich zorgen maken,	zigh **zorg**hen **mah**ken,
	ongerust zijn	onghe**rust** zaiyn
worth, worthless	waard, waardeloos	wahrd, **wahr**deloas
wound	wond	wond
wounded	gewond	ghe**wond**
wrist (watch)	pols(horloge)	pols(hor**lo**zhe)
wrong	verkeerd, onjuist	ver**kehrd**, on**jœst**
wrong, be	ongelijk hebben	**on**ghelaiyk **heb**ben

X

xerox	fotokopie	fotoko**pee**
x-rays	röntgenstralen	**runt**ghen-**strah**len

Y

yacht	(zeil-/motor)jacht	(**zaiyl**-/**mo**tor)yaght
yachting	watersport	**wah**tersport
year	jaar	yahr
yellow	geel	ghayl
yellow pages	Gouden Gids	**ghow**den ghids
yesterday	gisteren	**ghis**teren
yet	toch, [still] nog, [already] al	togh, nogh, ahl
young	jong	yong
youth (hostel)	jeugd(herberg)	**yøghd**hairbairgh

Z

zebra crossing	zebrapad	**zay**brahpahd
zip(per)	ritssluiting	**rits**slœting
zoo(logical garden)	dierentuin	**dee**rentœn

ENGLISH - DUTCH

A

aanbevelen - to recommend
aanbieden - to offer
aanbieding - special offer
aangebrand - burnt
aangenaam - pleasant, agreeable
aangenaam! - pleased to meet you!
aangetekend - registered
aanhangwagen - trailer
aankomen - to arrive, to gain weight
aankomst(tijd) - arrival (time)
aannemen - to suppose, to accept
aanrijding - crash, collision
aansteker - lighter
aantal - number
aantrekken - to wear, to attract
aanvraagformulier - application form
aanvragen - to apply
aanwijzen - to indicate, to point out
aardappels - potatoes
aarde - earth, soil
aardewerk - earthenware
aardig - kind, friendly
accu - battery
achter - behind, at the back
achteraf - remote
achterkant - back, rear (side)
achterlopen - to be slow, to lose time
achternaam - surname, family name
achteruit - backwards
adem - breath
ademnood - breathlessness
adres - address
advocaat - lawyer
afdalen - to descend
afdeling - department
afdruk - print

afgesloten (versperd) - blocked
afgesloten (beëindigd) - finished
afgesproken - settled, fixed
afrekenen - to pay
afspraak(je) - appointment, date
afspreken - to arrange, to fix (a
   time/date), to agree
afstand - distance
afvaart - sailing, departure
afval - waste, litter
afwijken - to deviate
afzeggen - to cancel
afzender - sender
agent - policeman, policewoman,
   constable, agent
alarmnummer - emergency number
algemeen - general
alleen - single, alone, only
alles - all
alstublieft - here you are, thank you,
   please
altijd - always
ambassade - embassy
ambtenaar - civil servant
ambulance - ambulance
ander(e) - other
anders - different
anders, ergens - somewhere else
anders, iemand - someone else
andersom - the other way around
angst - fear
angstig - afraid
ansichtkaart - postcard
antenne - aerial, antenna
antiek - antiques
antiquair - antique dealer
antivries - antifreeze

antwoord - answer
antwoorden - to answer
apotheek - dispensing chemist's
appel - apple
appelsap - apple juice
arm - poor, arm
armband - bracelet
as - ash, axle
asbak - ash tray
auto - car
automatisch - automatic
autosnelweg - motorway
autoweg - A road
avond - evening, night
avondeten - dinner, supper
avonds, 's - at night
azijn - vinegar

B

baai - bay
baard - beard
baas - manager
baby - baby
babyvoeding - baby food
bad - bath (tub), swim
baden - to take a bath
badhanddoek - bath towel
badkamer - bath room
badpak - swimsuit
badschuim - bath foam
bagage - luggage
bagagedepot - left luggage (office)
bagagekluis - (luggage) locker
bagagerek - luggage rack
bagageruimte - boot
bakken - to fry, to bake
bakker - bakery
bal - ball
balkon - balcony
balpen - ball pen
band - tyre, tie, bond, band
bang zijn - to be afraid
bank - bank, bench, couch

bankbiljet - banknote
barst - crack
barsten - to crack
batterij - battery
bed - bed
bedanken - to thank
bedienen - to serve
bediening (inbegrepen) - service (included)
bedoelen - to mean
bedoeling - intention
bedorven - bad, off
bedrag - amount
been - leg
beest - animal
beet - bite, I've got a bite!
beetje, een - a little (bit)
begane grond - ground floor
begin - start
beginnen - to begin, to start
begrijpen - to understand
behalve - except
behandeling - treatment
beide - both
bekend - (well-)known
bekeuring - ticket
bel - bell
belangrijk - important
Belg - Belgian
België - Belgium
Belgisch - Belgian
bellen - to ring, to phone, to call
belofte - promise
beloven - to promise
benauwd - short of breath, stuffy
benauwdheid - distress, stuffiness
beneden - down, below
benzine - petrol
benzinestation - petrol/filling station
benzinetank - petrol/fuel tank
berg - mountain
bergafwaarts - downhill

bergketen - mountain range
berglandschap - mountain scenery
bergschoen - mountaineering boot
bericht - message
berm - verge, roadside
beroemd - famous
beroep - profession, occupation, appeal
beschadigd - damaged
beschadigen - to damage
beschadiging - damage
besmettelijk - contagious, catching,
  infectious
bespreken - to book, to reserve,
  to discuss
best(e) - best
beste ... - dear ...
bestek - cutlery
bestellen - to order, to deliver
bestelling - order
bestemming - destination
betalen - to pay
betekenen - to mean
beter (dan) **-** better (than)
beter worden - to recover
betrouwbaar - reliable
bevolking - population, people
bewaakt - guarded
bewaker - guard
bewaking - surveillance, security
bewijs - proof
bewijsje - receipt
bewolkt - cloudy
bewusteloos - unconscious
bezichtigen - to (pay a) visit (to), to tour
bezienswaardigheid - place of interest,
  sights
bezoek - visit
bezoeken - to visit
bezwaar - objection
bezwaar - drawback
bezwaarschrift - objection
bieden - to offer

bier - beer, draught
bij - near, bee
bijna - almost, nearly
bijten - to bite
bijzonder - special
biljet - poster, ticket, (bank)note
binnen - within, inside, indoors
binnenkomen - to enter
binnenlands - domestic
binnenplaats - court(yard)
binnenweggetje - byroad
binnenweggetje - short cut
bioscoop - cinema
bitter - bitter
blaar - blister
blad - sheet, magazine
blad - leaf
blauw - blue
blauwe plek - bruise
bleek - pale
blij - happy, cheerful
blijdschap - happiness, high spirits
blijven - to stay
blik - look, glance, glimpse, tin (plate),
  can
blikgroente - tinned/canned
  vegetables
blikopener - tin/can opener
blind - blind
bloed - blood
bloem - flour, flower
bloot - naked
blussen - to extinguish, to quench
bocht - bend, curve
bochtig - winding
bodem - soil
boek - book
boeken - to book
boekhandel - bookshop
boer - farmer, peasant
boerderij - farm
boete - fine

boodschap - message
boodschappen - to shop
boom - tree
boomgaard - orchard
boord, aan - aboard, on board
boot - boat, ship
bonen - kidney beans, haricot beans
bonen - baked beans
bord - blackboard, sign, plate
borst - breast
borstel - brush
bos - wood, forest
bosweg - forest road
bot - blunt, bone
boter - butter
boterham - sandwich
botsing - collision, crash
bouwen - to build
boven - on top of, above, up(stairs)
bovenop - on top
braden - to roast, to fry
braken - to vomit
brand - fire
brandblusser - fire extinguisher
brandmelder - fire alarm
brandweer - fire brigade
brandwond - burn
brandwondenzalf - ointment for burns
breed - wide
breedte - width, breadth
breken - to break
brengen - to bring, to take
breuk - fracture
brief - letter
briefje - note
briefkaart - postcard
briefpapier - notepaper
brievenbus - postbox, letter box
bril - glasses
broek - shorts, trousers
broeder - male nurse
broer - brother

bromfiets - moped
brood - bread
broodje - (filled) roll
brug - bridge
brugwachter - bridgemaster
bruiloft - wedding
bruin - brown, tanned
buik - belly, stomach
buikpijn - stomachache
buiten - in the country(side), outside
buitenland - foreign country
(in het) buitenland - abroad
buitenlander - foreigner
buitenverblijf - country house
bumper - bumper
bureau - office, desk
burgemeester - mayor
bus - bus, coach, tin
bushalte - bus stop
busstation - bus station
buurt - neighbourhood, district
buurt van, in de - near, around, about

c

cadeau - present
café - coffee bar/shop, café
cake - cake
camera - camera
campingwinkel - camp site shop
caravan - caravan
carburateur - carburettor
carrosserie - body, coachwork
centimeter - centimetre
centrale - central
centrale verwarming - central heating
centrum - centre
chartervlucht - charter flight
chassis - chassis, frame
chef - manager
chocolade - chocolate
citroen - lemon
compleet - complete
compliment - compliment

concert - concert, gig
condoom - condom
conducteur - ticket collector
confectiekleding - ready-to-wear (clothes)
contract - contract, agreement
controle - supervision, check
corresponderen - to correspond
couchette - berth
coupé - compartment

D

daar - over there
daarna - afterwards, next
daarom - therefore
dadelijk - at once
dag - day
dag! - hallo!, goodbye!
dagschotel - today's special
dal - valley
dam - dam
dames - women, ladies
damestoilet - ladies' (toilet)
dank - thanks, gratitude
dansen - to dance
darm - intestine, bowel
darminfectie - intestinal infection
das - tie, scarf
dat - that
datum - date
deel - part
defect - faulty, defect
deken - blanket
demonstratie - presentation, protest march
dependance - annexe
dessert - dessert, sweets
deur - door
deurknop - doorknob
deze - this, these
dia - slide
diaprojector - slide projector
diarree - diarrhoea
dicht - closed

dicht bij - close to, near
dichtbij - nearby
die - that, those, who, which
dieet - diet
dieetvoeding - diet food
dief - robber, thief
diefstal - robbery, theft
dienstregeling - timetable, schedule
diep - deep
diepte - depth
diepvries - deep-freeze
diepvries - frozen food
diepvriezer - freezer
dier - animal
dierentuin - zoo
dierenvoedsel - pet food
dieselolie - diesel oil/fuel
dik - thick, fat
ding - thing
direct - direct, immediately
dit - this
dochter - daughter
dodelijk - deadly, lethal
doek - cloth, fabric, rag
doel - purpose, aim
doen - to do
dokter - doctor
dood - dead
doodlopend - dead-end
doof - deaf
door - through, because of
doorgang - way through
doos - box
dop(je) - cap, top
dorp - village
dorst hebben - to be thirsty
douane - customs
douche - shower
draad - thread
draaien - to turn
dragen - to wear, to carry
dringend - urgent

drinken - to drink
drinkwater - drinking water
drogen - to dry
droog - dry
druk - pressure
druk hebben, het - to be busy/occupied
drukken - to press, to print
dubbel - double
duiken - to dive
duikplank - diving board, springboard
duim - thumb
Duits - German
Duitser - German
Duitsland - Germany
duizeligheid - dizzyness
dun - thin
duren - to last
durven - to dare
duur - duration, expensive

E

echt - real
echtgenoot - husband *m*, wife *v*
eenpersoonskamer - single room
eenrichtingsverkeer - one-way traffic
eenvoudig - simple
eergisteren - the day before yesterday
eerlijk - honest
eerste - first
eetbaar - edible
eeuw - century
ei (hard gekookt) - (hard-boiled) egg
ei (zacht gekookt) - (soft-boiled) egg
ei (gebakken) - (fried) egg
eigendom - property
eigenaar - owner
eiland - island
eind(e) - end
eindpunt - terminus
elastiekje - rubber band
elektrisch - electric
elk - every, each
elleboog - elbow

emmer - bucket
Engeland - England
Engels - English
Engelsman - Englishman *m*,
  Englishwoman *v*
enige - only, sole, some, any
enkele reis - single, one way (ticket)
envelop - envelope
erg - very, awful, terrible
ergens - somewhere
ergens anders - somewhere else
etalage - (shop) window
eten - to eat
eten(swaar) - food
even - even
even(tjes) - a little while
evenwijdig aan - parallel to
excuses - apologies
expresse, per - by express delivery
ezel - donkey

F

fabriek - factory, works
familie - family
familie zijn van - to be related to
feest - party
feestdag - holiday
feestvieren - to celebrate, to party
fel - fierce, sharp
feliciteren - to congratulate
fiets - bicycle
fietsenmaker - bicycle repair man
fietspad - bicycle track
fietsroute - bicycle route
fietstocht - bicycle tour
fijn - nice, pleasant, fine
file - tailback
film - film
filmcamera - film camera
filmrolletje - film
filter - filter
filterkoffie - filter coffee
filtersigaret - filter-tipped cigarette

flat - apartment building
flauw - bland, insipid
flauwte - faint
flauwvallen - to faint
fles - bottle
flets - pale, dull
fluiten - to whistle
fontein - fountain
fooi - tip
formaat - size
foto - photo, picture
fotograaf - photographer
fotokopie - photocopy, xerox
fototoestel - camera
fout - wrong, mistake
foutloos - impeccable
frame - frame
frankeren - to stamp
Frankrijk - France
Frans - French
Fransman - Frenchman, Frenchwoman
fris - fresh, chilly
frisdrank - soft drink
fruit - fruit
fruitstalletje - fruit stand

G

gaan - to go
gaar - done, cooked
gal - bile
gang - corridor, hall(way), gait, walk
gans - goose
garage - garage, service station
garantie - guarantee
garantiebewijs - certificate of guarantee
garderobe - cloakroom
garen - thread
gas - gas
gasfles - gas cylinder
gast - guest
gastheer - host *m*, hostess *v*
gastvrij - hospitable
gat - hole

gauw - soon
gebakje - pastry, cake
gebakken - fried
gebergte - mountain range
gebied - area, field
geboortedatum - date of birth
geboren - born
gebouw - building
gebraden - roasted
gebroken - broken
gebruik - use, custom
gebruiken - to use
gebruiksaanwijzing - directions
gedachte - thought
gedeelte - part
geduld - patience
geel - yellow
geen - no, none
gehakt - minced meat
geheel - total, whole
gehoor - audience, hearing
gehoorapparaat - hearing aid
gehuwd - married
geit - goat
gekoeld - refrigerated, cooled
gekookt - boiled
geld - money
gelijk - equal, similar
gelijk hebben - to be right
gelijkvloers - on the ground floor
geluid - sound
geluidshinder - noise
gemak, op zijn - at ease, comfortable
gemakkelijk - easy, comfortable
gemeente - municipality, congregation
gemeentehuis - city/town hall
gemeenteraad - city/town council
gemengd - mixed
geneesmiddel - medicine
genezen - recovered
genieten - to enjoy

genoeg - enough
genoegdoening - satisfaction, atonement
genoegen - pleasure
gepast geld - exact money
gepensioneerd - retired
gerecht - dish, course, court
gereedschap - tools
gereserveerd - booked, reticent
gering - small
gerookt - smoked
geroosterd - grilled, roasted
gescheiden - separate, divorced
geschenk - present, gift
gesp - buckle
gestreept - striped
getal - number
getij - tide
getuige - witness
geur - smell, odour
geurig - fragrant
gevaar - danger
gevaarlijk - dangerous
gevel - front
geven - to give
gevoel - touch, feeling
gevoelig - sensitive
gevogelte - fowl, poultry
gevolg - result
gevonden - found
gevuld - stuffed
gewicht - weight
gewond - wounded, hurt, injured
gewonde - casualty
gewoon - normal, ordinary
gewoonte - habit
gezellig - cosy
gezicht - face
gezicht op - view of, overlooking
gezin - family
gezond - healthy
gezondheid - health
gids - guide

gif - poison
giftig - poisonous, toxic
glad - slippery, smooth
gladheid - black ice, ice on the road
glas - glass
goed - good, well
goedkoop - cheap
gordel - belt
gordijn - curtain
goud - gold
gouden - gold
graag - gladly, with pleasure
graag! - thank you, yes please, that
would be fine
graat - fish bone
graden - degrees
gras - grass
grasveld - lawn
gratis - free
graven - to dig
grens - border
griep - flue
grijs - grey
groen - green
groente - vegetable
groentehandelaar - greengrocer
groep - group, party
groet - greeting
groeten uit - best wishes from
groeten doen aan iemand - to give someone's regards to someone
grond - soil, land, reason, floor
grondzeil - ground sheet
groot - large, big
Groot-Brittannië - Great Britain
grootte - size
grot - cave
gunstig - favourable

H

haai - shark
haak - hook
haar - hair

haarlak - hair spray
haarspeldbocht - hairpin bend
haast - hurry
hagel - hail
hak - heel
hakken - to chop
hal - hall, lobby
halen - to fetch
half - half
hals - neck
halte - stop
ham - ham
hamer - hammer
hand - hand
handdoek - towel
handel - trade
handig - practical, useful, skilful
handleiding - manual
handrem - handbrake
handtasje - handbag
handtekening - signature
handwerk - needlework
handwerk - handiwork, handicrafts
hard - fast, loud, firm
hardhandig - rough, harsh
hart - heart
hartig - savoury, spicy
hartpatiënt - someone with a heart
   condition
haven - harbour, port
hebben - to have
heel - whole, entire, complete,
   undamaged, intact
heer - gentleman
heerlijk - lovely
heet - hot
hek - fence
helder - clear
helemaal - entirely, completely
helft - half
helling - slope
hemd - shirt, vest, singlet

hemel - heaven
herfst - autumn
herhalen - to repeat
herhaling - repetition, repeat, rerun
hersenschudding - concussion
herstellen - to mend, to repair, to recover
hetzelfde - the same
heuvel - hill
hier - here
hierheen - (over) here
hoe - how
hoed - hat
hoek - corner
hoe lang - how long
hoesten - to cough
hoeveel - how much/many
hond - dog
hondsdolheid - rabies
honger - to be hungry
hoofd - head, chief
hoofdstraat - main street
hoofdweg - main road
hoog - high
hoogte - height
hoogte, op de - in the know, informed
hoogtevrees - fear of heights,
   vertigo
horen - to hear
horens - horns
horloge - watch
houdbaar tot - best before
houden - to keep, to hold
houden van - to like, to love
hout - wood
houtskool - charcoal
huid - skin
huilen - to cry
huis - house
huisarts - general practitioner (GP)
huishoudelijke artikelen - household
   appliances
huishouding - housekeeping

huisvrouw - housewife
huiswerk - homework
hulp - help
huren - to hire, to rent
hut - hut, shack, cabin
huur - rent
huurauto - rented car
huwelijk - marriage

I

ideaal - ideal
identificatie - identification
identiteitsbewijs - identity card
ieder - every, each
iedereen - everyone, everybody, all
iemand - someone, somebody, anyone, anybody
iets - something, anything
ijs - ice, ice cream
ijsblokjes - ice cubes
ijzel - glazed frost
ijzer - iron
ijzerdraad - (iron) wire
ijzeren - iron
imitatie - imitation
imperiaal - roof rack
inbegrepen - included
indeling - division
inderdaad - indeed
ineens - suddenly, all of a sudden
inenten - to vaccinate, to inoculate
infectie - infection
informatie - information
informatiebureau - information office
informeren - to inform
informeren naar - to inquire about, to ask for
ingewanden - bowels, entrails
inhaalverbod - no overtaking
inhalen - to overtake
inham - bay, inlet
inheems - indigenous, endemic, native

injectienaald - hypodermic needle
inkopen doen - to go shopping
inkt - ink
inktvis - squid, octopus
innemen - to take, to swallow
in orde! - OK!, All right!
inrijden - to drive into
inschenken - to pour
inschepen - to embark
inschrijven - to register, to enter, to enroll
insect - insect
insectenbeet - insect bite
instappen - to get in/on
interessant - interesting
interlokaal - intercity
interlokaal - trunk/long, distance (call)
internationaal - international
invalide - disabled
invalidenwagen - wheelchair
invoeren - to introduce, to implement
invoeren - to import
invoerrechten - import duty, customs
invullen - to fill in, to complete
inwendig - internal

J

jaar - year
jaarlijks - annual
jacht - hunt(ing), yacht
jam - jam, marmelade
jammer, het is - it's a pity
jarig (ik ben) - (today's my) birthday
jas - coat
jack - jacket
jasje - jacket
jeugdherberg - youth hostel
jeuk - itch
jeuken - to itch
jodium - iodine
jong - young, cub, puppy
jongen - boy
juist - correct, right

jurk - dress
juweel - jewel
juwelier - jeweller, jewellery

K

kaak - jaw
kaars - candle
kaart - map, postcard, playing card
kaarten - to play cards
kaartje - ticket
kaas - cheese
kabel - wire, cable, flex, cable
kachel - stove, heater
kade - quay
kader - executives, management, frame
kakkerlak - cockroach
kalfsvlees - veal
kam - comb
kamer - room
kamermeisje - chambermaid
kamp - camp
kampeerterrein - camp(ing) site
kampeeruitrusting - camping equipment/
  gear
kampeerverbod - no camping
kampeervergunning - camping license
kamperen - to camp
kampkaart - camping permit
kampvuur - campfire
kampwinkel - camp site shop
kan - jug
kanaal - channel
kano - canoe
kans - chance
kant - edge, side, way, direction, lace
kantoor - office
kantoorbehoeften - office supplies,
  stationary
kap - bonnet
kapot - broken (down)
kappen - to cut down, to do one's hair
kapper - hairdresser
kar - cart, barrow

karaf - decanter
karnemelk - buttermilk
kassa - cash register
kast - closet, cupboard
kasteel - castle
kat - cat
kater - hangover
kathedraal - cathedral
katholiek (rooms-) - (Roman) Catholic
katoen - cotton
kauwen - to chew
kauwgom - chewing gum
keel - throat
keelpijn - sore throat
kelder - basement
kennis - knowledge, acquaintance
kennismaken - to meet
kennismaking - acquaintance,
  introduction
kerk - church
kerkdienst - (church) service
kerkhof - cemetery, churchyard,
  graveyard
ketting - chain
keuken - kitchen
kies - molar, tooth
kiespijn - toothache
kiezen - to choose, to vote
kijken - to look
kin - chin
kind - child
kinderbedje - cot
kinderstoel - highchair
kinderwagen - pram
kiosk - newsstand
kip(penvlees) - chicken
kist - case, crate
klaar - ready
klacht - complaint
klachtenformulier - complaints form
klagen - to complain, to moan
klasse - class

klederdracht - traditional dress/costume
kleding - clothes
klein - small
kleingeld - (small) change
kleinkind - grandson *m*, granddaughter *v*
klep - valve
kleren - clothes
klerenhanger - coat hanger, peg
klerenkast - wardrobe
kleur - colour
kleuren - to blush
klimaat - climate
klip - cliff, rock
klok - clock
klokkentoren - clock/bell tower
klontje - lump
kloof - gorge, crevice
klooster - monastery, convent
kloosterling - monk *m*, nun *v*
kloostergang - cloister
kloostertuin - convent/monastery garden
kloosterzuster - nun, sister
kloppen (op de deur) - to knock
(at the door)
klopt, het - that's correct
klosje - reel
knie - knee
knieschijf - kneecap
knippen - to cut
knipperlicht - indicator, blinker
knoflook - garlic
knoop - knot, button
knop - knob, bud, button, switch
koek - cake
koekje - biscuit
koel - cool, chilly
koelkast - refrigerator, fridge
koers - (exchange) rate
koers - course, direction
koffer - suitcase
koffie - coffee
koffieboon - coffee bean

koffiepot - coffee pot
kok - cook, chef
koken - to cook (a meal)
komen - to come
kompas - compass
koning - king *m*, queen *v*
kool - cabbage
koop, te - for sale
koorts - fever
kopen - to buy
koper - buyer, copper, brass
kopje - cup
koppeling - clutch
kort - short
korting - discount
kortsluiting - short circuit
kosten - costs, expenses
kosten - to cost
kostuum - suit
koud - cold
kousen - stockings
kraag - collar
kraamkliniek - maternity ward
kraampje - stand, booth
kraan - tap
kraan(wagen) - breakdown van/truck
krab - crab
krant - newspaper
kreeft - lobster
krijgen - to get
krik - jack
kruiden - herbs
kruidenier - grocer
kruidenierswaren - groceries
kruik - pitcher, jug
kruis - cross
kruising - crossing, junction
kuil - pit, hole
kuit - calf
kunnen - to can, to be able to
kunst - art
kunstenaar - artist

kunstgebit - false teeth, dentures
kunstmatig(e ademhaling) - artificial (respiration)
kurk - cork
kurkeik - cork oak
kurkentrekker - corkscrew
kus - kiss
kussen - to kiss, pillow
kussensloop - pillow case
kust - coast
kustwacht - coast guard
kwaal - ailment, illness
kwal - jellyfish
kwaliteit - quality
kwalijk nemen - to blame
kwalijk, neem mij niet - excuse me
kwalijk, neem mij niet - I am sorry
kwart - quarter
kwartier - quarter
kwijt zijn - to have lost
kwijtraken - to lose
kwijtschelden - to acquit
kwitantie - receipt

L

laag - low, layer
laars - boot
laat - late
laatst - recently
laatste - last, final
lachen - to laugh
laken - sheet
lam - paralysed
lam(svlees) - lamb
lamp - lamp
land - land, country, nation
landelijk - rural
landen - to land, to touch down
landing - landing, touchdown
landkaart - map
landschap - landscape
lang - tall, long
langdurig - lengthy, protracted, prolonged

langs - along
langzaam - slow
langzamerhand - gradually
lantaarn - streetlamp
lap - length/piece (of cloth)
lap grond - piece of land
lassen - to wcld
last - load, burden
last, ik heb last van - I am suffering from
lastig - awkward, inconvenient
lastigvallen - to trouble, to hassle
lauw - tepid, lukewarm
lawaai - noise
lawaaierig - noisy
laxeermiddel - laxative, purgative
leeg - empty
leeglopen - to go flat
leer - leather
leggen - to lay/put (down)
legitimatiebewijs - identification (card)
lek - leak
lekke band - puncture(d tyre)
lekker - nice, tasty
lelijk - ugly
lenen aan - to lend
lenen van - to borrow
lengte - height, length
lens - lens
lente - spring
lepel - spoon
lepeltje - teaspoon
leren - to teach, to learn, to study
leuk - nice, jolly, amusing
leunen op - to lean on/against
leuning - back, armrest, rail, bannisters
leve ... - long live ...
leven - to live, life
levend - living, live
levensmiddelen - food(stuffs)
lezen - to read
lichaam - body
lichamelijk - physical**

lichamelijke opvoeding - physical education (PE)
licht - light, easy, bright
lichting - collection
lief - sweet, dear
liefde - love
liefhebberij - hobby, pastime
liegen - to lie
liever hebben - to prefer
lift - lift, elevator
lift geven - to give a ride
liften - to hitchhike
lifter - hitchhiker
liggen - to lie (on), to be situated/located
ligstoel - deckchair
lijm - glue
lijmen - to glue (together)
lijn - line, rope, string
likken - to lick
links(af) - (to the) left
linnen - linen, cloth
linnengoed - linen
lint - ribbon
lip - lip
lippenstift - lipstick
liter - litre
logeren - to stay
logies en ontbijt - bed and breakfast
loket - counter, window
long - lung
lopen - to walk, to run
los - loose, untied
losmaken - to release, to untie
lossen - to discharge, to unload
lucht - sky, air
luchtballon - hot air balloon
luchtbed - air mattress
luchten - to air
luchthaven - airport
luchtpost, per - by airmail
luchtvaart - aviation
luchtziek - airsick

lucifer - match
luciferdoosje - matchbox
lui - lazy
luid - loud
luier - napkin, nappy
luisteren - to listen
luis - louse
lunch - lunch
lunchpakket - packed lunch

M

maag(pijn) - stomach(ache)
maagzuur - heartburn
maand - month
maandverband - sanitary towel
maat - size
machtiging - authorization
mager - slim, lean
magneet - magnet
makelaar - estate/house agent
maken - to make, to mend
makkelijk - easy
man - man, husband
mand - basket
mank - lame
marmer - marble
massief - solid, massif
mast - mast
matras - mattress
maximumsnelheid - maximum speed
mededeling - announcement
medicijn - medicine
meel - flour
meer - lake, more
meer dan - more than
meisje - girl
melk - milk
melkpoeder - dehydrated milk
meloen - melon
mes - knife
mevrouw - madam, miss
middag - afternoon
middageten - lunch

midden - middle
middernacht - midnight
mier - ant
minder - less
minder dan - less than
misschien - maybe
misselijk zijn - to be sick/queasy/
  nauseous
mist - fog
misverstand - misunderstanding
modder - mud
moe - tired
moeder - mother
moeilijk - difficult
moer - nut
moeras - swamp
moeten - to have to/be obliged to/
  must/need to
mogelijk - possible
molen - mill
mond - mouth
mondeling - oral
monnik - monk
monteur - mechanic
montuur - frame
mooi - beautiful
morgen - morning, tomorrow
morgens, 's - in the morning
mosterd - mustard
motor - engine
motorboot - motorboat, cabin cruiser
motorfiets - motorbike, motorcycle
motorkap - bonnet
motorpech - engine trouble
mouw - sleeve
mug - mosquito
muis - mouse
munt - coin
museum - museum
muur - wall
muziek - music

N

naaien - to sew
naald - needle
naam - name
naast - next to
nacht - night
nagel - nail
nagellak - nail polish/varnish
nagelschaartje - nail scissors
nagelvijltje - nailfile
nakijken - to check
namaak - imitation
nat - wet
nationaliteit - nationality
natuur - nature
natuurlijk - of course, natural
nauw - narrow
nauwelijks - hardly
nauwkeurig - painstaking, accurate
Nederland - Netherlands, Holland
Nederlander - Dutchman, Dutchwoman
Nederlands - Dutch
neef - cousin, nephew
neerzetten - to put down
negatief - negative
net - neat, tidy
net - net, just
neus - nose
nicht - cousin, niece
niemand - no one, nobody
niets - nothing
nieuw - new
nieuws - news
nieuwsblad - newspaper
niezen - to sneeze
nodig hebben - to need/want/require
nodig zijn - to be necessary
nog - still, yet
nogal - rather
noodrem - emergency brake
nooduitgang - emergency exit
noodverband - first-aid/temporary

dressing
nooit - never
noorden - north
noot - nut, note
normaal - normal, ordinary
nota - bill, account
noteren - to note, to jot down
nu - now
nummer - number
nummerplaat - numberplate

O

ober - waiter
ochtend - morning
oever - bank
of - or
officieel - official
officier - officer
ogenblik - moment
olie - oil
olijf - olive
olijfolie - olive oil
omdat - because
omgeving - environment, surroundings
omlegging/omweg - detour
omrijden - to make a detour
onbeleefd - impolite, rude
onberijdbaar - impassable
onbewaakt - unguarded, unattended
onder - under
onderbreken - to interrupt
onderbroek - underpants, knickers, panties
onderdeel - part
ondergronds - underground
ondergrondse - underground, tube
onder in - at the bottom of
onderkant - bottom, underside
onderschrift - subtitle, caption
ondertekenen - to sign
onderzoek - research
ondiep - shallow
oneerlijk - dishonest, unfair

oneven - odd
ongedierte - vermin
ongehuwd - single, unmarried
ongelijk hebben - to be wrong
ongeluk - accident
ongelukkig - unhappy
ongerust - worried, anxious
ongesteld zijn - to have one's period
ongeveer - approximately
ongunstig - unfavourable
onkosten - expenses
onmiddellijk - at once, immediately
onmogelijk - impossible
onschuldig - innocent
ontbijt - breakfast
ontbreken - to be absent/lacking/missing
ontdekken - to discover
ontmoeten - to meet
ontmoeting - meeting, encounter
ontsmetten - to disinfect
ontsmettingsmiddel - disinfectant
ontsteking - ignition, inflammation
ontvangen - to receive
ontwikkelen - to develop, to generate, to process
onvoldoende - insufficient, unsatisfactory
onweer - thunderstorm
oog - eye
oogarts - ophthalmologist
oogst - harvest
ook - too, also
oor - ear
oorsprong - origin
oorspronkelijk - original
oosten - east
opbellen - to call, to ring, to phone
opdienen - to serve
open - open
openen - to open
opeten - to eat
opgebroken - road works
opgeven - to give up, to abandon

oplichten - to cheat
oplichting - fraud
opmaken - to finish, to make out/draw up
oponthoud - stopover
oppas - baby-sitter
oppassen - to pay attention, to take care of
oppompen - to inflate
opruimen - to clean, to tidy
opruiming - sale
opschrift - caption, heading
opstaan - to get up, to rise
opstand - uprising, revolt
opstopping - traffic jam
optellen - to add
optillen - to lift
oud - old
ouders - parents
over - accross, over, above, finished
overbevolking - overpopulation
overdag - during the day(time)
overgeven - to vomit, to surrender
overhandigen - to hand (over), to present
overkant, overzijde - other side
overmorgen - the day after tomorrow
overstappen - to change, to transfer
oversteken - to cross (over)
overtocht - crossing, passage
overweg - level crossing

P

paal - post, stake, pole
paar - (a) few, (a) couple of
paard - horse
paardenkracht - horse power
paardenstal - stable
paardrijden - to ride
pad - path
paddestoel - toadstool, mushroom
pak - packet, package, suit
paleis - palace
pan - pan, pot
panne - breakdown, engine trouble
pannenkoek - pancake

panty - tights
papier - paper
papieren - papers, documents
papiergeld - (bank) notes
paraplu - umbrella
parasol - parasol, sunshade
pardon! - excuse me! I'm so sorry! I beg
your pardon!
parel - pearl
parfum - perfume
park - park
parkeergarage - car park
parkeerlicht - parking light, dimmer
parkeermeter - parking meter
parkeerplaats - car park
parkeerschijf - parking disc
parkeren - to park
pasfoto - passport photo
paskamer - fitting room
paspoort - passport
passen - to try on
pauze - break, intermission, interval
pech - bad/hard luck, breakdown, trouble
pen - fountain pen, ball(point) pen,
felt-tip pen
pension - guesthouse
peper - pepper
per - by, per, a
perron - platform
persoon - person
persoonlijk - personal
persoonsbewijs - identity card
pier - pier, jetty
pijl - arrow
pijn - pain, ache
pijnloos - painless
pijnstiller - painkiller, palliative
pijp - pipe
pil - pill, tablet
pilaar - pillar, column
plaat - print, picture, slab, sheet, record
plaats - place, point, location, seat

plaats bespreken - to book, to reserve
plaatskaartje - ticket
plaatsnemen - to take a seat
plak(je) - slice
plakband - adhesive/Scotch tape
plakken - to stick
plan - plan
plan zijn, van - to intend to
plank - board, shelf
plant - plant
plantaardig - vegetable
plastic - plastic
plat - flat
plattegrond - map
platteland - countryside
plein - square
pleister - (sticking) plaster
plezier - fun, joy, pleasure
poeder - powder
poes - (pussy)cat
poetsen - to polish, to brush, to shine
polis - policy
politie - police (force)
politieagent - policeman, policewoman, constable
politiebureau - police station
pols - wrist
pomp - pump
pont - ferry
poort - gate(way)
pop - doll
portefeuille - wallet
portemonnee - purse
portie - helping, share
portier - door, doorman, doorkeeper
porto - postage
post - post
postbode - postman
postbus - post office box, PO box
postkantoor - post office
postpakket - parcel
postzegel - stamp

pot - jar
potlood - pencil
prachtig - splendid, magnificent
precies - precise, exact
prijs - price, charge, prize, award
prijskaartje - price tag
prijslijst - price list
proberen - to try
procent - percent
proces-verbaal - report, record
proef - test
proeven - to try, to taste
proost! - cheers!
protest - protest, objection
protestant (hervormd) - Protestant
pudding - jelly, pudding
puist - pimple, spot
pyjama - pyjamas

R

raam - window
rand - edge, rim
rat - rat
rauw - raw, uncooked
rauwkost - raw vegetables
recept - recipe, prescription
recht - straight, justice
rechtbank - court (of law)
rechtdoor - straight on/ahead
rechter - judge
rechts - right-hand
rechtsaf - to the right
rechtuit - straight on
redden - to save
reddingsboot - lifeboat
reddingsvest - life jacket
rederij - shipping company
reep - bar
regen - rain
regenjas - raincoat
register - register
reinigen - to clean
reis - voyage, trip

reisbureau - travel agency
reisleider - (travel) guide
rem - brake
reparatie - repair
reserveonderdelen - spare parts
reservewiel - spare tyre
retourtje - return (ticket)
rib - rib
richting - direction
riem - belt, safety belt
rijbaan - lane
rijbewijs - driving license
rijden - to drive, to ride
rijp - ripe
rijst - rice
ring - ring
rioolbuis - sewer
risico - risk
riskant - risky
rit - drive, trip, ride
ritssluiting - zip
rivier - river
Rode-Kruispost - Red Cross post
roeiboot - rowing boat
roeien - to row
roeiriemen - oars
roepen - to call
roer - rudder
roest - rust
roesten - to rust
rok - skirt
roken - to smoke
roltrap - escalator
rond - round, around
rondrit, rondvaart - (sightseeing) tour
rondweg - ring road
rood - red
rookcoupé - smoking compartment
room - cream
roos - dandruff, rose
roosteren - to grill, to roast
rot (overrijp) - rotten

rots - rock, cliff
rotsachtig - rocky
rotsblok - boulder
route - route, way
routine - routine
rug - back
rugzak - rucksack
ruilen - to change
rundvlees - beef
rusten - to rest
rustig - peaceful
ruw - rough
ruzie - quarrel

s

salade - salad
salaris - salary
samen - together
sap - juice
saus - sauce
schaafwond - graze, scrape
schaap - sheep
schaar - scissors
schade - damage
schaduw - shadow
schakelaar - switch
schakelen - to switch
schaken - to play chess
scheef - crooked, slanting
scheepvaart - shipping
scheerapparaat - electric shaver
scheerlijn - guy (rope)
scheermesje - razor blade
schelp - shell
schep - scoop, shovel, spoonful
scheren - to shave
scherp - sharp
scherven - fragments, shards
scheur - tear, rip
scheuren - to tear, to rip
schilderij - painting
schip - ship
schoen - shoe

schoenlepel - shoehorn
schoenmaker - cobbler
schoenpoetser - shoeshine boy
schoensmeer - shoe polish
schoenveter - shoelace, shoestring
school - school
schoon - clean
schoonmaken - to clean
schotel - dish
schouder - shoulder
schouwburg - theatre
schroef - screw
schroevendraaier - screwdriver
schroeven - to screw
schuld - debt, guilty
seizoen - season
serveerster - waitress
serveren - to serve
servetje - napkin
sieraad - jewel, piece of jewellery
sigaret - cigarette
sinaasappel - orange
sinaasappelsap - orange juice
sla - lettuce
slaap - sleep
slaapwagen - sleeping car, sleeper
slaapzak - sleeping bag
slachten - to slaughter
slager - butcher
slagerij - butcher's (shop)
slagroom - whipped cream
slak - snail
slang - hose
slang - snake
slap - slack, floppy, limp
slecht - bad
slechthorend - hard of hearing
slechtziend - partially sighted
sleepkabel - towline, towrope
sleepwagen - breakdown truck/van
slepen - to tow
sleutel - key

sleutelgat - key hole
slijm - phlegm, slime
slingeren - to sway
slipje - panties, knickers
slippen - to skid
sloot - ditch
slot - lock
sluis - lock (gate)
sluiten - to close, to lock
sluitingstijd - closing time
smal - narrow
smalspoor - narrow gauge
smeermiddel - lubricant
smeren - to grease, to lubricate, to butter
smerig - dirty
snee - slice, cut, gash
sneeuw - snow
snel - fast, quick
snelheid - speed
sneltrein - express/intercity/through train
snoepgoed - confectionary, sweets
snoer - string
snor - moustache
snorkel - snorkel
soda - washing soda
sodawater - soda water
soep - soup
sok - sock
soort - kind, type
souvenir - souvenir
spannend - exciting, thrilling
spanning - suspense, tension
specialist - specialist
speelgoed - toys
speelkaarten - playing cards
speelplaats - playground
spek - bacon
speld - pin
spelen - to play
spellen - to spell
spelletje - game
spiegel - mirror

spier - muscle
spierpijn - sore muscles, myalgia
spijker - nail, tack
spijsvertering - digestion
spin - spider
spiritus - methylated spirits, meths
splinter - splinter
spoed, met - with dispatch
spoedbehandeling - emergency treatment
spoedgeval - emergency
spoedig - soon
spons - sponge
spoorboekje - (railway) timetable
spoorbomen - barriers, gate
spoorkaartje - railway ticket
spoorlijn - railway
spoorwegen - rail(way)
spoorwegovergang - level crossing
sport - sports
sportterrein - sports field
spreekkamer - surgery
spreekuur - surgery (hours)
springen - to jump
sproeien - to spray, to water
spuwen - to spit
staal - steel
staan - to stand
staan op - to insist (on)
stad - city, town
stadhuis - city/town hall
stal - stable
stallen - to store
standbeeld - statue
stank - smell
starten - to start
statief - tripod
statiegeld - deposit
station - station
steeds - continually
steeds meer - increasingly
steen - stone
steenpuist - boil, furuncle

steenslag - (loose) chippings
steil - steep
stekker - plug
stelpen - to stem, to stanch
stem - voice
stemmen - to vote, to tune
stempel - stamp, seal
stempelen - to stamp, to postmark
sterk - strong
sterkte - power
stevig - firm
stijf - stiff
stil - quiet
stilte! - quiet please!
stinken - to smell
stoel - chair
stoep - pavement
stof - cloth, dust
stok - stick
stomerij - dry cleaner's
stop! - stop, halt!
stop - fuse, plug
stopcontact - socket
stoplicht - traffic light(s)
stoppen - to stop
stoptrein - slow train
storen - to interrupt, to bother
storm - storm
straat - street
strak - tight, taut
straks - later, soon
straks!, tot - see you later!
strand - beach
strandstoel - deck chair
streek - area, region
streekgerecht - regional/local dish
streekwijn - regional/local wine
streep - line
strijken - to iron, to lower
strijkijzer - iron
strijkplank - ironing board
stromen - to flow

stromend water - running water
stroming, stroom - current
struik - bush
student - student
studeren - to go to college, to study
studie - studies
stuk - piece, broken, out of order, part
stuur - steering wheel, handlebars
stuur - helm
suiker - sugar
suikerpot - sugar bowl
suikerziekte - diabetes
supermarkt - supermarket

T

taai - tough, leathery
taal - language
taalgids - phrase book
taart - pie, pastry, cake
taartje - tart, cupcake
tabak - tobacco
tabakswinkel - tobacconist
tabletje - tablet
tafel - table
tafelkleedje - table cloth
tak - branch
tam (mak) - tame, domesticated
tampon - tampon
tand - tooth
tandarts - dentist
tandenborstel - tooth brush
tandpasta - tooth paste
tang - tongs *mv*
tank - tank
tanken - to fill up
tankstation - filling/petrol station
tarief - rate
tas(je) - (hand)bag
taxistandplaats - taxi rank
te - too, at, in
teen - toe
tegel - tile
tegelijkertijd - simultaneously,

at the same time
tegen - against
tegenover - opposite
tegenstander - opponent
tegenwoordig - today, at present
tegoedbon - voucher
teken - sign
tekenen - to draw, to sign
telefoon - telephone
telefoonboek - telephone directory
telefooncel - telephone booth/box
telefoonnummer - telephone number
telefoneren - to telephone, to call
telegram - telegram, cable, wire
televisie - television
televisienet - television network
tempel - temple
temperatuur - temperature
tennisbaan - tennis court
tennissen - to play tennis
tent - tent
tentharing - tent peg/pin
tentoonstelling - exhibition
terras - terrace, outdoor café
terug - back(wards)
terugkeer, terugreis - return (trip)
tevreden - satisfied/pleased with
thermometer - thermometer
thermoskan - thermos (flask)
thuis - home
thuiskomst - homecoming
tijd - time
tijdelijk - temporary
tijdperk - era
tijdschrift - magazine
tocht - draught, journey, trip
tocht, het - there's a draught
toegang - entrance
toegangshek - entrance gate
toegangskaartje - entrance ticket
toeslag - surcharge
toestaan - to allow, to permit

toestemming - permission
toilet - toilet, lavatory
toiletpapier - toilet paper
tolk - interpreter
tomaat - tomato
toneel - stage
toneelvoorsteling - theatrical performance
tonen - to show
tong - tongue
toosten (op) - to drink (to)
top - summit
toren - tower
touw - rope
trap - (flight of) stairs, kick
trein - train
treinkaartje - railway ticket
trekken - to pull, to travel (around)
trekkershut - hiking hut
trommel - drum, tin
trui - sweater
tuin - garden
tunnel - tunnel
tussen - between
tweedehands - second-hand
tweeling - twins *mv*
tweepersoonsbed - double bed
tweepersoonskamer - double room

U

ui - onion
uit - out
uitgaan - to go out
uitgang - exit
uitkijken - to watch/look out
uitlenen - to lend
uitrusten - to rest, to equip
uitrusting - equipment
uitspraak - pronunciation, verdict
uitspreken - to pronounce
uitstapje - trip, excursion
uitstekend - fine, excellent, protruding
uitstel - delay
uitverkoop - sale

uitwendig - external
uitwijken - to swerve, to turn aside
uitzicht op - view of
uitzien op - to face/look out on
uur - hour
uurwerk - clock

V

vaak - often
vaartuig - vessel, boat
vaarwel! - goodbye!
vaas - vase
vader - father
vakantie - holiday(s)
val - trap, fall
valhelm - helmet
vallen - to fall
van - from, of
vanaf - from, since
vandaag - today
varen - to sail
varken(svlees) - pork
vast - fixed, firm
vasten - to fast
vastentijd - Lent
vasthouden - to hold, to detain
vastmaken - to fix, to fasten
vee - cattle
veehouder - cattle breeder
veel - much, many, a lot
veel, te - too much
veemarkt - cattle market
veer - feather, spring
veerboot - ferry
vegen - to sweep
vegetarisch - vegetarian
veilig - safe
veiligheid - safety
veiligheidsgordel - safety belt
veiligheidsspeld - safety pin
veld - field, grounds
veldfles - flask
ver - far, a long way, distant

veranderen - to change
verantwoordelijk - responsible
verbaasd - surprised
verband (relatie) - relation, connection
verband met, in - concerning,
  in connection with
verband(gaas) - bandage, dressing
verbandkist - first-aid kit
verbazing - surprise, amazement
verbinden - to connect, to bandage,
  to dress
verblijfplaats - residence
verblijfsvergunning - residence permit
verblinden - to dazzle
verbod - ban, prohibition
verboden te .. - .. prohibited, no ..
verbranden - to burn
verder - further
verdergaan - to proceed
verdwalen - to get lost, to lose one's way
Verenigd Koninkrijk - United Kingdom
verf - paint
verfkwast - paintbrush
vergeten - to forget
vergezellen - to accompany
vergezeld van - accompanied by
vergiftiging - poisoning
vergissen, zich - to be wrong/mistaken
vergissing - mistake, error
vergoeding - refund, reimbursement
vergroting - enlargement
verguld - gold-plated
vergunning - permit
verhuizen - to move
verhuren - to let, to rent
verhuurbedrijf - leasing company
verhuurd - let, rented
verjaardag - birthday
verkeer - traffic
verkeerd - wrong
verkeersbord - road/traffic sign
verkering hebben - to go steady

verkopen - to sell
verkoper - salesman
verkouden zijn - to have a cold
verkoudheid - (common) cold
verlaten - to leave, desolate
verleden - past
verleden week - last week
verlichten - to light, to illuminate,
  to relieve
verlichting - light(ing), mitigation, relief
verlies - loss
verliezen - to lose
verloofde - fiancé *m*, fiancée *v*
verloving - engagement
verlopen (ongeldig) - to expire
verloren - lost
verminderen - to decrease, to reduce
verpleger - male nurse
verplicht - compulsory, obligatory
verrassing - surprise
vers - fresh, poem
verschil - difference
verschillend - different
versiering - decoration
versleten - worn out
versnelling - acceleration, gear
versperring - barrier, roadblock
verstaan - to hear, to understand
verstellen - to adjust, to adapt
verstopping - block(age)
verstopt - hidden, blocked, clogged
vertalen - to translate
vertaling - translation
verte, in de - in the distance, far off
vertraging - delay
vertrek - room, departure
vertrekken - to depart, to leave
vervangen - to replace
verwachten - to expect
verwachting - expectation
verwachting, in - pregnant
verwarming - heating

verwisseld - changed, swopped
verwonding - injury
verzekeren - to insure
verzekering - insurance
verzekeringsmaatschappij - insurance company
verzekeringspolis - insurance policy
verzenden - to send
verzoek - request
verzoeken (vragen) - to request
vest - cardigan
vestigen - to establish
vesting - fortress
vet - greasy, rich, fat
viaduct - flyover, overpass
vierkant - square
vies - dirty
vijl - file
vinden - to find, to think
vis - fish
visitekaartje - visiting card
visser - fisherman
Vlaams - Flemish
Vlaanderen - Flanders
Vlaming - Fleming
vlag - flag
vlak - flat, level
vlak bij - near
vlakte - plain
vlam - flame
vlees - meat
vleeswaren - meat products, cold cuts
vlek - stain, spot
vlekkenmiddel - stain/spot remover
vlieg - fly
vliegen - to fly
vliegtuig - (aero)plane
vliegveld - airport
vlo - flea
vloed - (high) tide
vloedgolf - tidal wave
vloeien - to flow

vloeistof - liquid, fluid
vloer - floor
vlooienmarkt - flea market
vlucht- flight, escape
vluchteling - fugitive, refugee
vluchtig - superficial, brief
vlug - fast, quick
vocht - liquid, moisture
vochtig - damp, moist
vochtwerend - dampproof
voedsel - food
voelen - to feel
voet - foot
voetbal - football, soccer
voetbalstadion - football stadium
voetganger - pedestrian
voetpad - footpath
vogel - bird
vol - full of, filled/stuffed with, no vacancies
volgen - to follow
volgend - next
volk - people
volkskunst - folk art
volkslied - national anthem
volledig - complete
vonk - spark
voor - to, in front of, before
vooraan - in front
vooraanstaand - prominent
voorbehoedsmiddel - contraceptive
voorbij - beyond, past, over
voorhoofd - forehead
voorkant - front
voornaam - first/Christian name, distinguished
voorrang - right of way
voorrang verlenen - to give right of way
voorrangsweg - main road
voorstel - proposition, proposal
voorstellen - to represent, to introduce, to propose, to suggest

voorstelling - performance, depiction, picture, image
voortdurend - continuous, constant
voortmaken - to hurry up
voortreffelijk - excellent
vooruit - ahead
vooruit! - let's get moving! come on!
voorwaarde - condition
voorwaardelijk - conditional
voorzichtig! - be careful!
vorige week - last week
vork - fork
vorm - shape
vorst - monarch, king, queen, frost
vraag - question
vragen - to ask, to request
vreemd - foreign, strange
vreemdeling - stranger, foreigner, alien
vreemdelingendienst - aliens registration office
vriend - friend
vriendelijk - kind, friendly
vrij - free
vrijen - to make love
vrijgezel - bachelor
vrijheid - freedom
vroeg - early
vroeger - in the past
vrouw - woman, wife
vrucht - fruit
vruchtensap - fruit juice
vuil - dirty
vuilnisbak - dustbin
vuilnisman - dustman, garbage collector
vulkaan - vulcano
vullen - to fill
vuur - fire
vuurwerk - fire works

w

waar - where, true, genuine

waar, het is - it's true
waarde - value
waardeloos - worthless
waarheen - where
waarheid - truth
waarom - why
waarschuwen - to warn
waarschuwing - warning
wachten - to wait
wachtkamer - waiting room
wagen - to dare, a car
wagenziek - carsick
wal - rampart, wall
wandelen - to walk
wandeling - walk
wang - cheek
wanneer - when, if
warenhuis - department store
warm - warm
warmte - warmth, heat
wasautomaat - washing machine
wasbenzine - benzine
wasgoed - laundry
wasknijper - clothes peg
waslijn - clothesline
wasmiddel - detergent
wasruimte - laundry room, washing facilities
wassen, zich - to have a wash
wassen - to launder
wastafel - washstand
wat - that, which, what, somewhat, slightly, a little
water - water
watersport - aquatics ·
waterskiën - waterskiing
waterval - waterfall, falls
watje - cotton wool
w.c. - toilet
wedstrijd - game
week - soft, week
weekeinde - weekend

weer - weather, again
weerbericht - weather forecast
weg - road, gone
wegdek - road surface
wegen - to weigh
wegenkaart - road map
wegenwacht - road patrol, AA/RAC patrol
weggaan - to leave
wegomlegging - diversion
wegsplitsing - fork
wegwijzer - signpost
weigeren - to refuse
weinig - little, few
wekken - to wake
wekker - alarm clock
welk(e) - who, which
welkom! - welcome!
welterusten! - good night! sleep well!
wens - wish
wensen - to wish, to desire
wereld - world
werk - work, job
werken - to work, to run, to operate
werkgever - employer
werknemer - employee
wesp - wasp
westen - west
weten - to know
wie - who
wieg - cradle, cot
wiel - wheel
wijd - wide, loose
wijk - district
wijn - wine
wijngaard - vineyard
wijnkaart - wine list
wijnkelder - wine cellar
wijzen - to point
wijzigen - to change, to alter
wijziging - alteration
wild - game, wild
willen - to want

wind - wind
windkracht - (wind) force
windscherm - windbreak, windscreen
windvaan - wind vane
winkel - shop
winkelcentrum - shopping centre
winkelwagentje - trolley
winter - winter
wisselen - to change
wisselkantoor - exchange office
wol - wool
wond - wound, injury
wonen - to live
woord - word
worst - sausage
wortel (boom, plant) - root
wortel (groente) - carrot
wrijven - to rub

Y

ij... (see i...)
yoghurt - yoghurt

Z

zaad - seed
zaal - hall
zacht - quiet, soft, smooth
zadel - saddle
zak - bag, pocket
zakdoek - handkerchief
zaklantaarn - torch
zakmes - pocketknife
zalf - ointment
zand - sand
zebra(pad) - pedestrian crossing
zee - sea
zeem - chamois/shammy (leather)
zeep - soap
zeer (erg) - very
zeer doen - to hurt
zeevis - marine/sea fish
zeewater - seawater
zeeziek - seasick
zeggen - to say

zeil - cloth, canvas, sail
zeildoek - canvas, sailcloth
zeiljack - windbreaker, windcheater
zeiljacht - yacht
zeilsport - sailing, yachting
zeker - securely, certainly, sure, safe, secure
zekerheid - safety, certainty
zekering - fuse
zelden - seldom
zeldzaam - rare
zelf - oneself
zelfde - similar, same
zelfs - even
zenden - to send
zicht - visibility
zicht op - view on
zichtbaar - visible
ziek - ill
ziekenauto - ambulance
ziekenfonds - National Health Service
ziekenhuis - hospital
ziekte - illness
ziektekostenverzekering - medical insurance
zien - to see
zijde - side, silk
zijdelings - sideways
zijstraat - side street
zilver - silver
zin in - to feel like, to fancy
zin - sentence, sense, point
zinloos - meaningless, pointless
zinvol - significant
zitplaats - seat
zitten - to sit, to be
zo - like this, so, as
zoeken naar - to search/look for
zoekraken - to get lost, to be mislaid
zoen - kiss
zoet - sweet, good

zoetjes - sweetener
zoetwaren - sweets
zoetwater - freshwater
zoetzuur - sweet-and-sour, pickled
zolder - attic
zomer - summer
zomertijd - summer time
zomervakantie - summer holidays
zon - sun
zonnebaden - to sunbathe
zonnebrand - sunburn
zonnebrandcrème - suntan lotion/cream
zonnebrandolie - suntan oil
zonnebril - sunglasses
zonnescherm - blind, shade, parasol
zonnesteek - sunstroke
zool - sole
zoon - son
zorgen voor - to look after, to care for, to take care of, to attend to
zout - salt
zoutarm - low-salt
zoutloos - salt-free
zoutpan - saltpan
zuiden - south
zuinig - economical, frugal
zuiver - pure
zuster - sister, nurse
zuur - sour, acid
zwaar - heavy, serious
zwager - brother-in-law
zwak - weak, feeble, poor
zwanger - pregnant
zwangerschap - pregnancy
zwart - black
zweer - ulcer, boil
zweet - sweat
zwembad - swimming pool
zwembroek - bathing/swimming trunks
zwemmen - to swim
zwemvest - life jacket

2e, 2de	tweede	second
afd.	afdeling	department
afz.	afzender	sent by
ANWB	---	Dutch automobile association
a.s.	aanstaande	next
a.u.b.	alstublieft	please
B, BG, P	begane grond, parterre	ground floor (Am.: first floor)
b.g.g.	bij geen gehoor	if there's no reply
blz., pag.	blad(zijde), pagina	page
BTW	Belasting Toegevoegde Waarde	Value Added Tax
b.v., bijv.	bijvoorbeeld	for example
b.v.	besloten vennootschap	private limited company
dhr./mevr.	de heer/mevrouw	Mr./Mrs.
dr.	doctor	Doctor (highest academic title)
drs.	doctorandus	academic title comparable to a Master's degree
EU	Europese Unie	European Union
EHBO	Eerste Hulp bij Ongelukken	first-aid organization
enz.	enzovoort	etcetera
excl.	exclusief	excluding
fa.	firma	company
i.p.v.	in plaats van	instead of
j.l.	jongstleden	last
km/u	kilometer per uur	kilometre per hour
NMBS	Nationale Maatschappij der Belgische Spoorwegen	Belgian national railways
NS	Nederlandse Spoorwegen	Dutch railways
n.v.	naamloze vennootschap	limited liability company
n.v.t.	niet van toepassing	not applicable
o.a., o.m.	onder andere(n), onder meer	among other things/persons
s.v.p.	s'il vous plaît (French!)	please
t.a.v.	ter attentie van	for the personal attention of
TCB	Touring Club van België	Belgian touring club
t/m	tot en met	up to and including
v.a.	vanaf	from
v. Chr.	vóór Christus	Before Christ
VTB	Vlaamse Toeristenbond	Flemisch tourist association
VVV	Vereniging voor Vreemdelingenverkeer	Dutch tourist information office
z.o.z.	zie ommezijde	please turn over